the God *whisperer* Daily Devotions

A Six-Month Devotional Plan for Christians Who Love Animals

Fred Bittner

Published by 2t2 Ministries, Parker, Colorado.
On the web at www.2t2ministries.org

ISBN: 978-0-9856992-0-8

Unless otherwise noted, Scripture references are taken from the NEW AMERICAN STANDARD BIBLE®, Copyright © 1960, 1962, 1963, 1971, 1972, 1973, 1975, 1977, 1995 by The Lockman Foundation. Used by permission.

Other versions are identified as follows:

NIV: The Holy Bible, New International Version, copyright © 1973, 1978, 1984 by International Bible Society.

Scripture quotations marked (NLT) are taken from the *Holy Bible*, New Living Translation, copyright © 1996. Used by permission of Tyndale House Publishers, Inc., Wheaton, Illinois 60189. All rights reserved.

THE MESSAGE: The Bible in Contemporary Language, copyright © 1993, 1994, 1995, 1996, 2000, 2001, 2002. Used by permission of NavPress Publishing Group.

Table of Contents

Introduction to *the God* whisperer *Daily Devotions*

Welcome to *the God* whisperer *Daily Devotions*. This book is filled with stories about animals. It is not, however, a book about animals. It is a book about deepening your relationship with Jesus. The stories are word pictures that help illustrate spiritual lessons much like the word pictures that Jesus used. When he used a tree in his story, he was making a spiritual point about people. He used fields, vineyards, coins, pearls, and even wineskins. All of his stories were word pictures: illustrations to teach us in engaging ways. The stories in *the God* whisperer *Daily Devotions* are true. The owners took the pictures of their pets. They have willingly allowed me to use their stories and they are praying that you will be blessed by the lessons you learn.

The God whisperer *Daily Devotions* is designed for five days of reading (Monday through Friday). Each week is centered around a common theme to help you focus on that subject. Saturday is designed to lead you through prayer over the weekly theme. There are no readings for Sunday. It is anticipated that you are attending your local church. You need to focus your attention by applying what you have learned in your work with the body of Christ.

About the Author

My wife, Kim, and I own Australian terriers, a fantastic breed of dogs, but a breed that is often very difficult to acquire. You will get to know them through many of the stories used in the book. We happily work with our dogs, and on occasion show them at various dog shows. It is a fun hobby—but it is just that, a hobby.

I wear several other titles, ones that are more important than that of dog owner. I am first a believer in Jesus Christ. He is my Lord and Savior and I wear His Name in all of life's circumstances. I am a husband, father, and grandfather. Kim and I have been married 37 years, we have three grown children (all married), and to date we have five grandchildren (a number which of course can change anytime within nine months of the writing of this book). I am also a pastor, educator, and author.

About 2t2 Ministries

2t2 Ministries is dedicated to providing the best small group Bible study material available. We do the work to evaluate the study materials and only recommend the best. We are constantly adding books that have been recommended and we have previewed. When 2t2 Ministries does not find quality materials on a subject, we create it and make it available to you.

While 2t2 Ministries does not endeavor to become a large scale publisher, we are interested in representing quality small group study books and devotional books. If your church has produced material you think should be shared with the greater body of Christ, contact 2t2 Ministries and inquire about submissions.

Please visit our website at: www.2t2ministries.org

Week 1: Spiritual Vitality

Monday: Lukewarm Is Not an Option

Meet Keziah, the newest member of Lisa's family. She is a beautiful example of a purebred Chocolate Lab puppy. The name means cinnamon in Hebrew and is the name of Job's second daughter after God blessed him the second time (Job 42:14). Like most puppies, Kessie (different spelling because it is easier to say) is soft, and cuddly like all puppies. She is learning to control her feet and legs, but is not always successful. She is small now, but very soon she will grow into a large dog.

Puppies begin their life contained in a small space. It may be a box, a whelping pen, or a small room. Their world is very limited, and their level of knowledge is even smaller. As they grow their environments expand. From a box they gain access to a whole room and, eventually, the house. We introduce them to the backyard and allow them to explore their new environment. With each stage of development, the puppy learns more and more. For dogs to grow up healthy we must provide them with ever expanding environments and richer challenges to keep them balanced.

When dogs get bored with their surroundings, they create their own ways of learning new things. They know their toys well enough, so they tear them up just to figure out what is inside. They become familiar with your garden and then start digging holes to discover what is underneath it. After they learn the confines of their backyard, they look for ways to get out onto the streets. When they are not allowed to grow and flourish, they become frustrated and get into all kinds of trouble.

Jesus said, "Truly I say to you, unless you are converted and become like children, you will not enter the kingdom of heaven" (Matthew 18:3). When we first meet Jesus our spiritual world is very small. We need to be sheltered in our new faith and "like newborn babes, long for the pure milk of the word, so that by it you may grow in respect to salvation" (1 Peter 2:2). As we grow, we are able to expand our spiritual environment. "But speaking the truth in love, we are to grow up in all aspects into Him who is the head, even Christ" (Ephesians 4:15).

When Christians do not expand their ministry, they become just as frustrated as a dog trapped in an enclosed backyard. Jesus calls such people lukewarm: neither hot nor cold. Lukewarm believers, whose growth have been stunted, start digging at others through criticism. They tear up relationships by their judgmental spirit. They don't see fruit in their own life, so they make themselves feel better by bringing others down. They cause trouble in the church and provide stumbling blocks for others. This is not the life the Lord has planned for us.

God wants us to grow and enjoy a fruitful ministry. He wants to expand our influence, and use us to bring others into a loving relationship with Christ. It is never too late to return to the "pure milk of the word" and reignite the process of "growing up in all aspects of Him."

The psalmist referred to some who struggled but found new vitality. He wrote, "Some of you wandered for years in the desert, looking but not finding a good place to live, half-starved and parched with thirst, staggering and stumbling, on the brink of exhaustion. Then, in your desperate condition, you called out to God. He got you out in the nick of time; He put your feet on a wonderful road that took you straight to a good place to live. So thank God for his marvelous love, for his miracle mercy to the children he loves. He poured great draughts of water down parched throats; the starved and hungry got plenty to eat" (Psalm 107:4, *The Message*).

Tuesday: Like a Boy and His Dog

A boy and his dog—does it get any better than this? They somehow have the ability to communicate without words. They are completely dedicated to each other even when it doesn't look like they are paying attention. When one hurts, they both hurt. It seems to be a part of how they are made.

The Bible says, "For we do not have a high priest who cannot sympathize with our weaknesses, but One who has been tempted in all things as we are, yet without sin. Therefore let us draw near with confidence to the throne of grace, so that we may receive mercy and find grace to help in time of need" (Hebrews 4:15–16). There is no better relationship than the relationship of Jesus and the one who trusts in him. He understands our needs, and is dedicated to us. He is there in our times of need. A look through the Psalms tells us that his righteousness, praise, righteousness, wealth, blessing, and provisions "endure forever."

So on this day, spend some time looking intently at the Lord. Climb into the Father's lap, and allow him to minister to you. "May the Lord direct your hearts into the love of God and into the steadfastness of Christ" (2 Thessalonians 3:5).

The Lord bless you, and keep you; The Lord make His face shine on you, and be gracious to you; The Lord lift up His countenance on you, and give you peace.

Numbers 6:24–26

7

Wednesday: Longing for Pure Milk

What happens when your beloved pet has a litter of puppies then gets sick and dies? That was Bibi's dilemma when her pet Chihuahua died shortly after giving birth to four cute little puppies. When that happened, Bibi, a high school student, sprang into action. She knew that if the puppies were to survive she would need to do all of the things that their momma would have done. She gathered up eyedroppers and began feeding the litter every two hours. She had to insure they were warm and clean. The jobs were tedious, time consuming, and often dirty, but she knew that the puppies needed her.

As the weeks passed, the eye drippers turned to baby bottles, eyes opened, and the growing puppies needed to begin stretching their legs. With that came new responsibilities of taking the dogs out of their whelping box and letting them struggle to walk. After five weeks of hard work, Bibi began to consider the fact that she was going to need to find her puppies a new home and let them go.

The process reminded me of the young Christians we come in contact with. God wants them to grow. To do that, they need spiritual milk. "Therefore, putting aside all malice and all deceit and hypocrisy and envy and all slander, like newborn babies, long for the pure milk of the word, so that by it you may grow in respect to salvation, if you have tasted the kindness of the Lord" (1 Peter 2:1–3).

Our job is to become like Bibi, to make sure they are being fed and spiritually loved in the Lord. We are to raise them up so that their growth is not stunted. Paul wrote, "I gave you milk to drink, not solid food; for you were not yet able to receive it. Indeed, even now you are not yet able" (1 Corinthians 3:2). What a sad commentary on those whose spiritual lives are in danger because of spiritual malnutrition.

Paul gave Timothy these words, "The things which you have heard from me in the presence of many witnesses, entrust these to faithful men who will be able to teach others also" (2 Timothy 2:2). This is what we call discipleship today: bringing new Christians to the word and helping them to take in scriptural teachings. Our job is to raise them up and help them to walk, to bring them to the point where they can stand on their own. If those under our care remain needy then we have not given them what they need to grow.

Our goal is to eventually let them go out on their own so they can find someone to support. We are then free to take on a new group of disciples. This is the way that God established for us "to grow up in all aspects into Him who is the head, even Christ" (Ephesians 4:15).

I am so proud of Bibi. Her dedication to the task of raising four puppies is very admirable. She is doing what is required to help the puppies thrive. Are you doing the same thing for a new believer? Are you putting in the time, helping them to learn, helping clean their messes, and teaching them to walk? Are Young Christians less important than four cockapoo–Chihuahua-mix puppies? We cannot afford to let them try to make it on their own. They need us, and God requires it of us.

Thursday: Imitation

It is rare to find a family dog that wants to do everything their master does, in the same way that their master does it. That, however, is the way Zero wants it. He wants to act human in every way possible. So when he sits on a chair, or the couch, he sits the way humans sit. Being upright on his backside is comfortable for Zero. He loves to sit next to those he loves, and will hold this position for hours on end. If his master does it, then it must be right, so Zero does his best to follow the example.

There is an interesting principle in the Scripture about imitating our master. The apostle Paul begins with this encouragement: "For if you were to have countless tutors in Christ, yet you would not have many fathers, for in Christ Jesus I became your father through the gospel. Therefore I exhort you, be imitators of me. For this reason I have sent to you Timothy, who is my beloved and faithful child in the Lord, and he will remind you of my ways which are in Christ, just as I teach everywhere in every church" (1 Corinthians 4:15–17).

Why imitate Paul? He is imitating Christ, and the best way to understand Christ in the early stages of our spiritual life is to follow those who know Christ well. Paul doesn't suggest that he is the only one who is worthy of being followed. "And we desire that each one of you show the same diligence so as to realize the full assurance of hope until the end, so that you will not be sluggish, but imitators of those who through faith and patience inherit the promises" (Hebrews 6:11–12).

Eventually we grow in our relationship with Jesus and are able to spend more time in the Word learning His ways. It is then that Paul wants us to make the switch. "Therefore be imitators of God, as beloved children" (Ephesians 5:1). By doing this we will "not imitate what is evil, but what is good. The one who does good is of God; the one who does evil has not seen God" (3 John 1:11).

Who do you know who represents Christ well? Follow their example. The actions will not make you righteous in themselves, but they will teach you a pattern of righteous behavior. Following their pattern will give you a longing to understand more. That longing will draw you to the Scripture where you will learn God's ways. Learning God's ways will make you more dependent on the Scripture and less dependent on the person whose example you are following.

The goal of imitation is not so that we will all become carbon copies of each other. Be an imitator "so that you will walk in a manner worthy of the Lord, to please *Him* in all respects, bearing fruit in every good work and increasing in the knowledge of God; strengthened with all power, according to His glorious might, for the attaining of all steadfastness and patience" (Colossians 1:10–11).

Remember, imitating Christ in this world is not easy. If it were, we could all just fake it. No, it takes time, sometimes getting it right and sometimes getting it wrong. But in these things we grow. This is why Paul also wrote, "The things you have learned and received and heard and seen in me, practice these things, and the God of peace will be with you" (Philippians 4:9).

Friday: A New Creation

It was a beautiful day outside, so she decided to have her quiet time on the patio. She was reading through Matthew 11 and had just come to the last verses in the chapter: "Come to Me, all who are weary and heavy-laden, and I will give you rest. Take My yoke upon you and learn from Me, for I am gentle and humble in heart, and you will find rest for your souls. For My yoke is easy and My burden is light" (Matthew 11:28–30).

These words drew her into deep reflection as she considered the burdens she was carrying, and she wondered how the burdens of Jesus could be so much lighter. She wanted to be yoked with Jesus and she thought she was, but it felt more like she was shouldering the weight on her own. Even prayer warriors can reach a plateau and she did not want to bear the burdens alone.

Bowing her head, she became lost in her conversation with her Lord. She praised Him, and told him about the needs she was bringing before him this day. Ending her prayer, she reaffirmed her faith and asked God that he would always share the yoke with her. When she opened her eyes, a butterfly had landed on her Bible, and was resting comfortably.

Jesus said to Nicodemus, "Truly, truly, I say to you, unless one is born again he cannot see the kingdom of God" (John 3:3). The butterfly began its life in a completely different form. It crawls, and wiggles to get around. It is considered a menace in a garden as it struggles to gain enough nourishment to move to the next phase of life.

Unless the caterpillar enters the cocoon and dies to itself, it cannot be born again as a beautiful butterfly. Once out of the cocoon, the butterfly cannot act again like a caterpillar. The DNA is the same, but the results are very different on either side of the cocoon. The same concept is true of the believer: "Therefore if anyone is in Christ, he is a new creature; the old things passed away; behold, new things have come" (2 Corinthians 5:17).

Ephesians 4 as translated in *The Message* says,

> And so I insist—and God backs me up on this—that there be no going along with the crowd, the empty-headed, mindless crowd. They've refused for so long to deal with God that they've lost touch not only with God but with reality itself. They can't think straight anymore. Feeling no pain, they let themselves go in sexual obsession, addicted to every sort of perversion.
>
> But that's no life for you. You learned Christ! My assumption is that you have paid careful attention to him, been well instructed in the truth precisely as we have it in Jesus. Since, then, we do not have the excuse of ignorance, everything—and I do mean everything— connected with that old way of life has to go. It's rotten through and through. Get rid of it! And then take on an entirely new way of life—a God-fashioned life, a life renewed from the inside and working itself into your conduct as God accurately reproduces his character in you.
>
> Ephesians 4:17–24

With this passage in mind, are you truly living the new way of life? Or are you still dragging along the struggles of your old way of life. You can be free, but it requires effort on your part. I tried to help a struggling butterfly to get out of its cocoon once. It was struggling for so long and I wanted to help the process along, so I created a larger hole in the cocoon and he dropped free. Unfortunately, the wings never straightened, the butterfly was not able to fly, and it died very quickly. I discovered that the butterfly needed to experience the struggle to become free. The struggle was what created the strength to live free and fly. So, how do we break free from our old ways?

It is here where we come full circle back to Matthew 11. To be free from our old life we must become yoked with Jesus. He can give you the strength to straighten our wings and fly.

Saturday: "Spiritual Vitality" Day of Prayer

In this, your first week with *the God* whisperer *Daily Devotions*, we explored the importance of building a relationship with God. "Truly I say to you, unless you are converted and become like children, you will not enter the kingdom of heaven" (Matthew 18:3). We are his children, and we desire to please him. This means taking time to be in the word and to worship, and to cultivate a desire to become like Christ.

Over the next six months we will explore many different aspects about our relationship with Christ. But the experience will mean little if we fail to take the proper steps to grow.

The apostle John wrote, "To the angel of the church in Laodicea write: 'The Amen, the faithful and true Witness, the Beginning of the creation of God, says this: "I know your deeds, that you are neither cold nor hot; I wish that you were cold or hot. So because you are lukewarm, and neither hot nor cold, I will spit you out of My mouth"'" (Revelation 3:14–16).

Lukewarm is not an option in a relationship with Jesus. He wants us to be like him. Remember what Ephesians 5:1, says: "Therefore be imitators of God, as beloved children." We dare not ignore these verses and hope that Jesus didn't mean what he said. So spend your time today praying about your spiritual life. Make a list of areas that you would like to surrender, and lay them at the foot of the cross today.

ek 2: Representing Christ

Monday: Different Is Good

Cats have always been a part of my life. They make me sneeze, but it doesn't really matter. I like cats, and they seem to like me. Friends with cats are always amazed that their cats immediately jump in my lap. I don't begin to understand why it happens. I look at my friends' animal pictures and save the ones that inspire me toward a biblical lesson. For some time now I have been saving up cat pictures. It all started with this photo.

Snarla is a very sweet cat that lives with my friend Caitlin. She is very dedicated to Caitlin and spends lots of time in her bedroom. Snarla is gentle spirited and can be very friendly, but she will not approach others if she feels at all nervous. Make a quick move toward her and she is gone. If she is not completely confident, you will have a difficult time finding her. She will to disappear, blend in, and not be noticed. She will still be around, but you won't even notice. She likes it that way.

Far too often, we act like Snarla. We have a relationship with God and we are secure enough in our salvation, but we fear standing out. We want to fit in and not be noticed, so we stay quiet about our beliefs, doing everything we can to be spiritually invisible. We hold tight to the joy of our salvation, but go about our business hoping not to be noticed. If there is a need, we consider helping, but retreat at the first sign of trouble. We say we don't know enough, or are afraid of being ridiculed. We don't want to be judged for our actions after people discover our faith.

Yet, we are called to be different, to stand up for our faith, and be noticed. Paul wrote, "Therefore, having these promises, beloved, let us cleanse ourselves from all defilement of flesh and spirit, perfecting holiness in the fear of God" (2 Corinthians 7:1). Permission to hide our faith is not found anywhere in the Scripture. Instead Peter urges, "Keep your behavior excellent among the Gentiles, so that in the thing in which they slander you as evildoers, they may because of your good deeds, as they observe them, glorify God in the day of visitation" (1 Peter 2:12).

Jesus' message comes through loud and clear when we read Matthew chapter five from *The Message*:

> Let me tell you why you are here. You're here to be salt-seasoning that brings out the God-flavors of this earth. If you lose your saltiness, how will people taste godliness? You've lost your usefulness and will end up in the garbage. Here's another way to put it: You're here to be light, bringing out the God-colors in the world. God is not a secret to be kept. We're going public with this, as public as a city on a hill. If I make you light-bearers, you don't think I'm going to hide you under a bucket, do you? I'm putting you on a light stand. Now that I've put you there on a hilltop, on a light stand—shine! Keep open house; be generous with your lives. By opening up to others, you'll prompt people to open up with God, this generous Father in heaven.
>
> Matthew 5:13–16

Don't hide. Stand out for Jesus. Being different from others is a good thing. It is, after all, what God wants.

Tuesday: Living a Life of Purpose

One day, Jesus said to the multitudes, "I must preach the kingdom of God to the other cities also, for I was sent for this purpose" (Luke 4:43).

Puppies are like children in so many ways. They are filled with curiosity as they experience new things. They put everything in their mouth. Puppies and children need lots of attention. Each one has a unique personality. Our pack of dogs grew from two to six when Jazzy had four puppies.

We named each of the puppies after famous big band leaders, and the songs that they made famous. One of the puppies, named Shim Sham Shimmy, became the dominant puppy of the litter. He played harder, rebelled more, and worked harder to control his three brothers. As he grew, his dominant behavior continued to express itself. If there was a problem, we knew that Shimmy would be in the middle of it. When the litter was old enough to be placed with other families, Shimmy was overlooked in favor of the other puppies. He was a good dog, but for some reason he didn't meet the needs of the families who wanted one of the dogs.

Shimmy was still with us at six months of age. He needed something that he wasn't getting with us. He needed a purpose. That purpose came when we received a call from a wonderful woman who was looking for a service dog to help with her disabilities. She was looking for a small dog that could ride on her electric scooter or sit on her lap, yet still be able to pick up objects, turn on lights, and support her daily functions. Shimmy and Elizabeth bonded well and she decided to take Shimmy home.

Elizabeth had two aging giant poodles that had served her well. For the first few days, Shimmy watched as the trusted poodles provided the needed services for their master. As the time passed, Shimmy became restless. When Elizabeth asked one of the dogs to do something for her, Shimmy sprang into action. He jumped up on the poodle and bit at the dog's collar in the same way he had controlled his brothers.

Unfortunately, this time Shimmy grabbed more than the collar and ended up drawing blood. Elizabeth isolated Shimmy from the rest of the family, convinced that she had made a mistake in bringing the puppy home. She called and informed us that Shimmy would be returned in the next few days. Later in the day, something amazing happened.

Shimmy had been locked in his kennel for several hours when Elizabeth realized that he should probably go outside to take care of business. When she opened the kennel door Shimmy shot out in a dead run, went to the back door, operated the mechanical opener, and headed out to the lawn. When he was finished he darted around to the bedroom door, grabbed the rope that operated that door, pulled it open, ran through the house, and put himself back into the kennel.

Elizabeth could not believe what she had witnessed. Shimmy had not been shown any of those mechanisms. He learned it all by watching the poodles. They decided that they needed to give Shimmy another try. He needed to fulfill his purpose of caring for Elizabeth.

In a very short time, he was picking up objects, doing work around the house, and making his master happy. Shimmy had found his purpose. He was a changed dog.

The apostle Paul said, "And we know that God causes all things to work together for good to those who love God, to those who are called according to His purpose. For those whom He foreknew, He also predestined to become conformed to the image of His Son, so that He would be the firstborn among many brethren" (Romans 8:28–29).

You have a purpose. God wants you to be conformed to the image of Christ. Just being around others who do the work will not bring fulfillment. In fact, you may find yourself as frustrated as Shimmy seemed to have been. Peter wrote, "For you have been called for this purpose, since Christ also suffered for you, leaving you an example for you to follow in His steps" (1 Peter 2:21). Our job is to fulfill our own purpose by following in the footsteps of Jesus.

What is your purpose? What have you been called to do? What are your talents? What brings you joy? Australian terriers were bred for two things.

They were bred to root out ground vermin on the farms and they were bred to ride on the wagons next to the women to provide protection as they traveled. Shimmy found his place riding on Elizabeth's scooter and meeting her needs. It was what he was born to do.

God has given us skills, gifts, and talents. He has called us to use those abilities to serve him and has offered us support as we step out on faith. "Now He who prepared us for this very purpose is God, who gave to us the Spirit as a pledge" (2 Corinthians 5:5). Find your purpose, and you will be a changed person. You will also be closer to God that ever before. It is what you were born to do.

Wednesday: Follow the Leader

Jazzy is the alpha dog in our pack. She commands respect from others by her presence. She puts up with a lot from the other dogs, but she lets them know when it's time to fall in line.

One Thanksgiving our three kids and five grand kids were at the house to enjoy the holiday. The dogs fascinated my grandson Will. He enjoyed watching them, but he loved following them. Will was particularly attracted to Jazzy. Whenever he was given the time and freedom, he would look for Jazzy. The two would then play a game of "follow the leader." Jazzy led and Will followed. Sometimes the process reversed itself and Jazzy would follow her little boy. For the most part, however, Jazzy was the leader.

Throughout the day, Jazzy led Will to various places that she liked to go. She showed him around the house, over and under furniture, and through several rooms. For a while, they played together in the Jazzy's kennel. Will brought toys from the kids toy bucket into the kennel, and tried to get the dog to play with them. When that got old, the two headed through the doggy door to explore the backyard.

Jazzy led Will around the patio furniture and through the gardens. She calmly and gently showed Will a rose bush, seemingly warning him not to mess with that one. Slowly, carefully and with almost no sound, the two played their "follow the leader" game as they explored Jazzy's world.

Jesus talked about "follow the leader" on several occasions:

- If anyone serves Me, he must follow Me; and where I am, there My servant will be also; if anyone serves Me, the Father will honor him. (John 12:26)

- And He was saying to them all, "If anyone wishes to come after Me, he must deny himself, and take up his cross daily and follow Me." (Luke 9:23)

- My sheep hear My voice, and I know them, and they follow Me. (John 10:27)

Jesus makes it very clear that he is our leader. He wants to lead us into his world and show us the Way of Life. The apostle Paul added to the "follow the leader" principle: "For you yourselves know how you ought to follow our example" (2 Thessalonians 3:7). He called Christians "imitators of us and of the Lord" (1 Thessalonians 1:6). The disciples followed Jesus. The early church followed the apostles.

We follow the principles of the Scripture, which teach us about Jesus and the apostles, the spreading of the gospel, and the work of the Holy Spirit. God has given us the church so that we can become both leaders and followers. We are to follow those who have wisdom and experience in serving Christ. We are also called to set an example that others can follow.

Who are you following? Is someone teaching you the principles of Jesus? Who is leading you to the rose bush to show you that you must be careful around it? Is a spiritual leader patiently working with you to help you explore the world of faith? We were not called to live in a spiritual vacuum. God gave us the church, with leaders who want to show us the way. It is biblical to play "follow the leader."

"Therefore, since we are surrounded by such a huge crowd of witnesses to the life of faith, let us strip off every weight that slows us down, especially the sin that so easily trips us up. And let us run with endurance the race God has set before us" (Hebrews 12:1, NLT).

Thursday: Let Your Light Shine

Participating in a dog show is a truly remarkable experience. A large dog show can have thousands of dogs gathered in one place. In that environment you may find a Great Dane walk past a Pomeranian without conflict. There may be dozens of dogs within feet of each other, yet no fights break out. Every size, color, age, and temperament gather together in the hopes of gaining the title of Best In Show.

The process of showing a dog fascinated me. I wanted to be able to make sense of the events I saw taking place at the dog show. When I considered the process it occurred to me that showing a dog could be divided into three distinct parts. The first part I will call the *Presentation*. This takes place when the ring steward calls your number to enter the ring. Once all participants are present the judge asks the handlers to walk the dogs around the ring. It is here that the handler must present his or her dog as the specimen that best meets the standard of its breed.

The second part of showing the dog I call the *Examination*. One by one, the judge physically examines every dog in the ring. Larger breeds remain on the ground, while smaller breeds are placed on a table. Judges expertly move their hands over the entire body of each dog. Once the judge has determined the quality of the dog it is ready for the third aspect of the show.

The last part can be called the *Demonstration*. The judge instructs the handler to walk the dog in a predetermined pattern. At this point, the handler wants to show the dog's best features. By showing the dog's best features the handler hopes to make a lasting impression in the mind of the judge. Jesus sent us out into the world to make a difference, to show it what being a Christian is all about.

Our goal is to match our lives to the standard (Christlikeness), and to represent Jesus to those who are without salvation. So we take part in the presentation. "Therefore I urge you, brethren, by the mercies of God, to present your bodies a living and holy sacrifice, acceptable to God, which is your spiritual service of worship" (Romans 12:1). We are also involved in the process of examination, which begins with us. "Test yourselves to see if you are in the faith; examine yourselves! Or do you not recognize this about yourselves, that Jesus Christ is in you—unless indeed you fail the test?" (2 Corinthians 13:5).

We know that everyone who knows of our faith will examine us as well. "But just as we have been approved by God to be entrusted with the gospel, so we speak, not as pleasing men, but God who examines our hearts" (1Thessalonians 2:4). Jesus came to be a demonstration of His Father's love: "But God demonstrates His own love toward us, in that while we were yet sinners, Christ died for us" (Romans 5:8). The apostle Paul saw himself as a demonstration of God's love as well: "Yet for this reason I found mercy, so that in me as the foremost [sinner], Jesus Christ might demonstrate His perfect patience as an example for those who would believe in Him for eternal life" (1 Timothy 1:16). "And my message and my preaching were not in persuasive words of wisdom, but in demonstration of the Spirit and of power" (1 Corinthians 2:4). This process continues with us since we have been called to go into all the world and make disciples (Matthew 28:19; Mark 16:15).

Here's another way to put it: You're here to be light, bringing out the God-colors in the world. God is not a secret to be kept. We're going public with this, as public as a city on a hill. If I make you light-bearers, you don't think I'm going to hide you under a bucket, do you? I'm putting you on a light stand. Now that I've put you there on a hilltop, on a light stand—shine! Keep open house; be generous with your lives. By opening up to others, you'll prompt people to open up with God, this generous Father in heaven.

Matthew 5:14–16, *The Message*

Friday: My Way

I want to do it *my* way!

These two dogs fascinate me. They could have taken turns, but they didn't. They could have waited for someone to open the big door. That would be too easy. Dogs naturally want what they want when they want it. The idea that both dogs couldn't fit through the doggie door obviously didn't occur to them. They both wanted to be first, and they wanted to do it their way.

The "my way" syndrome has been a part of our world since Adam decided to try the forbidden fruit. It has shaped society, and at times it has had a profound effect on the church. We want to pray our way, for our own wants. We exercise our faith "our way," and we defend ourselves should anyone point out inconsistencies in our actions. Too often, people enter a church with their opinions on their sleeves, only to drop out because everybody else is a "hypocrite" and *they* are the only ones who are "right."

Matthew 7 tells us that the way of God is like the door in this picture. "Enter through the narrow gate; for the gate is wide and the way is broad that leads to destruction, and there are many who enter through it. For the gate is small and the way is narrow that leads to life, and there are few who find it" (Matthew 7:13–14). This gate requires more than a "me first" attitude. It requires a Jesus-first approach. That's why Jesus said, "If anyone wishes to come after Me, he must deny himself, and take up his cross and follow Me. For whoever wishes to save his life will lose it; but whoever loses his life for My sake will find it" (Matthew 16:24–25).

Once we have received Christ, we are called to move away from the "me first" approach to life. First Corinthians 6 says, "Or do you not know that your body is a temple of the Holy Spirit who is in you, whom you have from God, and that you are not your own? For you have been bought with a price." Paul's conclusion is "glorify God in your body." We are also instructed to consider others as more important than ourselves. "Do nothing from selfishness or empty conceit, but with humility of mind regard one another as more important than yourselves" (Philippians 2:3). This cannot happen with a "me first" attitude.

I was raised on the acronym "JOY," which stands for Jesus, Others, and You. It is my constant reminder that it is not about me. My faith must be in keeping with Scripture, even if obedience to the word makes me uncomfortable for a time. It means that my public life is not about me. It is about serving others in the name of Christ, and giving preference to "one another in the fear of Christ." My family is not about me. Fulfillment comes from serving my family's needs.

Do you feel like you have your head jammed in the door? You can't get in, and you can't back out. You are just stuck, and there is no joy in your predicament. Maybe you need to take some time to reflect on how you got stuck. YOJ, isn't even a word. Neither is YJO. Those letters only go together one way. Our faith is like that as well. It only works one way. That's why it is a narrow gate.

Saturday: "Representing Jesus" Prayer Day

Chances are very good that your community has a number of churches. What you see are a number of locations where people can serve Jesus. What unbelievers see may be completely different. They may look at all of the buildings and names and think that Christians can't get along, or that they don't know how to agree on who God really is. If an unbeliever does not attend church, then he or she little opportunity to see Jesus at work. That is, unless Jesus is at work in you.

"Test yourselves to see if you are in the faith; examine yourselves! Or do you not recognize this about yourselves, that Jesus Christ is in you—unless indeed you fail the test?" (2 Corinthians 13:5). The test we fail may be more than about our own salvation. It may be the test of others who are looking at you to see if God is real. You may be the most important Christian presence in their life. Is your lack of obedience causing others to turn away from a relationship with Jesus? This is a scary thought, but it is entirely possible.

The JOY acronym we looked at this week is very important as we represent Jesus in the world. People know what is important to you, and if you are all about yourself then they will come to understand that Jesus doesn't really matter. Serving Jesus first is essential. Taking the time to focus on others as your sacrifice of praise is also important. They will respond when Jesus shines through your life and makes a positive impact on them. They will want to have what you have.

What needs should you meet this week? How can you represent Jesus at work in a way that will not be offensive but will still let people know where you stand? Does a co-worker have a need that you need to meet? Does your family represent Jesus in a way that causes your neighbors to know you are believers? Do not expect them to know you are Christians just because your car leaves the driveway on Sunday mornings.

Pray that God would open your eyes to the opportunities he will place before you this week. Ask God to challenge you to serve, and ask him for victories

Week 3: God's Blessings

Monday: The Humble Will Be Lifted

Lady belongs to my young friend Beto, a somewhat typical teenager. Beto is trying to find his way in life. He has good days and challenging ones. He is growing up, but he suffers the same bumps that other high school students face. Though Beto is not perfect, you wouldn't know it by how devoted Lady is to her master. She loves her master and is completely devoted to him. She follows her master, waits patiently, watches his moves, and responds when he gives her attention. In return, Beto freely admits his love for Lady.

In the book of James we read the words, "Humble yourselves in the presence of the Lord, and He will exalt you" (James 4:10). This concept was not new to James, but it is a consistent biblical principle:

> Pride goes before destruction, and a haughty spirit before stumbling.
> It is better to be humble in spirit with the lowly than to divide the spoil with the proud.
> He who gives attention to the word will find good, and blessed is he who trusts in the Lord.
>
> Proverbs 16:18–20

These days, we live by the "squeaky wheel gets the grease" philosophy. Make noise until we get what we want. Don't take a back seat to anyone. Humility is a foreign concept in today's society. Yet, humility is actually the means to gain what we try to get by making all kinds of noise. Our call is to feast at God's table, to give attention to his word, so that we can find good.

The good news for the believer is that our God is perfect. He does not shift with the changing winds. He is worthy of our honor and "is able to do far more abundantly beyond all that we ask or think, according to the power that works within us" (Ephesians 3:20).

"A man's pride will bring him low, but a humble spirit will obtain honor" (Proverbs 29:23).

Tuesday: So Blessed!

Laredo has a great life. He has a loving family, and a great little boy to care for. He has a great home, a purpose, and new challenge every day. If a dog can tell you how it feels by the look on its face, then Laredo is saying, "I am so blessed!"

Some may question this blessing. After all, he walks on all four of his legs. Without functioning hands to serve himself, he is dependent on his master for food and has to stick his face in a bowl to eat. He requires help to go in and out of the house and never has a day off. How could he possibly feel blessed? Yet, look at him! That is the face of a blessed dog.

If you are in Christ and you are living in obedience to the Scripture, then you too can say, "I am so blessed!" In fact, Jesus told us nine times in ten verses that ours is a blessed life. If we follow his word, and seek his will then we are blessed indeed.

> He opened His mouth and began to teach them, saying, "Blessed are the poor in spirit, for theirs is the kingdom of heaven. Blessed are those who mourn, for they shall be comforted. Blessed are the gentle, for they shall inherit the earth. Blessed are those who hunger and thirst for righteousness, for they shall be satisfied. Blessed are the merciful, for they shall receive mercy. Blessed are the pure in heart, for they shall see God. Blessed are the peacemakers, for they shall be called sons of God. Blessed are those who have been persecuted for the sake of righteousness, for theirs is the kingdom of heaven. Blessed are you when people insult you

and persecute you, and falsely say all kinds of evil against you because of Me. Rejoice and be glad, for your reward in heaven is great; for in the same way they persecuted the prophets who were before you."

Matthew 5:2–12

Some may be tempted to look at these verses and question their blessing. How can you be blessed when you are poor in sprit and you have to mourn? You are supposed to be hungry and thirsty for righteousness, and you are bound to gentleness and mercy. And what is this part about being persecuted for righteousness' sake? Blessed? I don't think so!

To those, however, who live the blessed life we recognize that the first half of each verse is a joy because it leads to the last half of the verse. Ours is the kingdom of heaven, and we shall be comforted. We will inherit the earth, be satisfied, receive mercy, and see God. We will be recognized as sons of God, inheritors of the kingdom. The righteousness we live may be a stumbling block to others but we are the ones who will receive the great reward.

If this isn't blessed, then I don't know what is. So the next time you are discouraged, feel persecuted, or are filled with sorrow, go to the end of the verse, and refresh your spirit with the joy that is yours. Then like Laredo, sit back and joyfully proclaim, "I am so blessed!"

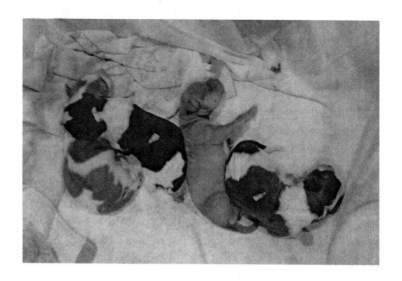

Wednesday: Untold Blessings

While working in East Los Angeles County, a dog approached Dan's friend. It was obvious that this dog was a stray and had been lost for a while. Her shaggy coat was filled with dirt. She was thin, and obviously needed help. When the man finished his work, he brought the dog home. When Dan first saw the dog he knew that she would not be fully saved until she was brought into his own family.

So just after Christmas, he adopted the dog and brought her home to be a companion for Valentine, his daughter's Chihuahua. He gave her the name Lucy and began nurturing her back to health. They wanted her to learn what it meant to be a part of their family, so they spent a lot of time working with her. Over the next few weeks the new family member became more and more plump. It became obvious that the dog they had saved was pregnant. Soon, four puppies were added to the household. They saved one dog—Lucy—and through the one, they saved four more.

Our world is full of people who are lost and wandering. They need a family to have compassion on them with the compassion of Christ. "But when he saw the multitudes, he was moved with compassion for them, because they were distressed and scattered, as sheep not having a shepherd" (Matthew 9:36). It would be easy enough to let them continue to wander, ignoring the fact that they are lost and need to be saved. But we are the ones who have been charged with the task of bringing them into the household of faith. "Therefore, we are ambassadors for Christ, as though God were making an appeal through us; we beg you on behalf of Christ, be reconciled to God" (2 Corinthians 5:20).

The Apostle Paul urged Timothy, "And the things you have heard from me in the presence of many witnesses, entrust these to faithful men who will be able to teach others also" (2 Timothy 2:2). We don't need to win the world all at once. One at a time will get the job done, because the person who finds salvation through you will have the opportunity to reach others.

I served on a jury pool where I began a conversation with a young lady who was seated near me. Since we had the time, we began to talk, general conversation at first, but it moved to spiritual things. She made a commitment to Christ that day, and was baptized the next Sunday. Within three week, seven more came to Christ through my relationship with her.

Like Jesus, we are to seek and save that which is lost. One lost woman at a well, drawing water, made a huge impact on her city because she met Jesus. One jailor came to Christ through Paul, and by the end of the night his whole household had made a decision to follow Jesus.

Win just one person and you may be opening the doors to untold blessings. That one may become five and grow to ten. Conversely, it may also be true that because we left the one, all ten could be lost. As appointed ambassadors for Christ, are we willing to let that happen?

Thursday: Our God Knows

Ginger is an amazing chocolate Labrador retriever that belongs to my friend Lisa. She is featured in several photographs in my book, *The God Whisperer*. Ginger is a champion obedience dog, an avid swimmer, and one of the best companions one could ever find. She enjoys meeting new friends, and gets along with every dog she meets.

On Ginger's tenth birthday Lisa threw a birthday party. All of Ginger's friends from their dog park were invited to attend. Like any party, there were games, and cake, goodies and gifts. The difference was that everything was designed for the dogs. It wasn't a party for people with dogs. It was a party for Ginger and her canine friends.

Last week, Ginger let Lisa know that she wasn't feeling well. There had been no signs prior, but it was clear that something was wrong. The vet confirmed that there was indeed a problem, and the next day Ginger was at the veterinary hospital having a tumor removed along with her spleen. When the pathology came back, Lisa was given the news: *hemangiosarcoma*— a fast moving form of cancer.

Ginger has a great life with someone who is committed to her. She has known love and companionship. Ginger has a master who prepared for all of her needs. Lisa had the foresight to purchase health insurance with a cancer policy. Since Lisa is off work right now, she has extra time to spend with Ginger. Lisa will continue to be with Ginger for as long as her life is extended by treatments.

We have a master who loves us and has prepared for us. He knew our need even before we were born and made a way that we could have a relationship with him. "For while we were still helpless, at the right time Christ died for the ungodly" (Romans 5:6). He continues to understand our needs every day of our lives. Several times in the gospels Jesus reminded us, "your Father knows what you need before you ask Him" (Matthew 6:8). This is an awesome promise when difficulties come our way. Paul summed it up in the first chapter of Ephesians by saying, "In him we have redemption through his blood, the forgiveness of sins, in accordance with the riches of God's grace that he lavished on us with all wisdom and understanding" (Ephesians 1:7–8, NIV).

We can explain God's blessings by using synonyms for the word "lavish." God's love and provisions for us are plentiful, extravagant, heaping, generous, abundant, and bountiful. That's like a birthday party to the tenth power! These are blessings for when everything is going right and tools for when things seem to be going wrong. This is why Romans tells us that God gives us the ability to persevere through life's trials because he is standing with us through the Holy Spirit (Romans 5:3–5).

Perhaps it would be easier to return to a promise that God made a long time ago, a promise he has never forgotten: "I will cause showers to come down in their season; they will be showers of blessing" (Ezekiel 34:26).

Friday: A New Name

When our granddaughter Elyse was four she decided that she wanted a dog of her own. She enjoyed coming over to visit our Aussies, and she loved the giant poodle at her other grandparents' house. But those dogs were not hers. She wanted one that lived at her house.

So Katie (our daughter) began taking Elyse to pet stores to look at puppies. Very soon, she found a puppy she wanted to bring home. She decided that the puppy would be named Hardy. Since their house was not ready to take a puppy home, they agreed to leave Hardy at the pet store. But Elyse never forgot the joy of claiming that puppy and giving it her special name. So, every few weeks Elyse would ask to visit another store to see the puppies. With each visit, she found a puppy that she liked and gave it the name Hardy. For two years, Elyse visited pet stores, looking forward to the day when one of her Hardys would be able to come home with her.

Recently, Katie noticed an advertisement for a three-year-old poodle. The owner was ill and could no longer take care of her dog. The need of one family became the opportunity for another. Boogee found a new home with Elyse, but something else was necessary. Boogee needed a new name, the name that Elyse had planned to use for two years. Boogee is learning to answer to his new name, Hardy.

The Bible tells us that Jesus came to seek and to save that which was lost. We were lost because we lived in a world that was sick. We needed a new home, and a new name. "See how great a love the Father has bestowed on us, that we would be called children of God; and such we are For this reason the world does not know us, because it did not know Him" (1 John

3:1). Through the sacrifice of Jesus, we have been given the name *Christian* (one who belongs to Christ). We are called by a name so awesome that those who stood against Jesus were afraid to even speak it. "But so that it will not spread any further among the people, let us warn them to speak no longer to any man in this name" (Acts 4:17).

The name we wear is our reminder that we have a new home, and a new master. "And if children, heirs also, heirs of God and fellow heirs with Christ, if indeed we suffer with Him so that we may also be glorified with Him" (Romans 8:17). "But if anyone suffers as a Christian, he is not to be ashamed, but is to glorify God in this name" (1 Peter 4:16). We serve a God who sought us out, and gave us his name. Let's get used to that name and wear it in a way that brings our Savior glory.

Saturday: "God's Blessings" Prayer Day

A praise song by Bill and Gloria Gaither swept the church world in the seventies:

> We are so blessed, by the gifts from Your hand
> We just can't understand why You loved us so much.
> We are so blessed, we just can't find a way or the words that can say
> Thank You, Lord, for Your touch.
>
> CHORUS:
> When we're empty You fill us 'til we overflow
> When we're hungry You feed us, and cause us to know.
> We are so blessed, take what we have to bring,
> Take it all, everything, Lord, we love you so much.
>
> We are so blessed by the things You have done,
> The victories we've won and what You've brought us through.
> We are so blessed, take what we have to bring, Take it all everything,
> Lord, we bring it to You.[1]

It was a catchy song, and people enjoyed singing it, but I wonder how many people actually felt what they were singing? It is easier to see how God is blessing others than it is to recognize his blessing in our own lives. Perhaps it is because we don't expect that it will happen. Or we attribute good things to be the result of our own efforts.

Seek God's blessing this week. What will you be going through in the next few days? Ask God to intercede. Entreat him to show you his blessings. Make sure that you are looking so that you will see his hand, and not "luck."

Week 4: Parenting

Monday: Influence

Dogs have always been a part of my life. My parents adopted a dog before I was born, so living with a pet was the only thing I knew. Tippy was a mixed-breed dog, resembling a small terrier. I watched my parents interact with him and learned from their example how to care for a pet. When it was time to adopt a pet of my own I chose a small dog. Kim and I have had dogs throughout our entire marriage, and all of them were small-breed dogs.

Recently, I began to question the desire to have small dogs in my life. Why not big dogs? I have friends who only like large-breed dogs. Why not small ones? Curiosity caused me to ask friends on Facebook about their childhood pets and their current ones. What I discovered was very enlightening.

People who grew up with small dogs want small dogs as adults. Others had large dogs as children. Now as adults they prefer large-breed dogs. Joy wrote, "We had a dachshund. And it obviously influenced me: we have two of them now." Marilyn wrote, "Cocker Spaniels were my first dogs and I have one now. I love them!" Terry added, "American Eskimo—love 'em! Last three dogs have been Eskies." Over and over, people testified that the breed they grew up with was the breed they have now. Even those who have changed breeds have remained true to the size of dog that they had growing up.

The apostle Paul recognized the influence of family when he wrote to Timothy: "I thank God, whom I serve, as my ancestors did, with a clear conscience, as night and day I constantly remember you in my prayers. Recalling your tears, I long to see you, so that I may be filled with joy. I am reminded of your sincere faith, which first lived in your grandmother Lois and in your mother Eunice and, I am persuaded, now lives in you also" (2 Timothy 1:3–5).

So often we hear parents say, "I don't want to influence my children to believe in Jesus. I want them to grow up and make their own decision." What they don't realize is that by avoiding faith, they have already taken a stand. They are showing by their actions that faith is not important. When their children grow up, faith is not important to them either. The reality is, parents have influence whether they think about it or not. Small dogs are important to me because they were important to my parents. Jesus is important to me because the ones I trusted the most modeled faithfulness. So much of who we are is a reflection on the influence we received as very young children. Our beliefs are sometimes taught, but they are more often caught without our knowing that learning is taking place. Paul had faith because his ancestors had faith. Timothy had faith because his mother, Eunice, and his grandmother, Lois, were believers.

The size and breed of dogs we have is only an illustration of the influence that parents have on their children. We teach lessons by what we say, but we shape lives by the things we do. Failing to speak teaches a lesson. Saying the wrong thing leaves a lasting impression. Staying home from church, not reading your Bible, and not standing up for Jesus are all influencers that will shape the beliefs and actions of our children when they are grown. If our interests shape what size and breed of dog our children will desire as adults, just think about the powerful faith they will develop when our lives are centered in the love of Jesus Christ.

Here is your reality check: Everything you do and say is shaping your children. Every priority, every possession, and every loyalty in your life has an impact on what your children will become. If this is true, then we need to take the words of Joshua 24:15 seriously: "'If it is disagreeable in your sight to serve the Lord, choose for yourselves today whom you will serve: whether the gods which your fathers served which were beyond the River, or the gods of the Amorites in whose land you are living; but as for me and my house, we will serve the Lord.'"

Tuesday: They Start Out So Innocent

Pit bull puppies. You can't stop yourself from looking at them. Their unique shape and coloration identifies them immediately. Their breed name conjures up mental images and plays with your emotions. You may think, "Oh, they are so cute. I want one." Or you may say, "Great, another litter of menacing pit bulls to terrorize our society!" Polarizing ideas, all from the same picture.

Yet, there is something we have to understand about these little guys. They are born just like all other dogs. They are innocent and playful. They are sweet and loving. They are curious and energetic. There is so much they need to learn. Sure, like all dogs they have the capacity to turn out mean. But, they also have the capacity to turn out loving and gentle. The difference between the two is how we train them.

Think for a moment about mankind. God said, "Let Us make man in Our image, according to Our likeness; and let them rule over the fish of the sea and over the birds of the sky and over the cattle and over all the earth, and over every creeping thing that creeps on the earth. God created man in His own image, in the image of God He created him; male and female He created them" (Genesis 1:26–27). Like the litter of puppies, babies are a beautiful sight. We love to look at them, hold them, and kiss them. We love the way they smell, and we are in awe of the miracle of their birth. Perhaps the reason we are so impressed with babies is that they are sweet, innocent, and the most like God.

Romans 5 reminds us that we are born to die because of the sin of mankind. Though they all face the penalty, babies are still born innocent. Otherwise Jesus would not have "called a child to Himself and set him before them, and said, 'Truly I say to you, unless you are converted and become like children, you will not enter the kingdom of heaven. Whoever then humbles himself as this child, he is the greatest in the kingdom of heaven'" (Matthew 18:2–4). Jesus viewed us as innocent, playful, sweet, loving, curious, and energetic. So, how do some people end up so lost? The difference is in how we are trained.

The world is filled with sinners, some who have become very adept at finding new ways to defy God. It is hard to live in this world without being tainted by these things. Is it any wonder that Peter wrote, "like newborn babies, long for the pure milk of the word, so that by it you may grow in respect to salvation" (1 Peter 2:2). We need to seek Christ so that "the peace of God, which surpasses all comprehension, will guard [our] hearts and [our] minds in Christ Jesus" (Philippians 4:7). We have the capacity to grow into a life of holiness—or a life of depravity.

It all begins with parents. "Train up a child in the way he should go, even when he is old he will not depart from it" (Proverbs 22:6). Teach faith, love, and hope. Show your kids what loving Jesus looks like. Help them to apply the fruit of the spirit to their lives. You will be blessed by the result, and even if they stray for a time, they will never forget.

Wednesday: Be a Small "C"

A prominent commercial several years ago showed a man and his son in a park. Everything the father did, the son tried to emulate. The final scene showed the father lighting up a cigarette and laying the package on the ground. The boy watches his father and picks up the pack. The commercial is a vivid example of how our children watch our actions and follow our lead.

A puppy instinctively follows the example of its mother or father. Whatever one dog does, the puppy does also. Until the puppy is adopted into another family it lives as an example of what it learns from the older dog.

Jesus said, "Take My yoke upon you and learn from Me, for I am gentle and humble in heart, and you will find rest for your souls" (Matthew 11:29). As believers, we are to be yoked with Jesus. Sharing the yoke means that we do what Jesus does, and we go where Jesus leads. Then Jesus said to His disciples, "If anyone wishes to come after Me, he must deny himself, and take up his cross and follow Me" (Matthew 16:24). Not only are we to be yoked with Jesus, but also we are to follow his lead. Our lives must be a reflection of who Jesus is. His heart should be our heart. His love has to live through us into the lives of our children.

Peter reminded us, "For you have been called for this purpose, since Christ also suffered for you, leaving you an example for you to follow in

His steps" (1 Peter 2:21). Paul also wrote, "Therefore be imitators of God, as beloved children; and walk in love, just as Christ also loved you and gave Himself up for us, an offering and a sacrifice to God as a fragrant aroma" (Ephesians 5:1–2).

So, if Jesus asks us to be like him, then we need to take it seriously. We have been called to be small "c" Christ-representatives to this world. More than this, we have been called to show our children what being like Christ means. If we want them to grow up knowing and serving Jesus then they need to see what it looks like though our example. We cannot tell them unless we are willing to also show them what the Christian life is all about.

Our kids learn from us. They are growing up in our shadow. They will be a reflection of what we have taught them. We must make sure that we are showing them the right things.

Throughout this day, reflect on your actions and attitudes. Are they Christlike? Do they show your family what serving Jesus looks like? Would you be pleased if they did the same things and shared the same thoughts?

Thursday: Parents Are Teachers

Duncan is a very active dog. Being a Jack Russell terrier gives him the right to be active. He is very committed to his owner, Danica, and is attentive to her when she is home, but she is not home all of the time. Danica was concerned with him being alone while she was at work. Duncan had nothing to capture his attention. So Danica found Chloe a cute little puppy to be Duncan's "mini me."

The two dogs became instant friends. Yet, there was a difference in age, size, and ability between the two dogs. There were things Duncan could do that Chloe had no knowledge of yet. So Duncan set out to teach his new companion the ropes. They began slowly at first, but as Chloe caught on, Duncan was able to add new dimensions to the training. It was important that Duncan raised his new friend to be a true protégé, who reflected his personality and approach to life.

Proverbs 22:6 says, "Train up a child in the way he should go, even when he is old he will not depart from it." I had a conversation recently with a couple that decided not to take their children to church. "We believe in God, and we believe we are Christians, but we don't want to force religion onto our children. They should be able to make their own decision," they said. I tried to convince them that by doing nothing they were already making a decision for their child, who will grow up doing nothing as well. Our children grow to become a reflection of our behavior.

The Bible is very clear about the role of the parent: "These words, which I am commanding you today, shall be on your heart. You shall teach them diligently to your sons and shall talk of them when you sit in your house and when you walk by the way and when you lie down and when you rise up. You shall bind them as a sign on your hand and they shall be as frontals on your forehead" (Deuteronomy 6:6–8). We are to teach our children so diligently that our faith and beliefs are like a sign printed on our forehead.

We need to think hard about the things we do in front of them. "Only give heed to yourself and keep your soul diligently, so that you do not forget the things which your eyes have seen and they do not depart from your heart all the days of your life; but make them known to your sons and your grandsons" (Deuteronomy 4:9). Children say amazing things at the most inopportune time. I remember vividly the day I stood in a long line at a supermarket. In front of me was a mother whose three-year-old daughter was seated in the cart. As time went by, the child became more restless. Finally when she could stand no more, she shouted a series of swear words followed by a series of racial slurs. Everyone was shocked. The mother tried to pass it off saying she had no idea where the ideas came from. Yet, it was clear that the child was innocently voicing her mother's opinion. She was taught to swear, and her racial hatred was modeled for her.

Your children are a gift from God. It is your job to teach them and to raise them up to know Jesus. Help your children see the importance of knowing God and seeking God in everything. "You shall teach [these words of mine] to your sons, talking of them when you sit in your house and when you walk along the road and when you lie down and when you rise up" (Deuteronomy 11:19). When you fail to teach them, you may just be teaching them to fail.

A former student of mine confessed, "I am becoming my mom." Are your children becoming a younger version of you? Are you teaching them your habits and mistakes, or are you showing them the way to freedom and roadmaps around mistakes? Don't leave them to decide for themselves. They will have plenty of time to follow their own course. While you have them, teach them. Teach them gently at first and add new teaching as they grow. Consider what your child might say in a supermarket line. Would it bring you satisfaction or embarrassment? You are the key. "Come, you children, listen to me; I will teach you the fear of the Lord" (Psalm 34:11).

Friday: They Won't Forget

Basie is a fine specimen of an Australian terrier. He was the last of Jazzy's four puppies to be placed in a good home. In fact, Basie remained with us for sixteen months. The early months are very important in the life of a dog. During Basie's puppyhood, we worked with him to master the basics like housebreaking. We invested in Basie's discipline, spending time to help him learn commands, and sharpening his skills as an obedient dog.

Basie grew attached to us, but we knew that he would be a much happier dog as the only pet in a household. Bobbi and Don took him in and have provided a great home. From time to time they send anecdotal stories about Basie's experiences. Recently, Bobbi related that Basie enjoys watching television.

Our dogs have always known when another animal shows up on the television screen. They don't seem to pay any attention to the TV except for when an animal enters the picture. For a while, Jazzy loved watching a show about a family of meerkats. She would watch every episode from beginning to end. When they ran off of the screen, Jazzy would run around to the back of the TV to see where they went.

Basie apparently took his television watching to his new home. However, his focus has not necessarily been on other animals, but something else. For a long time, Bobbi watched as Basie reacted to different events that happened on the screen, and it recently began to make sense.

Basie keeps watch for a man who comes onto the television screen every now and then. The man has white hair, and a white beard on his chin. Every time Basie see's that person he gets all excited and rushes to the side of the screen. Why is that significant? I have white hair, and a white beard on my chin. Basie thinks that the man in the screen is his old master, who taught him what it meant to be a good dog. He also reacts to a woman who resembles my wife, Kim. Does he still remember us?

Studies have shown that animals have a good memory. One recent study has revealed that horses can remember voices and events as much as eight years after the event happened. They remember people, and react to them long after the people believe the event is no longer relevant.

The Bible says, "Train up a child in the way he should go, even when he is old he will not depart from it" (Proverbs 22:6). God makes it very clear that the early years of child development are very important. He wants us to make the investment to teach children how to be godly people. "You shall teach them diligently to your sons and shall talk of them when you sit in your house and when you walk by the way and when you lie down and when you rise up" (Deuteronomy 6:7).

Sure they grow up and leave us. They may struggle for a season but they definitely remember. Perhaps this is why Paul wrote, "Fathers, do not provoke your children to anger, but bring them up in the discipline and instruction of the Lord" (Ephesians 6:4).

Basie reminds us of how important it is to invest in young people, teaching them, and setting an example of Christlike behavior. The early years are so vital in building belief systems and establishing a foundation for future behavior. These are the lessons that are never forgotten. If you want to make a difference in this world, invest in kids. Teach them, love them, and show them how to be obedient to Christ. It is an investment that will provide rewards for an entire generation.

Saturday: "Parenting" Prayer Day

Praying Over Our Children

Children are a blessing, but some blessings require more effort on our part than others. Kids are that kind of blessing. We receive them and love them, but we dare not stop there. We have a lifetime of work ahead of us.

People often say, "My home is the one place where I can let down my guard and relax." Often the result is that our children see two different people, and sometimes three. They see the work-a-day person with one approach to life. Then, there is the church person who may look different from the mid-week person. Finally, there is the person we are when we think nobody is looking. The problem is, our kids are looking, and all too often they are confused by what they see in us.

Popeye was known for saying, "I am what I am, and that's all I am. I'm Popeye the sailor man." That was a fun cartoon, but the comment sounds strangely familiar. Maybe that is because God said it first. "I AM who I AM" (Exodus 3:14). God wants us to know that he is the same in every situation. There are no shadows, no changes, and no situational ethics with God. What you see is what you get.

While some may see this as limiting, God sees it a freeing. You are the same person in church and on the job as you are in your home. Your kids see a person of faith who models Christ even when hitting your thumb with the hammer. They see you praying your finances, tithing your firstfruits to the Lord, making biblical life decisions, reading your Bible, and discussing the Lord's will in your life.

This week you read, "You shall teach them [God's principles] to your sons, talking of them when you sit in your house and when you walk along the road and when you lie down and when you rise up" (Deuteronomy 11:19). This is God's call for you, this week, and on into the future. Take time today to pray over your children. Pray for their lives, decisions, and beliefs. Pray that God would use you to shape their lives. Look at their heart, and pray for their soul. Make the focus of this week a new direction in your lifestyle.

Week 5: Fellowship

Monday: Together

Our pack began with just one puppy. Jazzy, our black and tan Australian terrier, became a vital part of our lives She was loyal, playful, and fun to have around. As time went on, however, it became evident that she was not very happy while we were at work. She needed another dog around because she was lonely. So we went looking for another Aussie to add to the pack. We found Satchmo (the red one on the right), and the two became great companions.

We didn't start out to add a third dog. Jazzy and Satchmo did that without our help. In fact, they had a litter of four puppies. All of them went to good homes, but one, Major, ended up back in our pack. All three are great dogs, with fantastic personalities, but together they are a dynamic pack. They discipline each other, play together, provide companionship when we are not home, and keep each other warm at night.

As a dog becomes lonely all by itself in a back yard, so Christians become lonely without fellowship. Ecclesiastes says, "Furthermore, if two lie down together they keep warm, but how can one be warm alone? And if one can overpower him who is alone, two can resist him. A cord of three strands is not quickly torn apart" (Ecclesiastes 4:11–12). The easiest explanation of this passage is that there is strength in numbers. Proverbs adds, "Iron sharpens iron, so one man sharpens another" (Proverbs 27:17).

As I read through the book of Acts, I am struck by the fact that the early church was most successful when the believers worked together. In fact, the word "together" occurs thirty-five times in the New American Standard Version. If something is referred to once in the Bible, I take notice. Mention it twice and the concept becomes very important. But, thirty-seven times? There is no way to overlook what God wants from us. He wants us to be together, in fellowship, in worship, and in ministry.

Another consistent picture comes when we look at all of the "one another" passages. We are told to serve, have fellowship with, love, forgive, and stimulate one another to love and good deeds. We are warned not to forsake assembling together. All of these commands explain what the book of Acts meant by the word "together."

God knew from the very beginning that "it is not good for man to be alone" (Genesis 2:18). We need others around us. We need to be challenged, encouraged, and loved. We need to find our place in the Kingdom of God. Fulfillment comes as we help each other grow in our relationship with God. Conversely, our relationship with God grows as we help others to find fulfillment in Christ.

Let God sharpen you *together* with the body of Christ.

Tuesday: Comfort One Another

Life can be tough. The pressures of life can be overwhelming at times. The traps of sin are deceiving and the results can be tragic. According to a Duke University study, 25 percent of people feel lonely, having no one to discuss their problems with. Add the number of those who feel lonely a majority of the time, and the number grows to 29 percent. There are many reasons why a person might experience these feelings. These reasons range from genetic causes to social and relational causes.

Our three Australian terriers stay very close to each other. They are a pack, and they do everything together. When one is excited, they are all excited. When one acts inappropriately, the other two do the correcting. When one gives the impression of being discouraged, tired, or alone, the others gather around and provide comfort. The result is that we have three very healthy, balanced dogs.

David wrote, "Answer me, O Lord, for Your lovingkindness is good; According to the greatness of Your compassion, turn to me, And do not hide Your face from Your servant, For I am in distress; answer me quickly. Oh draw near to my soul and redeem it; Ransom me because of my enemies! You know my reproach and my shame and my dishonor; all my adversaries are before You. Reproach has broken my heart and I am so sick. And I looked for sympathy, but there was none, and for comforters, but I found none. They also gave me gall for my food And for my thirst they gave me vinegar to drink" (Psalm 69:16–21).

We crave to be comforted. We will suffer any number of physical pains if we feel emotionally comforted by others. This kind of relief does not come through social media, the television, or the mall. A person could be in the midst of thousands of people, yet still feel alone. So, where can we go to find comfort?

The apostle Paul wrote about a certain man who had caused some problems in church at Corinth. The result was that the church withdrew from that man. Paul wrote, "The punishment inflicted on him by the majority is sufficient. Now instead, you ought to forgive and comfort him, so that he will not be overwhelmed by excessive sorrow. I urge you, therefore, to reaffirm your love for him" (2 Corinthians 2:6–8, NIV). The church, as God's "pack," accomplished the task of discipline. The man, left alone, needed something different. He needed to be comforted and brought back into the pack. This is why Paul returned to his encouragement near the end of his letter: "Finally, brethren, rejoice, be made complete, be comforted, be like-minded, live in peace; and the God of love and peace will be with you" (2 Corinthians 13:11).

Are you feeling lonely, isolated, or discouraged? God wants something better for your life. He wants you to live in relationship with him. He also wants you to live in relationship with others, to find peace, friendship, and support. You need someone to nuzzle up to you, to weep with your weeping, and laugh with your laughter. Paul said that Titus was filled with joy "because his spirit has been refreshed by you all" (2 Corinthians 7:13).

You need God and you need others if you are going to live a happy life. Let God do his work in you through fellowship with his pack, the church. If you have felt isolated in the past, it is time to return. God desires it for you, and the church is ready to comfort you.

Wednesday: The Power of a Buddy

Lotus embraced the role of being Paul's buddy from the moment the infant came home from the hospital. If Paul is accessible, his dog is not far away. Lotus protects his human buddy, plays with him, and helps him learn new things. Sure, they are different, but that doesn't seem to matter. They both belong to Sarah and Daniel and are both a part of the same family, and with that comes a special bond. In his infancy, Paul was not able to do much so they would just stay close to each other. But, as Paul grew, they were able to do more and more things together, teaching each other new things, and sharing their toys in common. As Paul continues to grow, their roles will change, but they will still be there for each other. Theirs is a relationship that will last through all of life's changes.

The Scripture talks a lot about buddies as well—only the biblical word is "brothers." For example, "A man of too many friends comes to ruin, but there is a friend who sticks closer than a brother" (Proverbs 18:24). Jesus defined a brother by saying, "For whoever does the will of My Father who is in heaven, he is My brother and sister and mother" (Matthew 12:50).

Paul relied on his brothers for many things: "As to all my affairs, Tychicus, our beloved brother and faithful servant and fellow bond-servant in the Lord, will bring you information" (Colossians 4:7). His brothers helped him, spent time with him, and comforted him in times of need. "For I have come to have much joy and comfort in your love, because the hearts of the saints have been refreshed through you, brother" (Philemon 1:7).

As believers, we need relationships like this. Call them brother or sister, prayer partner, or accountability partner. Whatever name you decide to use, you need a buddy who will be there for you. A buddy will know you well and be able to do things in your life that others cannot do. "If your brother sins, go and show him his fault in private; if he listens to you, you have won your brother" (Matthew 18:15). We rarely accept correction from someone we barely know. But our closest friend can tell us the truth and lead us to a better path. Buddies understand and can identify with how you feel: "Rejoice with those who rejoice, and weep with those who weep. Be of the same mind toward one another" (Romans 12:15–16a).

Who fills this role for you? We are not supposed to walk this path of faith alone. We need each other. Sure, a buddy may be different from you, but because of the blood of Jesus, you are a part of the same family. And with this comes the beginning of a relationship. If you don't have a relationship with someone who will "stick closer than a brother," then find a Bible Study to join or get involved in a ministry where you can build relationships. Find your buddy so that you can help each other grow in the Lord. Then make this statement be your goal: "Yes, brother, let me benefit from you in the Lord; refresh my heart in Christ" (Philemon 1:20).

Thursday: Better When We're Together

Parties can be a great experience. A birthday cake may taste good, but it tastes great when others enjoy it with you. A party helps you remember that you are not alone, and that there are others like you out there.

When Kessie turned one, her master, Lisa, threw her a party at the dog park. Instead of serving human food, Lisa prepared lots of doggy treats. One of the favorites of the day were frozen treats that were prepared for each dog. They loved the treat, but the fact that they could enjoy it together made it that much better.

The psalmist understood the joy of doing things together when he wrote, "We who had sweet fellowship together walked in the house of God in the throng" (Psalm 55:14). The blessing of being with like-minded people in the house of God is very important to our happiness and spiritual growth. This is why Acts 2:42 reported that "they were continually devoting themselves to the apostles' teaching and to fellowship, to the breaking of bread and to prayer."

What are the benefits of spending time with the body of Christ? We are able to grow in the understanding of the apostles' teaching. We come to understand the importance of the Lord's Supper when we gather together. We come to know each other's prayer needs when we are together. 1 Corinthians 1:9 adds, "God is faithful, through whom you were called into fellowship with His Son, Jesus Christ our Lord."

The church is called to come together weekly to celebrate what God has done in us, through us, and for us. "Therefore if there is any encouragement in Christ, if there is any consolation of love, if there is any fellowship of the Spirit, if any affection and compassion, make my joy complete by being of the same mind, maintaining the same love, united in spirit, intent on one purpose. Do nothing from selfishness or empty conceit, but with humility of mind regard one another as more important than yourselves" (Philippians 2:1–3).

Faith is just better when we are together. Please get together with your local church this weekend.

Friday: Happy Feet

In 2006 Warner Brothers produced a movie about a young penguin who was different from all other penguins. He was different because he had happy feet. He tapped and danced his way into people's lives. Perhaps the title was wasted on an animated penguin because twelve paws, attached to three Mastiff puppies, are the epitome of happy feet.

Mastiff puppies are big, but their feet are huge. Coordination and gracefulness don't visit the Mastiff until they have a lot more experience at life. As puppies, however, they are just fun to watch. The way they run forces even the grumpiest person to smile. Happy feet. That's a name that fits.

My father was in the shoe business his entire life. He used to joke that people with big feet had a firm "under standing." I laughed every time he said it, if for no other reason than he was my dad. I worked my way through Christian college fitting shoes in my dad's stores. I have seen every kind of foot there is and I am fairly certain that the size of one's foot has nothing to do with a firm understanding.

The Bible, however, has something very important to say about feet. God cares about what we do with our feet. Proverbs 4:26 warns to "Watch the path of your feet and all your ways will be established."

There seems to be two kinds of feet. There are happy feet and unhappy feet. Unhappy feet follow the wrong path. "For their feet run to evil and they hasten to shed blood" (Proverbs 1:16). Unhappy feet are always in the dark. Feet that live in darkness are always bumping into painful things. Quite often the blood that is shed is their own as they run into one painful thing after another.

So how does God define happy feet? They are feet that walk in the light. King David said, "Your word is a lamp to my feet, and a light to my path" (Psalm 119:105). "But if we walk in the Light as He Himself is in the Light, we have fellowship with one another, and the blood of Jesus His Son cleanses us from all sin" (1 John 1:7). Happy feet live in the light and surround themselves with people of the light. They not only walk in the light, they show others the way to the light. Isaiah 52:7 says, "How lovely on the mountains are the feet of him who brings good news, who announces peace and brings good news of happiness, who announces salvation, and says to Zion, 'Your God reigns!'"

Sometimes we get so wrapped up in the big picture that we lose our way. We look at the things we cannot do and we draw back. We remember the times that we slipped and fell, and are apprehensive to get up and try again. We consider the business of our lives and think that we could not possibly do anything else, and pass over opportunities that God places before us. With all that we face, how do we develop happy feet? Proverbs 4:26 answers the question very simply: "Watch the path of your feet and all your ways will be established."

Happy feet can be large or small. They can be young or old. They can have bunions, bumps and bruises and still be happy feet. They may bear the scars of broken toes from years of walking in darkness and still enjoy the fruit of happiness. If we use our feet to walk in the footsteps of Jesus then our feet can be happy feet. Like David we can say, "My steps have held fast to your paths. My feet have not slipped" (Psalm 17:5).

What do your feet and the path that you walk say about you?

Saturday: "Fellowship" Prayer Day

We sometimes hear the phrase, "No man is an island." John Donne wrote that in the poem by the same name. We understand the point, but we live quite often as though Donne was wrong. I hear people I speak with say, "I don't know how to get involved in church. It is difficult to get plugged in. I don't know anybody, so I just go to church and then go home." This sounds so much like it is the church's fault. Yet, when we give them options for small groups or involvement in ministry they say, "I just don't have time for that."

Are you living on a spiritual island? Is it possible that very few know you at church because you don't really want to let them in? You are living the island life. Jesus reduced the entire law of God to two commands: "You shall love the lord your God with all your heart, and with all your soul, and with all your strength, and with all your mind; and your neighbor as yourself" (Luke 10:27).

The people down the street are your neighbors. The people you shop with are your neighbors. The people in the pew behind you are your neighbors. The people who believe differently than you are also your neighbors. Jesus wants us to love them all, and that means being open to them.

We need fellowship! It is that simple. Spend some time today praying over the people you know and the church where you attend. How does God want to include you in the fellowship of the body, your neighborhood, and your community? Pray, formulate a plan, and begin to carry it out today. If God wants something different, he will close the doors, but in the meantime, you are doing something.

Week 6: Following Jesus

Monday: A Special Invitation

Laredo has been Renee's companion, friend, and protector for most of his eight years of life. Renee adopted Laredo, a yellow Labrador retriever, as a puppy. He went through college with her. He moved wherever she moved and adapted to whatever circumstances that Renee found herself in. He was there when she began her career in the almond industry. He provided love and strength during the long hours of harvest. He remained vigilant during her absence, longing for her return at the end of the day. When Renee met Wade, Laredo adapted yet again, accepting Wade as a member of the pack. Through all circumstances, Laredo remained faithful to his master, ready and willing to perform any duty that was given to him.

Because Laredo was such a loving companion, Renee knew that he had to be a part of the most important event of her life. While most wedding parties have a maid of honor, and a best man, Renee decided to create a new position for Laredo. He became "best dog." Laredo helped Doug walk Renee down the aisle. When asked, "Who brings this bride to marry this man?" Laredo let out a joyful bark. Then he sat quietly as Wade and Renee exchanged vows, and he accepted his new role as the follower of two masters.

If Laredo had been just an average dog, he would not have been invited to the wedding. He was there because of his amazing faithfulness and his eagerness to adapt to any circumstance that Renee placed him in. He was a part of the wedding because of his unending love and loyalty to his master. He was "best dog" because he willingly assumed any role he was given as long as that role supported his master.

Jesus spoke very clearly in Matthew 25:1–13 about a wedding feast. He identified you and me as his bride. "Then the kingdom of heaven will be comparable to ten virgins, who took their lamps and went out to meet the bridegroom" (v. 1). We have the invitation to be the bride of Christ. But, the story does not stop there. Jesus revealed that some of the virgins were prepared and others were not. Some accepted their role and the rest gave it no thought. When it finally became clear that they were unprepared, they tried to borrow from the successes of those who were prepared. When their lamps went out and while they were away trying to purchase more oil the bridegroom came. "Later the other virgins also came, saying, 'Lord, lord, open up for us.' But he answered, 'Truly I say to you, I do not know you'" (vv. 11–12).

We are not called to be casual followers of Jesus Christ. Instead we are to be vigilant, ready to serve in whatever circumstance Jesus leads us to. We are to eagerly serve and faithfully represent the master of our souls. We need to be prepared, as Jesus said at the end of the bridegroom parable: "Be on the alert then, for you do not know the day nor the hour" (v. 13).

Serving Jesus does not mean running your lamp on empty. We have the Word of God, and the body of Christ to keep us full. We have the Holy Spirit to enable our ministries. We have been given the tools to be faithful. Like Laredo, we serve the Lord with the desire to hear the words of Matthew 25:23 spoken to us: "His master said to him, 'Well done, good and faithful slave. You were faithful with a few things, I will put you in charge of many things; enter into the joy of your master.'"

Take a moment to inventory your spiritual life. If the bridegroom came today, would you be invited to walk down the aisle, standing in your appointed spot next to Jesus? Or would you be left behind, like the rest, in the lonely confincs of an empty backyard?

Tuesday: God's Tea Party

It is impossible to look at this picture without smiling. In the photo, taken in 1880, are three Australian terriers having a tea party. At a time, when people took pictures with somber faces, someone thought to set up a photo that shows off the personality of their Aussies.

This week, our younger daughter and family came for a visit. Grandma was excited to spend time with her two youngest grandchildren. We had a lot of exciting events planned, but none of those things could happen until she took part in their plans. Within an hour of their arrival, Grandma and the two grandkids were having one of their traditional tea parties. Whether pretend, or using cookies and water, the tea party has been an important part of their relationship. It is a tradition that has been worth keeping.

Paul wrote, "Now I praise you because you remember me in everything and hold firmly to the traditions, just as I delivered them to you" (1 Corinthians 11:2). He made the same point to Timothy when he wrote, "Retain the standard of sound words which you have heard from me, in the faith and love which are in Christ Jesus" (2 Timothy 1:13).

Holding to tradition is very important in our relationship with Jesus. But we need to distinguish between biblical tradition and man's tradition. We know this to be true because of a conversation that Jesus had in Matthew 15: "Then some Pharisees and scribes came to Jesus from Jerusalem and said, 'Why do Your disciples break the tradition of the elders? For they do not wash their hands when they eat bread.' And He answered and said to them, 'Why do you yourselves transgress the commandment of God for the sake of your tradition?'" (Matthew 15:1–3).

The traditions they wanted to hold to were the traditions they designed for themselves. Well- meaning as they may have been, Jesus let them know they were holding on to the wrong things. In fact, Paul was very forceful on the subject in his letter to Timothy: "If anyone advocates a different doctrine and does not agree with sound words, those of our Lord Jesus Christ, and with the doctrine conforming to godliness, he is conceited and understands nothing; but he has a morbid interest in controversial questions and disputes about words, out of which arise envy, strife, abusive language, evil suspicions" (1 Timothy 6:3–4).

There are practices we may enjoy, but are they biblical, or just our preferences? There are traditions we hold to, but did Jesus prescribe them? We may want to reach out for the newest activities, but what Jesus may want is for us to long for his tea party. "In pointing out these things to the brethren, you will be a good servant of Christ Jesus, constantly nourished on the words of the faith and of the sound doctrine which you have been following" (1 Timothy 4:6).

"It was for this He called you through our gospel, that you may gain the glory of our Lord Jesus Christ. So then, brethren, stand firm and hold to the traditions which you were taught, whether by word of mouth or by letter from us" (2 Thessalonians 4:14–15).

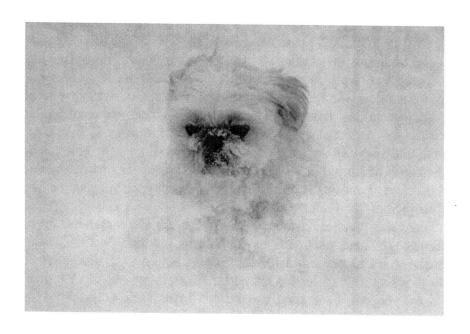

Wednesday: Never Too Dirty for God

Look hard. The rest of Dodger's body is there somewhere in and around the snow. During other seasons, Dodger has the ability to get muddy, track in dirt, and require a lot of grooming. But during the winter, when he enters the house he is white with snow. The picture reminds me of King David in Psalm 51. The king had been through a difficult season of his own. He had tracked in the mud of his sin with Bathsheba, and he was feeling very dirty. When Nathan pointed out his sin, David was cut to the heart. He needed a new season in his life. He needed restoration. So, David removed himself to pray: "Purify me with hyssop, and I shall be clean; Wash me, and I shall be whiter than snow. Make me to hear joy and gladness, Let the bones which You have broken rejoice. Hide Your face from my sins and blot out all my iniquities. Create in me a clean heart, O God, and renew a steadfast spirit within me. Do not cast me away from Your presence and do not take Your Holy Spirit from me. Restore to me the joy of Your salvation and sustain me with a willing spirit. Then I will teach transgressors Your ways, and sinners will be converted to You" (Psalm 51:7–13).

It is hard to fathom what it means to be whiter than snow until you find yourself in the middle of a snow pack. Everything is white. The trees bow low with the covering of snow. Impurities of the land disappear, and the noise of life is muffled by the sweet silence that comes with a fresh blanket of white. If the sun manages to emerge, everything glistens with the radiant glow. What God did for David, he can do for you.

You are not so dirty that the blood of Jesus cannot make you whole again. There is no sin that cannot be made clean when you fall on your face and seek God's forgiveness. Is it any wonder that God spoke through Isaiah, saying, "'Come now, and let us reason together,' says the Lord, 'though your sins are as scarlet, they will be as white as snow; though they are red like crimson, they will be like wool'" (Isaiah 1:18). Have you fallen victim to the lie that you are too far gone to be forgiven? Don't believe it. God wants to reason with you today, and make you whiter than snow. The next move is yours.

Thursday: Jesus, Take the Wheel

Samson is generally a compliant poodle. When at home with his owners, Brad and Debbie, he listens and follows their commands. He is fine in the yard, and he is great on a leash. But get him in the open, and he fights the call to become a different dog.

Recently, Samson accompanied the family on vacation. They went to a lake to enjoy the water and spend time motoring around in a boat. Sampson could see a whole host of things he had never experienced. He wanted to take control and go. Though his master was at the wheel, Samson wanted to guide his own course.

This picture draws my attention back to Samson of the Bible. We read of his birth in Judges 13:24: "Then the woman gave birth to a son and named him Samson; and the child grew up and the Lord blessed him." From the very beginning, Samson was blessed. What a wonderful concept, to know that you are blessed from the beginning. Yet, it didn't take long for Samson to alter his course.

In the very next chapter, we read, "Then Samson went down to Timnah and saw a woman in Timnah, one of the daughters of the Philistines. So he came back and told his father and mother, 'I saw a woman in Timnah, one of the daughters of the Philistines; now therefore, get her for me as a wife.'

Then his father and his mother said to him, 'Is there no woman among the daughters of your relatives, or among all our people, that you go to take a wife from the uncircumcised Philistines?' But Samson said to his father, 'Get her for me, for she looks good to me.'"

There is an interesting difference between dogs and humans. Dogs are run first by their nose. The power of scent is very strong, and it is their primary sense at birth. After a while their eyes open, and they are able to look around. Lastly, the ears open and begin to work. It should be no surprise that we have a difficult time getting our dogs to hear us, since we are appealing to the least dominant of the three senses. For a human, however, the eyes are the most dominant sense. Notice what Samson said, when he got out in the open. He said, "I saw a woman," and, "she looks good to me." This is not the only time that Samson suffered from wandering eyes. He visited a prostitute for the same reason. In the end, it was his eyes coupled with his pride that led to his downfall. Fortunately, he recognized his failure, and died with God's power, but how much more could have been done to the glory of God if he had let his master run his life.

Isn't it amazing how fast we can let our eyes wander and end up steering a course away from God's will for our lives? The temptation may be different, but the results can be just as tragic. Where have you pulled a Samson, and taken the wheel from your master? Yet, which would you rather have: the knowledge that the Lord has blessed you, or the realization that you have taken the wheel and charted your own course to destruction?

Perhaps Carrie Underwood's powerful song "Jesus Take the Wheel" needs to become our prayer.

> Jesus, take the wheel
> Take it from my hands
> 'Cause I can't do this on my own.
> I'm letting go
> So give me one more chance
> To save me from this road I'm on.[2]

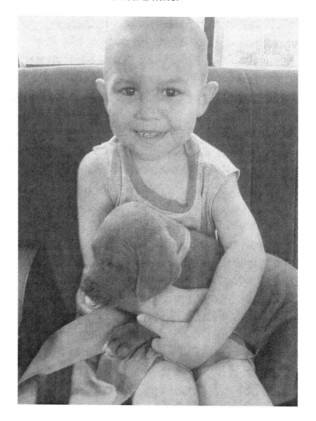

Friday: In His Arms

He has his mother's eyes. The evidence of joy on his face takes me back to a young eighth grader named Yesenia who shared that same joyful expression. When I see Andrew, I remember his mother, a former student and now a friend. If you know Yesenia, you understand what I am saying. If not, then look at the picture of Andrew and you will see what his mother is like.

Recently, Yesenia announced that she and Andrew needed to run some errands, Andrew decided that his puppy, Blue, needed to go along. As they drove down the street, Andrew said, "Mommy, take a picture." Yesenia grabbed her phone, pointed it over her shoulder and complied with her son's request. What she captured was this image of a happy little boy, loving and caring for his puppy.

I am reminded of the words of Jesus about his Father: "If you had known Me, you would have known My Father also; from now on you know Him, and have seen Him" (John 14:7). "I and the Father are one" (John 10:30). You see, we have the ability to look at Jesus, to throw ourselves into his lap and to find rest in his presence. By knowing Jesus, we come to know the Father. David understood this concept. He wrote, "I've thrown myself headlong into your arms— I'm celebrating your rescue. I'm singing at the top of my lungs, I'm so full of answered prayers" (Psalm 13:5, *The Message*).

Where can joy be found? Where do we go to find answers to prayer? What kind of faith would cause us to sing at the top of our lungs? The answer to all three questions is the same, since it is all found in the arms of Jesus. David continued, "We pondered your love-in-action, God, waiting in your temple: Your name, God, evokes a train of Hallelujahs wherever it is spoken, near and far; your arms are heaped with goodness-in-action" (Psalm 48:9, *The Message*).

When challenged about his relationship with Jehovah, David wrote, "'I've already run for dear life straight to the arms of God. So why would I run away now when you say, "Run to the mountains; the evil bows are bent, the wicked arrows aimed to shoot under cover of darkness at every heart open to God. The bottom's dropped out of the country; good people don't have a chance'?" Psalm 11:1–3, *The Message*). The fact is that there is no safer place than in the mighty arms of God.

The photograph caught a glimpse of a happy boy loving his puppy. The picture is only a moment in time. Yet, when we place our trust in Jesus, resting in his arms, we come to know the Father in a whole new way. That is a picture which never changes. Jesus said, "All things have been committed to me by my Father. No one knows the Son except the Father, and no one knows the Father except the Son and those to whom the Son chooses to reveal him. Come to me, all you who are weary and burdened, and I will give you rest. Take my yoke upon you and learn from me, for I am gentle and humble in heart, and you will find rest for your souls" (Matthew 11:27–29, NIV).

Before moving on, pray through Psalm 91, as interpreted in *The Message*:

> You who sit down in the High God's presence, spend the night in Shaddai's shadow, Say this: "God, you're my refuge. I trust in you and I'm safe!" That's right—he rescues you from hidden traps, shields you from deadly hazards. His huge outstretched arms protect you—under them you're perfectly safe; his arms fend off all harm. Fear nothing—not wild wolves in the night, not flying arrows in the day, not disease that prowls through the darkness, not disaster that erupts at high noon. Even though others succumb all around, drop like flies right and left, no harm will even graze you. You'll stand untouched, watch it all from a distance, watch the wicked turn into corpses. Yes, because God's your refuge, the High God your very own home, evil can't get close to you, harm can't get through

the door. He ordered his angels to guard you wherever you go. If you stumble, they'll catch you; their job is to keep you from falling. You'll walk unharmed among lions and snakes, and kick young lions and serpents from the path.

Psalm 91:1–13, The Message

Saturday: "Following Jesus" Prayer Day

Many worship services today use the Chris Tomlin song, "I will follow." Read through the words, and if you know the melody, sing it as a prayer to God.

I Will Follow

Where you go, I'll go
Where you stay, I'll stay
When you move, I'll move
I will follow

All your ways are good
All your ways are sure
I will trust in you alone
Higher than my side
High above my life
I will trust in you alone

Where you go, I'll go
Where you stay, I'll stay
When you move, I'll move
I will follow you
Who you love, I'll love
How you serve I'll serve
If this life I lose, I will follow you
I will follow you

Light unto the world
Light unto my life
I will live for you alone
You're the one I seek
Knowing I will find
All I need in you alone, in you alone

In you there's life everlasting
In you there's freedom for my soul
In you there's joy, unending joy
and I will follow

Week 7: The Church

Monday: No Distinctions

Bret and Molly live with my friend Velma in Montana. When I saw this picture of the dogs peering out of the back of Velma's SUV, I was struck by the relationship between the two dogs. Their size and breed are different. It is obvious that coloring is different, hair is different length, and they have different skill sets. With all of those differences they are still buddies, and the differences are not important to them. What is important to them is that they are both dogs and they both belong to Velma. From my earliest memory of Sunday school and children's church, I remember singing, "Jesus loves the little children, all the children of the world. Red and yellow, black and white, they are precious in His sight. Jesus loves the little children of the world." The idea that God's love spanned all colors, sizes, and cultures was ingrained in my belief system.

Yet, when I looked around the church, everyone seemed to look alike. Today's church, however, has done a much better job of mirroring the spiritual culture in which God created the church. Romans 2:11 gives a clear prescription God's design for the church: "For there is no partiality with God." Galatians 3:27–29 says, "For all of you who were baptized into Christ have clothed yourselves with Christ. There is neither Jew nor Greek, there is neither slave nor free man, there is neither male nor female; for you are all one in Christ Jesus. And if you belong to Christ, then you are Abraham's descendants, heirs according to promise."

We have experienced the words of Colossians 3:11: "a renewal in which there is no distinction between Greek and Jew, circumcised and uncircumcised, barbarian, Scythian, slave and freeman, but Christ is all, and in all." We can have this kind of fellowship because we are all humans "made in His image," and we all belong to God. "But now in Christ Jesus you who formerly were far off have been brought near by the blood of Christ. For He Himself is our peace, who made both groups into one and broke down the barrier of the dividing wall, by abolishing in His flesh the enmity, which is the Law of commandments contained in ordinances, so that in Himself He might make the two into one new man, thus establishing peace" (Ephesians 2:13–15).

The Scripture is very clear. Worship has no nationality, culture, gender, or class. We are simply God's people expressing our love for what He has done for us, in us, and through us. We live in exciting times because "there is no distinction between Jew and Greek; for the same Lord is Lord of all, abounding in riches for all who call on Him" (Romans 10:12).

Tuesday: Different, Yet the Same

Minnie and Daisy were sisters, born in a litter of four puppies. I brought them both home with the idea of introducing them to the family. I figured that if everybody had a vote we could select the right one to join our family. However, the family was divided as to which puppy fit best with the family. Unable to decide, both dogs remained in our home.

After several years of life, Minnie developed cancer and could not be saved. Daisy was left alone for the first time in her life. The two dogs had never been apart. They played together, fought with each other over trivial things, kept each other company during the day, and kept each other warm at night. One did not move without the other responding. But all of that was gone when Minnie died. Daisy was left to figure out what the next stage of her life would be like.

Within the same time frame, our next-door neighbor passed away. Scamper, one of his four cats found himself outside and unwanted. Very soon, Scamper adopted me. He was at the door in the morning waiting for a welcome scratch, and he was back on the porch waiting for me to come home. As he heard the car come around the corner, he would run out into the street, and slowly lead me into the driveway. Then, of course, I would have to spend a few minutes with him before I could go inside.

These two animals, which before this time did not see eye-to-eye, found comfort in becoming friends. They moved cautiously at first, but soon became good friends. Their differences no longer mattered and the past was forgotten. Scamper and Daisy shared their days and nights happily for several years. When they stopped looking at their differences, they discovered that meeting common needs far outweighed the struggles.

One Sunday morning I was looking out over the congregation as they worshipped. Things seemed normal, except for one incredible exception. Near the back was a homeless man with ragged clothes. He lived under a nearby underpass. I knew him well. Next to him sat a county sheriff's deputy. They were sharing a book together, singing praises to the Lord, and enjoying one another's company.

Outside of the church building, the deputy may have needed to deal harshly with my homeless friend. But inside of the church, they were brothers in Christ. It reminded me of the equality that is shared through Christ Jesus: "There is neither Jew nor Greek, there is neither slave nor free man, there is neither male nor female; for you are all one in Christ Jesus" (Galatians 3:28). Romans confirmed this idea by saying that equality is for, "all those who believe; for there is no distinction" (Romans 3:22).

We all struggle with needs, losses, and moments of crisis. When those times arrive, we need fellowship and the support of friends who will support us. The good news is that we can always turn to the church. It is the one place where the cats and dogs, homeless and sheriff, men and women, and every culture under the sun can find equal acceptance. "Every item of your new way of life is custom-made by the Creator, with his label on it. All the old fashions are now obsolete. Words like Jewish and non-Jewish, religious and irreligious, insider and outsider, uncivilized and uncouth, slave and free, mean nothing. From now on everyone is defined by Christ, everyone is included in Christ" (Colossians 3:10–11, *The Message*).

It is easy to focus all of the problems in the world. People have differences, and at times they can seem insurmountable. But God created all of us. He wants to bless us. He wants us to learn from each other, to enhance each other's lives, to look past the differences and discover that we are not alone.

Wednesday: The Power of Friendship

"Spencer was a great dog. He died way too soon." This tribute was given by my friend Mike who, along with his wife Judy, owned Spencer. They recognized, however, that Spencer was really the neighborhood's dog. Spencer was close to several of his neighbors and, contrary to normal opinions, the neighbors loved it when Spencer spent time in their yard. Spencer was a great dog, and everyone who knew him loved him.

One day, Mike went out to find Spencer, but the dog was nowhere in sight. The only thing out of place in the neighborhood was a UPS truck parked on the street. As Mike approached the truck, he found the driver sitting on the floor of his truck eating his lunch. Lying next to the driver was Spencer, enjoying a snack of his own. As it turned out, the driver had come to know Spencer very well. Each day, the driver would look at his itinerary. If his deliveries brought him anywhere near Spencer's neighborhood, he would bring a second sandwich with him. The second sandwich was for Spencer. Sharing his lunch with Spencer was a tradition that he had carried on for a long time. When he drove into the neighborhood, Spencer, who recognized the sound of his truck, would run over and climb into the truck to visit his lunch buddy.

Do people go out of their way to see you? That may be a difficult question to answer honestly. Yet, the fact remains that you may be the only gospel that your friends and neighbors will ever see. This is why Jesus called us "the salt of the earth." In Matthew 5 Jesus said, "You are the salt of the earth; but if the salt has become tasteless, how can it be made salty again? It is no longer good for anything, except to be thrown out and trampled under foot by men" (v. 13).

The warning of Jesus is that we guard ourselves to ensure that we do not become tasteless or unsalty. Why would he urge us to be salt? Salt makes people thirsty. As a result they seek out something to quench that thirst. We are called to be salt so that people around us will want what we have to quench their spiritual thirst. That is why Jesus added this statement found in Mark's gospel: "Salt is good; but if the salt becomes unsalty, with what will you make it salty again? Have salt in yourselves, and be at peace with one another" (Mark 9:50).

Spencer was just a dog, but his personality and temperament were such that people wanted to be around him. Neighbors sought him out. The UPS man planned his schedule around being able to spend time with Spencer. If we are truly salty as Jesus commands, then we will be at peace with others and they will want to go out of their way to spend time with us.

Using another word picture Jesus said, "You are the light of the world. A city set on a hill cannot be hidden; nor does anyone light a lamp and put it under a basket, but on the lamp stand, and it gives light to all who are in the house. Let your light shine before men in such a way that they may see your good works, and glorify your Father who is in heaven" (Matthew 5:13–16).

Whether it is salt or light, the command is the same: Represent Christ. Be the kind of person who others want to be friends with. Invest some of your precious time in others. For them to want to be your friend you must be available and accessible. For them to want to remain your friend you must exhibit the principles described in Galatians 5:16–23. I want to encourage you to look up this text and pray through these verses. Become salt. Make someone you know thirsty.

Thursday: Forgiveness

Being the pack leader of a multiple-dog household, I am struck by a quality found in dogs that is not always found in humans. It is the quality that allows a pack to remain a pack while operating as a team. It is the quality that allows dogs within the pack to forgive, forget, and move on. We call it living in the moment.

One evening, our dogs were given a treat to chew on. Each one grabbed its treat and headed to a corner to enjoy the reward for being good. Our dogs eat at different speeds. Jazzy is always done first. Satchmo finishes second after Jazzy, and Major is always last.

When one of the dogs finishes its own treat, it invariably tries to appropriate the unfinished portion of one of the other dogs. This is usually met by a warning growl. If the growl is unheeded, an angry bark follows, and possibly a warning bite to show that it means business. Strangers might think that our dogs don't get along. Yet, nothing could be further from the truth. They can get frustrated with each other one minute, and be perfectly happy with each other the next. They can growl, and then lie next to each other content to keep each other company.

Since dogs live in the moment, they have no interest in hanging onto old bitterness. Hanging onto anger is not a part of who they are. Holding grudges makes no sense to them. Once the disagreement is finished, they move on. God is this way. Micah asked, "Who is a God like You, who pardons iniquity and passes over the rebellious act of the remnant of His possession? He does not retain His anger forever, because He delights in unchanging love" (Micah 7:18). Several times in the Scripture God reminds us, "I will remember their sins no more."

The ability to forgive and move on is a mark of an obedient Christian. "Be kind to one another, tender-hearted, forgiving each other, just as God in Christ also has forgiven you" (Ephesians 4:32). This means that we are called to forgive others in the same way God has forgiven us. Forgive, forget, and move on.

People are going to rub each other the wrong way. We will disagree on things we feel are important. Others will invade our space and try to steal our happiness. All people have the ability to get frustrated, even angry, with others around them. What do we do with that anger? God forgives and moves on, then calls us to do the same. He expects us to do this with people inside the church, with those we work with, our family, and the people down the block. In fact, the call to forgive, forget, and move on is extended to everyone. "If possible, so far as it depends on you, be at peace with all men" (Romans 12:18).

Do you live in the moment, or chain yourself to the past? Do you hold grudges and keep lists of wrongs, or can you forgive, forget, and move on. A balanced dog can lie down and fall asleep anywhere. Do you stay awake at night tossing and turning because you can't get over your anxiety? Ask God to give you a heart of compassion. Seek to live in the moment, finding the best in others, while living at peace with those around you.

"Finally, brethren, rejoice, be made complete, be comforted, be like-minded, live in peace; and the God of love and peace will be with you" (2 Corinthians 13:11).

Friday: Value Differences

Shimmy is learning to be a guide dog. A few weeks ago he was posted in a photo riding on his master's scooter. Being a service dog is such an honor. Very few dogs could qualify to be a service dog. He picks up things from the floor if his master drops them. He can turn on lights and open and close the doors in their house. He is learning very quickly, but there are so many things that he still cannot do.

When Shimmy first began his training, he became part of a team. He was placed with two giant poodles. He was young and had no experience, while they were older and very capable. His enthusiasm toward his new job forced him into a power struggle with the whole family. When there was a need, Shimmy wanted to be the one to take care of it. He resented the older dogs and even lashed out at one of them.

As time went on, however, Shimmy came to trust the other two service dogs. He watched their actions and learned from their experience. They were not his competition but his partners in service to their master. Each of them had different rolls based on experience, size and abilities. When they stopped competing with each other and started working together, they became a powerful team.

The church is filled with people of different ages, experiences, and abilities. It would be easy to view ministry as a competition, wanting to be the one who stands out. Yet, we are not merely individuals, but a part of a team. "In his grace, God has given us different gifts for doing certain things well. So if God has given you the ability to prophesy, speak out with as much faith as God has given you. If your gift is serving others, serve them well. If you are a teacher, teach well. If your gift is to encourage others, be encouraging. If it is giving, give generously. If God has given you leadership ability, take the responsibility seriously. And if you have a gift for showing kindness to others, do it gladly" (Romans 12:6-8, NLT).

> Yes, the body has many different parts, not just one part. If the foot says, "I am not a part of the body because I am not a hand," that does not make it any less a part of the body. And if the ear says, "I am not part of the body because I am not an eye," would that make it any less a part of the body? If the whole body were an eye, how would you hear? Or if your whole body were an ear, how would you smell anything? But our bodies have many parts, and God has put each part just where he wants it. How strange a body would be if it had only one part! Yes, there are many parts, but only one body. The eye can never say to the hand, "I don't need you." The head can't say to the feet, "I don't need you."
> 1 Corinthians 12:14–21, NLT

There is no need for competition within the body of Christ. Churches with different names are not competing. Members of a local church do not need to challenge each other for dominance. We are all on the same side. Whether it is in the same church or between churches, Christians are providing service for the same Master. It is not about us. It is about Him. When we commit to being a part of a team, begin celebrating each other's abilities, and start valuing differences, then we will truly make an impact on our world. Sure we are different, but God made us that way. "All of you together are Christ's body, and each of you is a part of it" (1 Corinthians 12:27, NLT).

Saturday: "Church" Prayer Day

Prayer for the Unity of God's Church

Throughout history the church has gone through many transitions. Political unrest and war have created changes within the church. Social changes have had a big impact. With each generation comes change as they move into leadership. Yet the message remains the same.

When the church began at Pentecost, many struggled through persecution. Slaves and free people began to worship next to each other. Women were included in worship as Christ gave them new status. Talk about change!

In early America, the church was the moral compass of the community, guiding in ways no other institution could. There were times when the church reflected social norms instead of setting them. During those times, the church suffered greatly, but that does not seem to be the case today.

In today's worship, you will find different ages, life circumstances, opinions, races, and home languages. I was touched by the worship of an elderly woman not long ago. The service was loud, the lights were flashing, and the music was rocking. It was hardly the church that this woman was used too. But she was singing at the top of her lungs, praising Jesus and swaying to the music. She was committed to valuing worship instead of criticizing it. She was embracing differences instead of questioning them. She was reaching out to those who were much different than her, and she loved it!

Galatians 3:28 says, "There is neither Jew nor Greek, there is neither slave nor free man, there is neither male nor female; for you are all one in Christ Jesus." Make it your prayer today that you will reach out to someone who is different than you. Learn from them, and teach them. Discover who they are, and broaden your perspective. God will bless you through it.

Week 8: Using Our Gifts

Monday: Gifts and Talents

One night, Jazzy heard a noise in the back yard and tore through the doggie door out into the cool night air. We had no idea what she heard or how she may have noticed anything with all of the commotion that was going on inside of the house. Satchmo and Major were asleep on the floor, and hardly noticed when Jazzy leapt to her feet and went outside. About fifteen minutes later, she returned. It took a minute for us to realize that she had brought something into the house with her. When I looked at my feet, I realized that had Jazzy killed a large rodent, brought it into the house, and laid it at my feet.

Our first reaction was to scold her for bringing something like that into the house. But shock quickly turned to rejoicing. Jazzy was bred to take care of rodents and animals that live under the ground. It is instinctual for her to do that job. She was merely doing what she was supposed to do. How could we complain about that? So we began to praise her for a job well done. We made a big deal about her accomplishment, and Jazzy enjoyed every minute of the praise she received. Kim offered Jazzy a doggie treat from the cupboard as a prize, while I disposed of the rodent.

Not wanting to be outdone, Major (who was not yet two years old) decided to go on a hunt, too. He ran into the backyard looking for something he could catch and bring back into the house. Within minutes, he bounded back through the doggie door carrying a large stick, which he happily dropped in the same location where Jazzy had placed the rodent. After we stopped laughing, we praised Major for the attempt and tossed the stick back outside.

The Bible says that each of us has been given specific gifts and talents. We are called to put them to use in works of service in building up the body of Christ. Doing what we are supposed to do brings glory to God when we lay the fruit of our efforts at his feet. You may sense a need that nobody else notices but if that is what God calls you to do, he will surely bless your efforts. Paul urged Timothy to "be sober in all things, endure hardship, do the work of an evangelist, fulfill your ministry" (2 Timothy 4:5). We could insert any other gift into this sentence and it would still apply. Do the work of an encourager, exhorter, or teacher. Pray for people, perform acts of service, or give as unto the Lord. Do God's work among the lost and the brokenhearted. Teach the children, care for the needy, and support those who are weak. Whatever your ministry might be, do it well, be sober, and endure hardship. Just remember, when all of us exercise our gifts, there is no telling what kind of people will be brought into the church.

But know this: when it happens, we will finally be fulfilling the words of Jesus who urged us to go out into the highways and byways and compel them to come in.

Tuesday: Gifts

What would it be like if dogs looked at each other with the same critical eye that we humans do?

"Look at those floppy ears—can you imagine?"
"Her legs are too short, and her body is way too long."
"That dog is huge, why isn't he on a diet?"
"Wow, that one is really cute."
"I'd like to be him."
"I would be more popular if I could be a friend of hers."

If dogs judged each other based on their looks, they might become critical or envious. They might be tempted to resent their own gifts, and long for the gifts other dogs have.

Dogs, like people, are very different. They are bred for specific purposes. Rawley is a basset hound. He is a beautiful specimen with short legs, long ears, and a nose that can pick up any scent. He doesn't look like other dogs but he is not supposed to look like them. He has a different gift than dogs bred to swim in the cold water, or dogs that run like the wind. By embracing his nose, ears, and body shape, he becomes the best that he can be.

The Bible tells us that God has made us in his own image. And he has gifted us for his purposes. Judging others for their gifts, or coveting the gifts others have, is frowned upon in the Scriptures. Romans 11:29 tells us that God's gifts are irrevocable—so we may as well embrace who we are and what we are able to do. "I pray that the eyes of your heart may be enlightened," wrote Paul, "so that you will know what is the hope of His calling, what are the riches of the glory of His inheritance in the saints" (Ephesians 1:18).

Writing to the Corinthians Paul said, "But now there are many members, but one body. And the eye cannot say to the hand, 'I have no need of you'; or again the head to the feet, 'I have no need of you.' On the contrary, it is much truer that the members of the body which seem to be weaker are necessary" (1 Corinthians 12:20–22).

The fact is we are all different. There is no need for jealousy or envy. We all have a purpose. The more we work together, the better the kingdom works. Ignoring your gift because you consider it less important means that something is missing in the vital function of the church.

Who you are is the person God wanted you to be. You may have messed that person up through poor choices, but that person is still there. Embrace your gift and let it shape your life and ministry. Find fulfillment in what you can do, instead of lamenting over what you are not able to do. You are important. Yes, you! Your gift is necessary. When you do what God has called you to do, you will understand yourself better, and you will gain fulfillment that you have not enjoyed before.

"To this end also we pray for you always, that our God will count you worthy of your calling, and fulfill every desire for goodness and the work of faith with power" (2 Thessalonians 1:11).

Wednesday: What Are You Known For?

Buffy is sitting just off my right side. Between us is the ball he wants me to throw for him. He watches my face, paying attention to my every movement, waiting for me to look in his direction. Each time I do, his face immediately drops to the ball. If he thinks I can't reach it, he moves it closer. If I ask, he will pick it up and place it on the chair beside me. He could chase his ball all day. Ask those who know Buddy to describe him and they will include the orange and blue ball jammed in his mouth or sitting in front of him.

I am connected to my coffee cup with the same dedication as Buffy is to his ball. It is rarely far away from me. If I misplace it, I have to stop what I am doing and find it. If the cup was left somewhere on campus, my students knew that the first order of business was to find Mr. Bittner's cup. Ask people to describe me, and they will include the insulated stainless steel cup dangling from my right hand.

What is your attention fixed on? Are you known for your attachment to food or your hobbies, the sports section or your knitting needles? Maybe you are focused on exercise or your job, clothes or your appearance. Ask people to describe you, and they will invariably include the thing you are fixed on in the description.

God wants us to focus on being like Christ. "Therefore be imitators of God, as beloved children" (Ephesians 5:1). "Walk in a manner worthy of the calling with which you have been called" (Ephesians 4:1). This means that we must invest ourselves in the study of the Scripture to find out what it means to be like Christ. In addition, we should be in church where we can watch other Christians to see how they represent Christ.

Hebrews tells us to "fix our eyes on Jesus, the author and perfecter of faith" (Hebrews 12:2). The Gospel of Luke can help us understand what it means to have our eyes fixed on Jesus. "And he [Jesus] closed the book, gave it back to the attendant and sat down; and the eyes of all in the synagogue were fixed on Him" (Luke 4:20). Those who were gathered were hanging on the silence, waiting to know how Jesus was going to interpret the Scripture for them. Nothing was more important to them at that moment.

This is a convicting concept when you consider the things that you might be known for. Do people include your faithful attitude and Christlike behavior in their description of you? Do people even know about your faith? A trusted friend once said, "There is no such thing as secret discipleship. Either the discipleship will drown out the secrecy, or the secrecy will destroy the discipleship. You cannot have both." Would anybody play ball with Buffy if he kept his ball hidden from people? A ball that is hidden quickly leads to a dog that doesn't play. It is his attention on the ball that causes people to respond to him. In the same way, it is your attention to Christ that causes people to respond to Jesus. So, think about it as you go through your week. What are you known for?

Thursday: Finding New Ways to Exercise Your Gift

Australian terriers are bred to hunt rodents. They go under the ground to capture animals that dig holes and destroy the farms and fields. Our Aussies have brought us many various gifts of rats, gophers, and moles. They are skilled and diligent to accomplish the task that has been bred into them.

What do Aussie terriers do when they do not live on a farm? What do they hunt when the few local rodents have been caught? They simply look for new and creative ways to exercise their gifts. Major has learned from his mother, Jazzy, that a special rodent is always lurking in their midst. This rodent does not look like other rodents and it is under water instead of underground. Their rodent of choice is the pool sweep.

The dogs are forever pulling the sweep out of the pool, tearing the rubber wheel and the leaf-catcher off. Once they have determined that the sweep is dead, they leave it on the side of the pool, spraying water all over the backyard. From time to time they alter their pursuits by throwing the rubber tires back into the pool so that I have to fish them out before reassembling their enemy.

What do you do when you see no opportunity to exercise your gift? Do you give up feeling justified that you can now sit back and do nothing? Or do you look for ways to creatively express your gift? I have always been involved in evangelism. It is a gift; a passion that I truly enjoy. But I have been struggling physically, and have been through two back surgeries and a knee replacement—which just happened this week. (I am writing from a hospital bed.). Can I give up?

The other day, my wife and I spent some time with a long-time friend in ministry. We learned about a world evangelism focus called, "Heart and Soul 90." This ministry asks for three commitments from people. First is a commitment to pray 90 seconds a day for a specific place where Christ needs to be preached. "And He was saying to them, 'The harvest is plentiful, but the laborers are few; therefore beseech the Lord of the harvest to send out laborers into His harvest'" (Luke 10:2).

The second call is to invest 90 cents a day to help those on the cutting edge of evangelism. "For I testify that according to their ability, and beyond their ability, they gave of their own accord" (2 Corinthians 8:3).

Third, the ministry promises to send 90 percent of what it receives directly to the missionaries doing the work.

I may not be able to actively participate in the evangelism process right now, but I can help spread the word for Heart and Soul 90. By doing this, I am exercising my gift of making evangelism happen. I am exercising my gift in a creative way so that those who are on the forefront of evangelism can accomplish the task.

(To learn more about this ministry, go to www.heartandsoul90.com)

Friday: Love Grows Here

If I were to pick a photograph to represent the church, it would be one like this. The sign over the door would read, "Love Grows Here." Believers would meet together and chew on a passage of Scripture until they have successfully applied it to their lives. There would be peace. Being together would be a blessing. People in attendance would rejoice in being a part of the body. Often times, however, this is not an accurate picture of the church.

While working on our family's genealogy, my wife read a history of a young Baptist church in Hopewell, New Jersey. The church began in a house in 1715. The historian, Isaac Eaton, kept very accurate records of the struggles that the church faced. In his own words, he recorded the "diverse difficulties attending the church sometimes unhappy differences and wasting discords seem to prevail and draw as it were a sable cloud of confusion over this church to the no small hindrance of the gospel comfort of its professors and wounding the credit of religion hardening sinners and so forth." He recorded every fight that took place among the brethren, and every split that took place for thirty years. There were a few additions by baptism, but losses kept pace with the additions and the church remained small. As she read aloud the words from the church historian, I was amazed that a group of people who came to America to practice their religious freedom would so quickly sink to the same level as the churches they left in

Europe.

This is not to say that the whole history of the church was this painful. In 1747 Mr. Eaton wrote that "a marked revival of enthusiasm and spirituality developed and many in the congregation seemed to seek the Lord, mourning and weeping as they go with their faces Zion-ward. The ministers preached with fervor and power and soon there was such an apparent revival in religion that there was in great measure a happy stop put to frolicking and gaming in the neighborhood. The joyful sight appeared of souls flocking to God as doves to their windows and joining with the church from time to time."

So, what happened that the church went from grumbling to growth? The members came together and prayed. They talked about problems, found solutions, and agreed upon a new direction. As a result, revival broke out and the whole community was changed. In short, they took the Scripture seriously.

Jesus said, "A new commandment I give to you, that you love one another, even as I have loved you, that you also love one another" (John 13:34). John repeated the command by saying, "Beloved, let us love one another, for love is from God; and everyone who loves is born of God and knows God" (1 John 4:7). Even Peter understood the unifying power of love: "Above all, keep fervent in your love for one another, because love covers a multitude of sins" (1 Peter 4:8).

Our job is to hang the "love grows here" sign over the door and practice the principles of the Scripture. When we love one another, God ushers in a time of revival. When the bonds of love are broken, "unhappy differences and wasting discords" follow. This is not to say that we accept everything and challenge nothing. Paul said, "Brethren, if any person is overtaken in misconduct or sin of any sort, you who are spiritual [who are responsive to and controlled by the Spirit] should set him right and restore and reinstate him, without any sense of superiority and with all gentleness, keeping an attentive eye on yourself, lest you should be tempted also" (Galatians 6:1, Amplified). A church committed to love will come together, talk over differences, agree upon a direction, and walk together in unity.

Your church can be transformed. Your church can experience revival. It can impact the community where you live. The Transformation of the church must start with you. "Let love be without hypocrisy. Abhor what is evil; cling to what is good" (Romans 12:9). Visualize a "love grows here" sign hanging over your head. Let love flow through you, and watch the revival begin, one relationship at a time. You may be the exact person that God is waiting for to help change the church you attend into a powerful force for the gospel.

Saturday: "Using Our Gifts" Prayer Day

"If you then, being evil, know how to give good gifts to your children," said Jesus, "how much more will your Father who is in heaven give what is good to those who ask Him!" (Matthew 7:11). It is clear that God blesses us with gifts and calls us to use those gifts in his service. How *many* gifts and what *kinds* of gifts may be up for debate—but the reality of gifts is not.

Throughout this week we have been urged to examine our gifts, dust them off and use them to build up the body of Christ. There are several man-made tests available to determine your gifts, but a great way to get started is to ask others. Chances are they can tell you what gift you have. They can see it in you even if you do not. Knowing your gift is not as essential as being willing to be used by God. Not knowing is not an excuse for a lack of action.

Get involved, join a ministry, volunteer for service, and God will reveal himself to you. Your gifts and strengths will become evident, and you will be blessed for using them. Use this prayer day to seek God about your ministry. Interview other believers about what they see in you. Allow this day to be a day of surrender.

Week 9: Spiritual Integrity

Monday: More Than a Pretty Face

Chance hasn't been on the dog show circuit for very long, but his presence in competition has been powerful. His AKC name is "Champion Suvans Yosemite Sam," and this bichon frise has been racking up championship points since he broke onto the scene. Darlene knows that her dog is a winner, but she also knows that Chance is more than just another pretty face.

While in the grooming area of the prestigious Purina Dog Show in Toronto, Canada, Chance decided to let his personality shine through. It is as though he said, "Oh, you want a picture? Take a shot of this!" Chance won best in breed at this show, and had a number of amazing pictures taken, but this is the one that captured my attention.

Though I have never had the option of saying this myself, how many times have you heard the phrase, "There is more to me than just a pretty face." Society places a premium on physical beauty. Billions of dollars are spent each year to insure that we have nipped and tucked all of the right things. Then we cover what is left with the latest products to insure that the rest of our blemishes are covered. A former student recently wrote, "I just started using make-up, because society has convinced me that I am not pretty enough without it." This student is currently in the eighth grade and she has already suffered the effects of social judgment. I know her well enough to know that she has no reason for concern. She has a radiance that glows from the inside, making her a beautiful person, make-up or no make-up.

Don't just say you are more than a pretty face. Be more than a pretty face. Peter wrote, "Your adornment must not be merely external—braiding the hair, and wearing gold jewelry, or putting on dresses; but let it be the hidden person of the heart, with the imperishable quality of a gentle and quiet spirit, which is precious in the sight of God" (1 Peter 2:2–4). We are urged in Job 40:9–11 to adorn ourselves with eminence and dignity, and to clothe ourselves with honor and majesty.

Solomon wrote, "By His knowledge the deeps were broken up and the skies drip with dew. My son, let them not vanish from your sight; Keep sound wisdom and discretion, so they will be life to your soul and adornment to your neck. Then you will walk in your way securely and your foot will not stumble" (Proverbs 3:20–23). What makes a person (man, woman, or child) beautiful is what comes out of that person. Those qualities may include their personality, wisdom, grace, gentleness, dignity, and the peace which surpasses all understanding. True beauty comes from the inside, because we "put on the Lord Jesus Christ, and make no provision for the flesh in regard to its lusts" (Romans 13:14).

Jesus said, "Let your light shine before men in such a way that they may see your good works, and glorify your Father who is in heaven" (Matthew 5:16). Looking good is important, but being godly is more important. Make the investment to nip and tuck the areas of sin in your life, covering the blemishes that are left with the blood of Jesus. Groom the inside so that, like Chance, you can say, "Oh, you want a picture? Take a shot of this!"

Tuesday: Inconsistencies

I must admit that I am a people watcher. I am fascinated by what people do and say. So often there are inconsistencies between actions and beliefs. As a sinner I know that those same behaviors are present in me. But some things just stand out and remind me of spiritual truths. I had some time on my hands, so I went to a public place to take in the sights and sounds. Very soon my attention was drawn to a young girl and her mother.

The girl was twelve years old—and just barely that. On her right wrist was a rubber bracelet indicating that she had invested five dollars to spread the word about a violent man. It is an honorable thing to want to end violence. Undoubtedly, she believes that her five-dollar investment will have an impact. Yet with the same right hand the girl was clutching a movie ticket for a film that is packed with violence. The ticket slid down each page, marking every line of the book that spawned the movie. Five dollars to say she is against violence and at least of twenty dollars to support products that graphically depict violence.

Out of curiosity, I asked her about the bracelet and the book. My observation was lost on both her and her mother. Perhaps my heightened awareness came from the fact that I was studying about the absolute consistency of Jesus. The Scripture is amazingly clear that Jesus said what he meant and lived what he said. "For even hereunto were ye called: because Christ also suffered for us, leaving us an example, that ye should follow his steps: Who did no sin, neither was guile found in his mouth: Who, when he was reviled, reviled not again; when he suffered, he threatened not; but committed himself to him that judgeth righteously"(1 Peter 2:21–23, KJV). Jesus didn't promote one thing and do something else. He didn't take positions simply because they were popular. In fact, to many his positions were unpopular even though they were correct.

No guile: an interesting concept that causes me to wonder. How often do I say one thing and promote something else? Are my inconsistencies apparent to those who do not know Christ? How blind am I to my own weaknesses, and how many people are discounting Christ because I am filled with inconsistency? Jesus wants us to be like him. He said, "Therefore you are to be perfect, as your heavenly Father is perfect" (Matthew 5:48). That means I must be consistent in all things.

As I pondered this newfound conviction, a woman sat down next to me. She was nervously mumbling to herself, digging through her purse trying to find something that was not there. Then, she started talking to me, trying to include me in her conversation. Her presence irritated me and I found myself wishing she would leave. After all, I was in the middle of a deep spiritual thought about discovering my own weaknesses.

That was when the word "guile" really hit me. I had it—big time! Turns out she was having a full-on panic attack. She sat next to me intentionally because I looked nice and might be able to help talk her off of the emotional cliff she was teetering on. I have no idea what might have happened had I rejected her needs while I was busy being spiritual. But a half-hour later the woman (whose actual name is Sassafras) let out a deep sigh and thanked me for being such a nice Christian man.

Inconsistencies abound. I am grateful for the lesson I learned, but I know that I will have to relearn the same lesson many times before any mastery can take place. How about you? Is God bringing people, circumstances, or issues before you to point out your inconsistencies? What are you learning? Or, more importantly, what are you not learning because you are missing God's point? Open your eyes to the lessons he has prepared for you today, and start a new path to spiritual growth.

Wednesday: Beauty Is in the Eye Of . . .

Take a look at various dog breeds and you will find very different features. Some are sleek and fast, while others are slow and chunky. Some breeds are very popular, while other breeds are hard to find. The Chinese crested seems to win all of the ugliest dog competitions. The shar–pei looks like he is wearing someone else's skin. Other breeds look like they were designed from spare parts. Yet each dog has a skill, an instinctual ability, and a purpose. There is a purpose for the way they are built.

People are even more unique. No two of us are exactly alike. We can be tall or short, have big ears or bulbous noses. We may have long, skinny feet, or short, stocky legs. Hair color varies, as does skin color. And though we are unique we try not to stand out.

We have bought into the belief that beauty is in the eye of the beholder. And since others are the "beholders," we concern ourselves with becoming what others will consider beautiful. This takes the focus off of uniqueness and places it on sameness. We feed the problem of self-image because we are using the wrong frame of reference.

Beauty is not in the eye of the beholder. Beauty is in the eye of the maker. The psalmist wrote, "For You formed my inward parts; You wove me in my mother's womb. I will give thanks to You, for I am fearfully and wonderfully made; Wonderful are Your works, and my soul knows it very well" (Psalm 139:13–14).

When you look in the mirror are you awestruck by the fact that you were fearfully and wonderfully made? The fact that God created you just the way he wanted you to be while you were still in your mother's womb is an amazing truth to grasp. God doesn't make junk. He made you the way he wanted you to be. You may not understand why God made you to look the way you do, but there is a reason. You may have the wrinkles of a shar–pei, or the frailty of a Chihuahua. You may be lean and strong or walk with a limp, but if that is the way you were created then that is what God wanted you to be like. And since God doesn't make junk, there is a purpose for you being you.

"Your hands made me and fashioned me; Give me understanding, that I may learn Your commandments" (Psalm 119:73). Instead of worrying about how others behold you, pray that the God who fashioned you with his own hands would give you understanding. He created you and gifted you for a purpose—His purpose. "For we are His workmanship, created in Christ Jesus for good works, which God prepared beforehand so that we would walk in them" (Ephesians 2:10).

The next time someone tries to devalue you, or you tear yourself down with negative self-talk, state boldly and with confidence, "Beauty is in the eye of the maker, and my maker loves me!"

Thursday: More Than Appearances

Shimmy was the largest puppy born in the litter. Though he was only about six ounces at birth, he was still larger than all of his siblings. Within days the difference between the puppies became evident. He grew quickly, and his small belly became round and plump. In fact, we jokingly began to call Shimmy "Sir Fatsalot."

We weighed the puppies daily to ensure that they were getting adequate nutrition and gaining appropriate amounts of weight. As time progressed we dropped to every other day, then weekly, as we documented their size and weight. Two of the puppies just wanted out of the plastic tub that was placed on the scale. They weren't the least bit interested in what we were doing. One of the puppies relaxed and settled into the bottom of the tub. Shimmy, however, was different. He didn't want to relax and accept his weight. He didn't want to climb out and avoid the scale. He wanted to know what the numbers were. He would climb far enough over the edge so that he could see his own weight. He fixated on the changing numbers of the digital scale.

Most of us fit into one of these three categories:

- We want to escape the truth about our lives.
- We surrender to our present reality and let things just happen.

- Or we fixate on our circumstances, constantly fussing over what is or isn't, what we are and what we want to be. We invest in how we appear and try hard to look like something else.

Amazingly, the Scriptures have some things to say about appearances. Jesus insisted that we "stop judging by mere appearances, and make a right judgment" (John 7:24). The psalmist wrote, "We justify our actions by appearances; God examines our motives" (Proverbs 21:2 *The Message*). We fixate on the things we do not like about ourselves, but Paul seemed to address this feeling: "These are matters which have, to be sure, the appearance of wisdom in self-made religion and self-abasement and severe treatment of the body, but are of no value against fleshly indulgence" (Colossians 2:23).

So what does God want from us? Peter offers these words: "Your adornment must not be merely external—braiding the hair, and wearing gold jewelry, or putting on dresses; but let it be the hidden person of the heart, with the imperishable quality of a gentle and quiet spirit, which is precious in the sight of God" (1 Peter 3:3–4). These are the things that do not show on a scale, or reflect in our diet. It does not reflect in a mirror, or change with our clothing. God looks at the heart. He values your spirit and your faith. He calculates your level of obedience, and your willingness to represent Him in this world.

Are you looking at the right things in your life? Being healthy is important, but being right with God is more important. Being physically attractive is a nice idea, but being beautiful in the Lord is much more inviting. Don't fixate on the scale. Focus on the Word of God. You can be God's person just the way you are, and, with a godly focus, you can become the person He wants to be. That person is will be happier, and more attractive than you could ever imagine.

Friday: Let Wisdom Speak for Itself Once in a While

One of the most quoted stories of *Aesop's Fables* is "The Boy Who Cried Wolf." It seemed that the boy enjoyed the reactions of others each time he cried wolf. However, each time he repeated his cry, fewer and fewer people reacted to his voice. Eventually the sound of the boy's voice had been heard so much that no one reacted to him. His voice was just another sound in the white noise of life. Eventually, a wolf did come by and scared the poor boy half to death. He cried and he cried, but nobody came. A yippy dog and the boy who cried wolf seem to have a lot in common.

People get tired of hearing them. This may be why I am so impressed with a dog like Tasha. She is a standard poodle, with a café mocha coat. She lives with my friend Jean, who calls Tasha her "Numero Uno." Her registered name is "Touch of My Heart Natasha Marie." You can tell when a dog is smart, but one look at Tasha in this picture and you see more than intelligence. It is more like a quiet wisdom. She does not need to yip, or bark, or cry wolf in any sort of way. She uses her voice sparingly and lets her quiet spirit speak for her. Proverbs 17 says, "He who restrains his words has knowledge, and he who has a cool spirit is a man of understanding. Even a fool, when he keeps silent, is considered wise; when he closes his lips, he is considered prudent" (vv. 27–28). Add this to Proverbs 10:19 and you have a formula for being viewed as someone who has a piece of God's heart. It says, "When there are many words, transgression is unavoidable, but he who restrains his lips is wise." We may have an opinion about every subject under the sun. That doesn't mean that we need to freely share them. Others will view us more like a yipping dog than as a wise follower of Jesus.

There are times to speak and times to be silent, according to Ecclesiastes 3:7. James tells us that our words can get us into trouble when shared too freely: "If anyone thinks himself to be religious, and yet does not bridle his tongue but deceives his own heart, this man's religion is worthless" (James 1:26). He advises that we be "quick to hear" and "slow to speak" (James 1:19). This isn't a mandate to keep our mouths shut all the time. That would merely be avoiding our responsibility as Christians to speak the truth in love. But holding our tongue until the time is right is a powerful tool. Ecclesiastes 9:17 says, "The words of the wise heard in quietness are better than the shouting of a ruler among fools."

Do you want to be viewed as one who has a piece of God's heart? Choose your words wisely. Wait until the time is right. Allow God to work in the hearts of those around you, preparing them for when it is your turn to speak. It is not the number of words we speak that makes us wise, but the power behind a few words well placed.

Saturday: "Spiritual Integrity" Prayer Day

The devotions of for the last five days have had a lot to do with our physical appearance and the way we view ourselves. The beauty industry makes billions of dollars annually. Billions more are made by the diet industry, plastic surgeons, tanning salons, and hair studios. Then there is the garment industry that tells what fashions are in or out, based on what they are currently making.

Some of the most attractive people you will ever meet do not follow the trends and cannot afford the latest beauty products. In fact, their beauty is not based on these things. They are beautiful on the inside, and people just love to be around them. A radiant smile and a warm heart are powerful tools in the hands of a righteous person. More important than being someone you want to look at, that person is one you really want to get to know.

How beautiful are you? How much do you spend on the outside, and how much do you spend on building your character? How much time do you spend in prayer, and how does it compare to the amount of time you take primping for the day? Your values are reflected in these comparisons.

God wants to change your "inner person" to make you the person that reflects his image and his grace. Make this a day of surrender. Reestablish your priorities and make sure that you are not just following the crowd in hopes that somebody will notice you. When you become the person God wants you to be, people will notice.

Week 10: Surrender

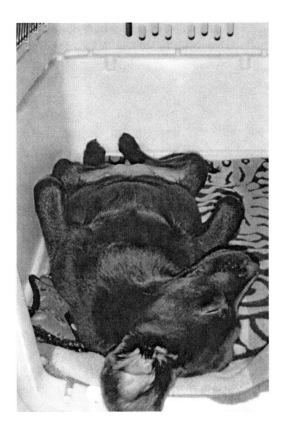

Monday: Settled

Don't you wish you could rest this comfortably? Kessie has settled into her new home with Lisa and is completely secure with her environment. The picture reminded me of something I wrote in *The God Whisperer*:

> Settling is a requirement of a good relationship between dog and master. It requires time, focus and patience. Shut off the television, ignore the phone, get down on the floor, and just be still. We want our dog to be comfortable in our environment. To accomplish this, they must feel comfortable with us in their environment. The essential idea is to demonstrate that you own both environments. When they accept your mastery, then they can become comfortable with their role in either environment. They learn to trust completely.

A settled dog will not only lie down in your presence but will roll over, exposing the most vulnerable part of his or her body—the underside. Every other part of the canine body is structured for protection. Muscles and bones work together to create a very solid frame around the essential parts of the dog. The one part that is dangerously exposed is the underside below the rib cage. A truly settled dog will willingly roll over and expose their underside. It is their way of saying "I trust you completely." That is a settled dog.

The God Whisperer, p. 62

God wants us to be settled before him. His desire is that we trust him so completely that we willingly expose our deepest hurts and most sensitive desires before him. When we are able to do this, then we will more fully understand the relationship the apostle Paul had when he wrote, "For this reason I bow my knees before the Father, from whom every family in heaven and on earth derives its name, that He would grant you, according to the riches of His glory, to be strengthened with power through His Spirit in the inner man, so that Christ may dwell in your hearts through faith; and that you, being rooted and grounded in love, may be able to comprehend with all the saints what is the breadth and length and height and depth, and to know the love of Christ which surpasses knowledge, that you may be filled up to all the fullness of God. Now to Him who is able to do far more abundantly beyond all that we ask or think, according to the power that works within us, to Him be the glory in the church and in Christ Jesus to all generations forever and ever. Amen" (Ephesians 3:14–21).

Until we are fully rooted and grounded in the love of Christ Jesus, we will only scratch the surface of his grace. Practice being settled before the Lord and you will go beyond the knowledge level. Be completely open to Jesus and find the strength and power you didn't even know could exist in your inner person. This is what God wants. It is what Paul prayed for, and it is what our souls desire.

Tuesday: Even God Rests

When Dakota was a puppy, he set the standard for rest and relaxation. Being a basset hound, Dakota comes by the concept of rest honestly. With their long bodies, short legs, floppy ears, and droopy eyes, the basset seems a prime candidate to teach us how to rest.

When they are awake, puppies are generally full of energy. They run at full speed, getting into everything. All of life is a new experience. They want to try everything, smell everything, and chew everything they can find. But very soon they run out of energy, lie down, and fall fast asleep. There are few things more precious than a baby (or a puppy) sleeping peacefully. I have been thinking a lot about the concept of rest because I need it and my doctors have ordered it.

Perhaps you feel a need to rest. Your body is giving every sign that you need a vacation. You need rest, but there doesn't seem to be any time. Yet it is essential that you find the time to rest and recharge. Rest now or your body will force it on you through sickness, stress, and physical pain.

God established the pattern of rest: "Thus the heavens and the earth were completed, and all their hosts. By the seventh day God completed His work, which He had done, and He rested on the seventh day from all His work, which He had done. Then God blessed the seventh day and sanctified it, because in it He rested from all His work which God had created and made" (Genesis 2:1–3). In the same way, he told us to work six days and rest on the seventh. Psalm 37:7 says, "Rest in the Lord and wait patiently for Him; Do not fret because of him who prospers in his way, because of the man who carries out wicked schemes." This verse is particularly important because it addresses our fear of taking vacations. We ignore days off because while we are gone someone else might undermine our work and profit from it. Yet we are told to trust the Lord even in our resting. God is still in control.

Jesus continued his Father's pattern of rest. In Mark 6:31 we find these words: "And He said to them, 'Come away by yourselves to a secluded place and rest a while.' (For there were many people coming and going, and they did not even have time to eat.)." I am sure Jesus found it just as difficult to take the time to rest his body. Nevertheless, he made the time and found places to get away from the crowds. Rest improves health, changes perspectives, and helps build new vision.

We may never be able to rest like Dakota, the basset puppy, but we all must find the time to stop and rest. Don't wait until you are ordered to rest or your body gives out. Make a commitment to rest because God rested. Find the time to rest because that's what Jesus did. Practice the ability to rest because there will come a time when God will want you to rest with Him. "So there remains a Sabbath rest for the people of God" (Hebrews 4:9). What a glorious day of rest that will be. Take care of the temple that is your body so that you may reap the great Sabbath reward.

Wednesday: Worry

One look at her new puppy, and Kay knew that her name should be Zureil, a fine Hebrew name from the Old Testament. Zureil is loving, friendly, and devoted to Kay. Like most good dogs, she wants nothing more than to please her master. She also loves to eat treats, and for that you have to understand her routine.

When Zureil was young, Kay taught her to perform all of the usual pet tricks. Each trick was rewarded with a treat. Soon, Zureil learned that tricks and treats were associated with each other. If she wanted the treat, she had to perform. After a while, she stopped waiting for command, and started performing the tricks on her own. The problem was that Zureil wasn't sure which command Kay was going to give. So, Zureil started combining tricks, which eventually included every trick in her repertoire. She sits, then lies down, spins around, tries to shake, speaks, and anything else she can think of, all in rapid succession. The more she tries, the faster the routine becomes until all you see is a whirl of motion, without completing a single trick. When she finishes she tilts her head and smiles, as if to say, "Did I do it yet?"

A dear friend named Alvin once said, "When I am faced with a problem, I consider the solutions, decide on a course of action, and try it. If that doesn't work I do something else, trying everything within my power to solve the problem myself. If that doesn't work then, and only then, do I ask God for help."

Alvin's approach to life was very much like Zureil's approach to treats. I have never agreed with his theology, but I always appreciated his honesty. He voiced what most of us actually do on a regular basis. We overlook the will of God, ignore His commands, sidestep prayer, and try our best to perform every trick we can think of to solve the issues we face. Then we look toward God and smile with pride as if to say, "Look God, I am a good Christian. Can I have the treat?"

Jesus never said go and do, then come back and tell me about it. Instead, he said, "Ask, and it will be given to you; seek, and you will find; knock, and it will be opened to you. For everyone who asks receives, and he who seeks finds, and to him who knocks it will be opened" (Matthew 7:7–8). Add this to what Jesus already said one chapter earlier: "And who of you by being worried can add a single hour to his life?" (Matthew 6:27).

Are you seeking God? Are you waiting on guidance from the Lord? Are you studying Scripture for direction? Or, have you settled into Zureil's life? In reality, we are more like Alvin than we care to admit.

Think about what you did today. How many decisions did you make on your own? How many actions did you follow through on with no thought of prayer? Or what struggle did you pray over, only to go off and do what you had already decided to do anyway? As you consider these questions, why not make Psalm 25:4–6 your constant prayer. Turn your worries into opportunities to be blessed.

> Show me the right path, O Lord; point out the road for me to follow. Lead me by your truth and teach me, for you are the God who saves me. All day long I put my hope in you. Remember, O Lord, your compassion and unfailing love, which you have shown from long ages past.
>
> Psalm 25:4–6, NLT

Thursday: What Would a Tail Say about You?

You can tell a lot about the attitude of a dog by paying attention to the way it responds to you. It may show its teeth and growl, or maybe even bark at you. If it does this, it's best to keep your distance. On the other hand the tail can say even more about how a dog is feeling. If the tail is up, the dog is uneasy and aggressive. If the tail is down, the dog is feeling fearful or discouraged. When the tail is flat the dog is calm. But, when the tail is wagging wildly, you know the dog is happy and open to interact with you.

Let's face it—life can be tough, even for Christians. Sickness, job loss, a bad economy, and other issues are not exclusive to one group of people. But in the midst of these things God wants us to experience joy. James encourages us to "consider it all joy, my brethren, when you encounter various trials, knowing that the testing of your faith produces endurance. And let endurance have its perfect result, so that you may be perfect and complete, lacking in nothing" (James 1:2–4).

Paul exhorts us to "exult in our tribulations, knowing that tribulation brings about perseverance; and perseverance, proven character; and proven character, hope; and hope does not disappoint, because the love of God has been poured out within our hearts through the Holy Spirit who was given to us" (Romans 5:3–5).

In the Sermon on the Mount, Jesus describes several circumstances in which we can find blessed happiness. Being poor, humble, and persecuted are included in those circumstances. Yet Jesus points out that we are *blessed*—which literally can be translated as "O the happiness of!"—when we go through those circumstances. The reason for our happiness is that we are promised tremendous growth and victory as we happily work through our circumstances. So here is the question: What would a tail say about you? Would it say that you are angry and aggressive? Would it say that you are defeated and discouraged? Or, would the tail be flat showing that you are at peace?

Would your tail wag at the chance to tell others about the peace that you have found in your circumstances? For the most part, we can hide our emotions as we make our way through the course of our day. But a tail would give those emotions away, revealing how we really feel.

Set a goal for yourself to check the attitude you might project. Seek the Lord about your attitude, and your circumstances, but in public where people are waiting to see how your faith makes you different, ask God to give you joy. Let this statement be your guide: BARK LESS, WAG MORE.

Friday: I Want to Be Where You Are

There are times when Kim and I need to travel to places where our dogs cannot accompany us. We usually have members of the family around who can care for our pack of Aussies. This was not the case a on a recent trip to another state. So we invited a family friend to come and care for them. Andrea knows our dogs well and we were happy that she was willing to come.

Four days is a long separation when you live in the moment and you don't know when your master will return. When one of us travels, the dogs do not eat as well. They pace the house hoping to find the missing master in some other room. We could only guess what they would be like when both of us were gone. We found out when Andrea snapped this photo and emailed it to us. The dogs dismantled the cushions on the couch, roughed up the pillows and settled in to wait for our return. The couch held our scent, and it was one place where they felt close to us. We were gone, and they just wanted to be with us.

Perhaps the psalmist had similar feelings when he wrote, "One thing I ask of the Lord, this is what I seek: That I may dwell in the house of the Lord all the days of my life, to gaze upon the beauty of the Lord and to seek him in his temple" (Psalm 27:4, NIV). Jesus knew that the disciples would experience the same sense of loss very soon. He tried to comfort them by saying, "Do not let your heart be troubled; believe in God, believe also in

Me. In My Father's house are many dwelling places; if it were not so, I would have told you; for I go to prepare a place for you. If I go and prepare a place for you, I will come again and receive you to Myself, that where I am, there you may be also" (John 14:1–3).

The early church had the same desire to be with the Lord. Paul acknowledged this when he wrote, "Therefore we are always confident and know that as long as we are at home in the body we are away from the Lord. For we live by faith, not by sight. We are confident, I say, and would prefer to be away from the body and at home with the Lord. So we make it our goal to please him, whether we are at home in the body or away from it" (2 Corinthians 5:6–9).

There are times when all of us want to ruffle up God's pillows and hide. We watch and wait for the time of his return. We long for the time we can be in his presence. These feelings intensify when we're lonely, hurt, or confused. The good news is that we have God's word to settle into during our quiet time where we can enjoy the sweetness of his presence. The Scripture reminds us that through these times we only see in part, but there will be a time we see him face to face. He has promised that he will come again and receive us and we will be where he is.

As I studied the photograph of the dogs sleeping on our couch I could not be upset, because I understood what they were feeling. Over the next two days, I found myself singing a very familiar Don Moen worship song:

> I just want to be where You are,
> dwelling daily in Your presence
> I don't want to worship from afar,
> draw me near to where You are.
> I just want to be where You are,
> in Your dwelling place forever
> Take me to the place where You are,
> I just want to be with You.[3]

Saturday: "Surrender" Prayer Day

It seems like we are always taught the "Go" passages in church. We rarely hear that there are times when God wants us to just sit by the still waters and rest. Hopefully, this week you heard that message loud and clear.

We would love to have a balance of work, faith, family, and relaxation in our life. But the reality is, balance is unachievable. Something will always require extra attention. The best we can hope for is that we can prioritize the pressures and separate the urgent from the important. God is pleased with our prayers in the fast lane on the way to work, but he desires more than your words. He wants your time and your undivided attention as much as your husband or wife and children do.

Take time today to just be with the Lord. Give him some words of praise, and then just relax in his presence. Saying nothing may bring him more honor today than all of your prayer lists. Let it all go, take a deep breath and just relax in his presence.

Week 11: Traditions

Monday: The More Things Change, the More They Stay the Same

Sandra works very closely with the Australian Terrier Club of America. She breeds Aussies, shows Aussies, and serves on the board of the association. Recently Sandra posted this photo of a woman holding her Australian terrier. It is estimated that the photo was taken in the 1870s. While we can enjoy the nostalgia of the picture, there is a lesson that needs to be learned.

It seems that the more things change, the more they stay the same. We are reminded all too often of Hollywood stars carrying their Chihuahuas everywhere they go. It is difficult to go out in public without finding people doing the same thing. The other day, I witnessed an elderly man and his wife as they walked through a high-end furniture store. They were noticeable because the man had a Yorkie tucked under his arm. Times have changed, so has our clothing, but our habits have remained the same.

Take a look at the church, ten, twenty, or a hundred years ago and you will recognize the same truth. Buildings have changed with the years. The way we dress on Sunday has definitely changed with time. Worship services do not look anything like they did years ago. Even the names on the buildings have changed as churches move away from denominational labels and toward more generic (and often obscure) names. Yet, the more things change, the more they stay the same.

No matter how much a worship service changes, Jesus is still the focus. He said, "I am the way, and the truth, and the life; no one comes to the Father but through Me'" (John 14:6). The plan of salvation has not changed either. Peter said, "'there is salvation in no one else; for there is no other name under heaven that has been given among men by which we must be saved" (Acts 4:12).

The goal of the body of Christ has not changed: "Now the Lord is the Spirit, and where the Spirit of the Lord is, there is liberty. But we all, with unveiled face, beholding as in a mirror the glory of the Lord, are being transformed into the same image from glory to glory, just as from the Lord, the Spirit" (2 Corinthians 3:17–18). In fact, the truth about life has not changed: "And inasmuch as it is appointed for men to die once and after this comes judgment" (Hebrews 9:27).

It is comforting to know that some things never change. The gospel has not—and will never be—changed. Practices might change, but that is only the public expression of the church as we attempt to keep truth relevant. The fact remains that "there is one body and one Spirit, just as also you were called in one hope of your calling; one Lord, one faith, one baptism, one God and Father of all who is over all and through all and in all" (Ephesians 4:4–6). This remains the same!

Therefore, since we have so great a cloud of witnesses surrounding us, let us also lay aside every encumbrance and the sin which so easily entangles us, and let us run with endurance the race that is set before us, fixing our eyes on Jesus, the author and perfecter of faith, who for the joy set before Him endured the cross, despising the shame, and has sat down at the right hand of the throne of God. For consider Him who has endured such hostility by sinners against Himself, so that you will not grow weary and lose heart.

Hebrews 12:1–3

Tuesday: Standing in the Doorway

Dogs are the keepers of the home. When we go to work or run an errand, they remain at home waiting for us. Since they have so little sense of time, we could be gone five minutes or five hours and they are still excited to see us. When I come home, three Australian terriers greet me. They wiggle gleefully and tell me how much they have missed me with squeals of joy. Our house is a much warmer place because the dogs have invested their lives to wait for us to come home.

Hudson lives in Texas with his loving master, Caro. When the door is open, Hudson has access to the outside world. He could dart out of the door and run down the street, but he doesn't. His world is inside of the house where his family lives. He does not hold a grudge when Caro is out too long. He does not keep a list of offenses or complain about what he can or cannot do. He simply waits expectantly for the return of his master, and then showers her with love and acceptance.

The words of Solomon seem to reflect Hudson's attitude: "Heed instruction and be wise, and do not neglect it. Blessed is the man who listens to me, watching daily at my gates, waiting at my doorposts. For he who finds me finds life and obtains favor from the Lord" (Proverbs 8:33–

35).

The one who is blessed is the one who stands in God's doorway, who leans against the doorpost and waits for the wisdom and guidance of the Lord. Sure there is a big world out there with countless temptations, but the wise believer knows that being in God's house is the most blessed place on earth. To be in the presence and fellowship of the Lord is worth the wait because we find favor with the Lord.

Hebrews 9:28 continues the concept of waiting at God's doorstep: "Christ was sacrificed once to take away the sins of many; and he will appear a second time, not to bear sin, but to bring salvation to those who are waiting for him." Are you waiting for Jesus? Are you standing at the gates of his temple waiting for the salvation that he has promised?

Perhaps you find that you have run down the street, chasing after some temptation that caught your eye. The good news is that all is not lost. Jesus will pursue you. He will leave the ninety-nine, and will follow after the lost one (Matthew 18:12). He wants to bring you back into his house and give you his blessing.

The old adage says, "Good things come to those who wait." The Scripture confirms this. Keep standing firm in the doorway of God. When Jesus returns you will find fellowship and blessing in his presence. If Hudson could talk he would tell you that perfect fellowship with our master is worth the wait.

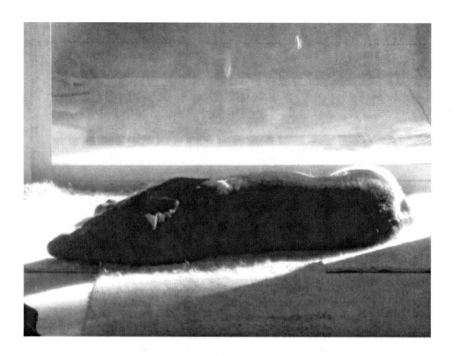

Wednesday: Follow the Light

Dogs have a natural inclination to seek out the light and warmth of the sun. The ray of light coming through the window may be nothing more than a thread, but our dogs will find it, and stretch out their body to absorb the most amount of light possible. This picture could be of any one of my dogs. You can probably picture your dog doing this as well.

The chocolate Lab in this picture is our friend Lisa's dog, Ginger, who was diagnosed with terminal cancer. She underwent surgery to remove a tumor. For a while Ginger improved, seeming to return to her old energetic self. On Monday of last week she took a turn for the worse and did not make it through the evening. Since then, this picture of Ginger has taken on new meaning.

Jesus said, "While I am in the world, I am the light of the world" (John 9:5). He continued, "I have come into the world as a light, so that no one who believes in me should stay in darkness" (John 12:46). As our dogs are naturally drawn toward to the light, so we are called to seek out the light of the world, and bask in his glory.

The Twenty-third Psalm is one of the best known and most memorized passages in the entire Bible. This psalm becomes even more amazing when we take into account what Jesus said about himself.

> The Lord is my shepherd, I shall not be in want. He makes me lie down in green pastures, he leads me beside quiet waters, he restores my soul. He guides me in paths of righteousness for his name's sake.
>
> Psalm 23:1–3, NIV

The beginning of this Psalm is discussed extensively in *The God Whisperer* (the book). The key to having a relationship with our shepherd, or pack leader, is that we willingly submit to the master. Down is a vital position in our relationship with Jesus. It is the place where we surrender to his leading. It is the place where we find restoration for our soul. These verses give us a beautiful picture of a successful quiet time. The motivation that makes our quiet time powerful comes in the portion that follows:

> Even though I walk through the valley of the shadow of death, I will fear no evil, For you are with me; Your rod and your staff, they comfort me.
>
> Psalm 23:4

The valley referred to here is literally the valley of darkness, gloom, or death. It is a valley we will all face at the end of our lives. Yet for the believer there is an added feature. For there to be shadows, light must be present. To identify distinct shadows as a feature, the light must come from a single source. Jesus is that single source of light. Jesus wants to be our master in the best times of life and in the darkest times of life. When life is at its darkest, he is there to lead us safely through the darkness and into his realm of glory. The promise of Jesus in John 12 becomes even more powerful by placing his words in the context of this Psalm. When we trust the shepherd of our souls and look for his light, even in the darkest of places, then we have his promise that he will not leave us in that dark place.

If you want to have your cup overflow, and you anticipate being in the house of the Lord forever, then you must seek and follow the Light of the World. Lie down before him. Stay in his presence. Sit at his feet. Become settled in his authority. And when the time comes for you to approach that valley, remember these words: "Walk toward the light."

Thursday: Choose What Lasts

Herman and Lily are smooth-coated dachshunds. They live with Caitlin, a former student of mine. They are named after Herman and Lily Munster (I had no idea that *The Munsters* could still be found on television). They are happy dogs, demonstrated by the fact that when they wag their tail, their whole body wags as well.

Dachshunds were originally bred to go underground and take on badgers. As a result, they have an amazing ability to focus on one thing, and will not give up until they have prevailed. Since Herman and Lily live in the city, they have had to find other areas on which to focus their attention.

Their passion is peanut butter. Caitlin feeds it to them by the spoonful, and even though it gets all over their mouths and noses, they will not quit until the spoon is clean. Then, of course, they lick and lick, trying to clean the peanut butter out of the roofs of their mouths. The experience may be a challenge, but once their mouths are clean they stare at the empty spoon until Caitlin scoops more out of the jar.

I attended Christian College with a pair of creative brothers who loved to play guitar, and sing praises to God. They were also talented songwriters. One song has rolled around in my head for more than forty years. Here is one verse from the silly song they performed in chapel: "Bacon and eggs in the morning will stick to your ribs. / Pabulum, pudding, prunes will stick to your bib. / Peanut butter soup will stick to the bottom of your bowl, / But the word of God will stick to your soul."

We need to think about where we focus our lives. Many pursuits will capture our attention. We focus on them and continually go back for more. Unfortunately most of those pursuits are merely peanut butter soup stuck to the bottom of the bowl. Life needs to be about more than winning the peanut butter battles. If in the end we are found hungry and thirsty, have we really won anything?

Jesus said, "I am the living bread that came down out of heaven; if anyone eats of this bread, he will live forever; and the bread also which I will give for the life of the world is My flesh" (John 6:51). Doesn't it make sense to seek after something that will last forever? Seeking Jesus, making his service our passion, and not turning away from him is choosing the one thing that stands the test of time. The writer to the Hebrews offered God's promise to those who choose him. "Therefore He is able also to save forever those who draw near to God through Him, since He always lives to make intercession for them" (Hebrews 7:25).

Let's make the Christian life a little more fun. Put things in perspective. Do you worry about that person who is never happy with you? Picture him or her as a prune. Troubled by the over-simplified philosophies of today's world? It is just Pabulum! The problems of your day are nothing more than wading through pudding, and the temptations that would draw you away are just sticky peanut butter. This is not to downplay the difficulties of life, but to illustrate that our value is infinitely greater than the junk that is stuck to our bib at the end of the day. Stop focusing on what you find hanging there and choose the one thing that will last forever: your salvation and the One who died to offer that amazing life to you.

"To Him who sits on the throne, and to the Lamb, be blessing and honor and glory and dominion forever and ever" (Revelation 5:13).

Friday: To Him Who Has Ears

Dogs have an amazing ability to hear sounds that their human owners could never hear. Their ears are actually the third of the sensory organs they rely on from birth. They begin with the nose, followed by the opening of the eyes. It takes many days for their little ear buds to develop and the ear canal to open. Cesar Milan points out that dogs always operate with their nose first, then eyes, and finally ears. One would think that they don't use their ears at all, especially when they are running down the street, leaving you calling after them. Actually, they hear you fine, but their nose and eyes are overpowering the ears. Actually they can block out sound easily, but they can hear the faintest sounds from far away locations.

Kim drives a Toyota Prius, a hybrid vehicle. After the car has warmed up, it is easy to drive at slower speeds under electric power only. In the evening when she arrives home from work, she turns onto our street, and coasts toward home. The engine shuts off as she rounds the corner and she drives under electric power only. It is in electric-only mode that the Prius becomes extremely quiet. It is easy to drive within a couple of feet of a pedestrian without them hearing you.

Our Australian terriers can be sleeping on the floor with the house closed up. I may even have music playing on the stereo. Yet, the dogs can hear when Kim is driving down the street. They wake from their sleep, and take their positions at the front window. Their short tails quiver wildly as they wait for the silent car to come into view from down the street. How do they know? What do they hear? How can they tell it is Kim's car? Amazingly, they know the sound of each of our cars, and are prepared for our arrival long before the car comes into view.

Young Samuel was serving Eli in the temple. When nighttime came Samuel heard someone calling his name. He raced to Eli to find out why he was called. Eli assured Samuel that he had not called, and he should go back to bed. No sooner had he returned to his bed, when the voice called out a second time. Even though Eli heard nothing, he believed that the Lord was calling Samuel. "And Eli said to Samuel, 'Go lie down, and it shall be if He calls you, that you shall say, "Speak, Lord, for Your servant is listening." So Samuel went and lay down in his place. Then the Lord came and stood and called as at other times, "Samuel! Samuel!" And Samuel said, 'Speak, for Your servant is listening'" (1 Samuel 3:9–10).

This story becomes more special when you understand the beginning of the chapter: "Word from the Lord was rare in those days, visions were infrequent" (v. 1b). How did Samuel hear a voice when no one else heard? It was rare. Very few people ever heard God's voice. Yet Samuel heard God. Jesus warned us about our ears by saying, "He who has ears to hear, let him listen" (Matthew 11:15). He also said, "Take care how you listen; for whoever has, to him more shall be given; and whoever does not have, even what he thinks he has shall be taken away from him" (Luke 8:18)

So how do you listen? More importantly, what are you listening for? If God spoke would you recognize it? You might be tempted to quote the words of 1 Samuel and say, "God rarely speaks these days, and visions are infrequent. He is not going to talk to me." Yet over and over the Scripture tells us to listen to God. Throughout the book of Revelation we are told, "He who has an ear, let him hear what the Spirit says to the churches." To those who hear come promises. We will be able to eat from the tree of life, which is in the Paradise of God. We will not be hurt by the second death. We will be given manna to eat, and we will have a new name written in stone.

"But blessed are your eyes, because they see; and your ears, because they hear" (Matthew 13:16).

Saturday: "Traditions" Prayer Day

Are You Keeping The Right Traditions?

This week we discussed the need to follow the right things, to choose the things which will last. Each of us holds on to our own set of traditions. Some of the things we call traditions are nothing more than habits, and, when pressed, we have no real idea why we still do them. I know a family that has taken the exact same vacation every year for nearly fifty years. Talk about a tradition!

The church is filled with things we hold dearly as traditions but are only our preferences. At times we hold onto the wrong things and make them a test of faith when they are not essential to the gospel. The blessing of spiritual maturity is that we can be tolerant of practices and beliefs that are not essential to the gospel. However, we can only do this when we know what the essentials are.

Over the weekend, create a list of the things that are *essential* as you understand them from the Scripture. Then use this list to start discussions with church leaders and people who you respect.

Week 12: Our Witness

Monday: The Toddler in 16D

The middle-aged lawyer in row 17 spent the first half of the two-hour flight pouring over a legal brief. As she read, she scribbled notes on a yellow legal pad. It was obvious that she was committed to understanding intricate details of the document. That is, until the toddler in 16D peaked around the edge of the seat, threw up her arms and said one of the only words she knew: "Hi!"

Suddenly the legal brief had no power. The lawyer tucked the document and the legal pad into the seat pocket and dedicated her attention to the toddler in front of her. For nearly an hour the two strangers played peek-a-boo around the edge of the seat. Her long brown hair, held by a pink bow flopped in her mother's face each time she leaned over and peered backwards at the totally engaged lawyer.

As I watched from 18C, I developed a whole new appreciation for Matthew 18:2–4. Jesus "called a child to Himself and set him before them, and said, 'Truly I say to you, unless you are converted and become like children, you will not enter the kingdom of heaven. Whoever then humbles himself as this child, he is the greatest in the kingdom of heaven.'"

The common application of this passage reminds us that God wants us to have a childlike faith. Such faith is completely dependent on the power and love of the father. We are happiest when we sit in our Heavenly Father's lap and trust his leading. But as I watched this child command the attention of the lawyer behind her, I realized that there was another important aspect of becoming like a child. God wants us to have a childlike presence.

One with a childlike presence understands Matthew 10:16: "Behold, I send you out as sheep in the midst of wolves; so be shrewd as serpents and innocent as doves." If we have a childlike presence we will have eyes that reflect Christ and hearts that reflect Christ.

A childlike presence is opposite of a childish presence. A childish presence draws attention to itself, while a childlike presence reflects the love of Jesus. A childlike presence makes people put down their busy-ness and focus on the God who shines through us. Salt, light, a city set on a hill that cannot be hidden—these are qualities of a childlike approach to life. It is the life that makes others thirst for the God we serve.

Though the toddler spoke only one word, she was more attractive than everyone else on the plane. As I watched, I realized that Jesus uses those who come to him with a childlike faith, and represent him to others with a childlike presence. It begins when we throw ourselves into the lap of our heavenly father. Can there be anything more attractive than that?

"Whoever then humbles himself as this child, he is the greatest in the kingdom of heaven."

Tuesday: Tolerance

Lily and Herman Munster are two of the most tolerant dogs you will meet. They will let Caitlin do just about anything to them. Although it looks like she is constantly tormenting them, it is not true. It only seems to be true because that is when they get their picture taken the most.

Recently, Caitlin took her dogs to the beach. Sounds like a safe event. What could happen at the beach? Well, they hadn't been there long when Caitlin decided to bury her precious dachshunds up to their ears in the sand.

For a dachshund to be underneath the ground is not a stretch. After all, they were bred to go underground following rodents into their den. But to be buried at the beach, sand fleas and all, that is a different story. Yet, Herman and Lily took what was given to them, trusted their master, and even seemed to find pleasure in the coolness of the moist sand. They appeared to be comfortable enough to even take a nap while buried in the sand.

There are plenty of times in life when someone might think it would be funny to bury us in the sand. This may be in good fun, a serious put down, or anything in between. When this happens there are two possible, yet opposing, reactions that we can take. We can be completely offended by it, or we can love the people doing it and try to find something positive in the situation. Over and over, the apostle Paul compares man's wisdom and God's wisdom with the comparative word "foolishness." Within the church, however, Paul pleads, "Therefore, accept one another, just as Christ also accepted us to the glory of God" (Romans 15:7).

"Be kind to one another, tender-hearted, forgiving each other, just as God in Christ also has forgiven you" (Ephesians 4:32). Kindness and tenderheartedness are listed in the same verses with forgiveness. Apparently there were those in the early church who were trying to bury each other. This makes sense in the light of Paul's words to the Christians at Colossae: "Bear with each other and forgive whatever grievances you may have against one another. Forgive as the Lord forgave you" (Colossians 3:13, NIV).

The alternative to bearing with others and forgiving them is to be offended. But to those who would follow this approach, I might remind you of what Peter discovered when he tried to be offended. "Then Peter came and said to Him, 'Lord, how often shall my brother sin against me and I forgive him? Up to seven times?' Jesus said to him, 'I do not say to you, up to seven times, but up to seventy times seven'" (Matthew 18:21–23).

Joseph of the Old Testament saw his share of sand fleas when his brothers threw him into a hole and later sold him into slavery. How did Joseph respond to his brothers when he next saw them? "[He] said to them, 'Do not be afraid, for am I in God's place? As for you, you meant evil against me, but God meant it for good'" (Genesis 50:19). How could he say this to the brothers who did something so rotten to him? He was "in God's place." This place was more than one of judgment, but was a place where Joseph could see God's heart.

Are you in God's place? Are you in the place where love, forgiveness, and tender-heartedness abound? You see things much differently when you view them from God's place. Who knows you may even be able to enjoy the coolness of the sand while others think they have you buried.

Wednesday: Not My Will But Yours Be Done

When Renee adopted Laredo, she was intent on training a service dog. Her goal was to make a difference in someone's life. So she contacted a reputable service organization and a cute little yellow Labrador was placed in her care.

Training a service dog is a twenty-four-hour-a-day job. Laredo accompanied Renee to college, slept through Renee's classes, and was well known for passing gas during lectures. Laredo became one of the most famous celebrities on the college campus. Through all of this, Renee worked, trained, corrected, and encouraged Laredo to be the best service dog he could be. After all, being a service dog was his intended purpose.

The day Laredo was returned to the organization was a difficult one. Renee had grown attached to her companion. Though it was hard, she turned Laredo over for the final test to see whether he would be an ideal service dog. Laredo passed every test but one. That one test disqualified him from certification.

So, what do you do with a dog that everyone expected to be a good service dog? Renee wasn't sure, but she knew that she loved Laredo and was eager to take him back into her life. Not long after, Renee married Wade, and Hunter was born. With the birth of Hunter, Laredo found his true calling. Guarding, guiding, and serving for Hunter has become his passion. Caring for his boy has proven to be Laredo's true calling.

You may have worked and trained for the ideal job only to discover it didn't work for you. You may have sought after the person you envisioned as the perfect mate, and the relationship failed. Or, you tried to serve in a ministry that looked like a good fit, only to discover that you were totally wrong for the task. If anything like this has ever happened in your life, you need to adopt the words of Jesus as he prayed in the garden: "Not my will, but yours be done" (Luke 22:42). Those were the words Jesus prayed in the garden before he was crucified. Though troubled by the events he knew were ahead of him, Jesus was confident that God's plan was better than any plan devised by man.

His ministry only lasted three years. He was in the prime life. To many who looked on, Jesus may have looked like a failure—but he knew better. He knew that God's plan was a victorious one, so he willingly surrendered to the Father's will.

The saying, "We tried it once, and it didn't work," seems to be a universal code. It is to say, "I have failed and I am unwilling to attempt anything else." The apostle Paul was the principal leader in bringing the gospel to the Gentiles, and yet he had a significant illness, which he called a "thorn in the flesh." He prayed that God would take it away, but that did not happen. Instead, God said to him, "'My grace is sufficient for you, for my power is made perfect in weakness.' Therefore I will boast all the more gladly about my weaknesses, so that Christ's power may rest on me" (2 Corinthians 12:9).

I searched the entire Bible looking for the word failure. The NIV never uses the word. It is used once in the NASB, but not in reference to Christians. What you will find in the Scripture is this promise: "Now to Him who is able to do far more abundantly beyond all that we ask or think, according to the power that works within us" (Ephesians 3:20).

When we face a struggle we need to say, "Not my will, but yours be done." When we reach a dead-end, we need to remember, "Not my will, but yours be done." When our plans don't work and we don't know where to turn—"Not my will, but yours be done." When you are at a crossroads, do you want to go your way or God's way? When others judge you, telling you that you can't do something, never forget the words of Jesus, "Not my will, but yours be done." Your greatest ministry is still ahead of you.

Thursday: Earning the Right

Australian terriers, like most canine breeds, need to be groomed. The method used for the Aussie is a technique called stripping. This is done in two ways. The first way is to use a stripping comb, which takes old weak hair out and leaves the new strong hair behind. The second way requires work done by hand, taking small amounts of hair between the thumb and forefinger and pulling. The strong hair remains and the old hair comes out. The process is not painful, but it makes a huge difference in the way the dog looks and feels.

One place where dogs are uncomfortable with this process is their ears. Australian terriers need to have their ears stripped of all long hair. Our mature dogs, Jazzy and Satchmo, are used to having their ears groomed. They have learned to trust Kim as she deals with their sensitive ears. They understand that the process may not be fun, but it will have positive results. Puppies, on the other hand, do not have the same level of trust. They don't understand what is happening and they are not willing to submit to the experience. One of the hazards of grooming the ears is that the dog can turn its head and bite. It happens so fast that it is very difficult to get out of the way. The result is painful and often draws blood. They don't intend to hurt you. They just want you to stop pulling at their ears.

Grooming our dogs' ears reminds me of a passage written by Solomon: "Like one who takes a dog by the ears is he who passes by and meddles with strife not belonging to him" (Proverbs 26:17). Christians have a belief system and a lifestyle that can be very different from others around us. Our moral standards and opinions may be dramatically opposed to theirs. It may be difficult to hear others' complaints, catch wind of people's problems, and be subjected to expletive-filled stories. We may want to intercede and try to solve problems or correct behaviors, but Proverbs warns us about the possible results.

We must earn the right to grab the ears of those around us. We need to gain their trust before we can speak to their issues. Move in too fast, and we will get bit hard. What kind of witness is that? They will not understand what you are doing, and they will do anything to get you to stop pulling at their ears. Give it time. Be patient. Earn the right. Help with the small things to show them you have their best interest at heart. The time will come when they will willingly give you access to the ears. Then groom away!

Friday: Discernment

We took Major to our local animal hospital. He needed his shots updated, and the doctor needed to look him over. The hospital is a large building which houses the clinic, a board-and-care facility, a doggy day care, and a reproductive clinic. As a result, different dogs continuously occupied the waiting room. They came in one door and disappeared through one of the other doors behind the counter. Since Major needed an exam room, we had to wait.

The first dog to arrive was a fluffy black and white dog. One look and Major was excited to meet this new friend. They enjoyed meeting each other, but the exchange was brief. Next through the door were two overweight Pekinese. Major took one look at them and turned away hoping to find something more interesting to occupy his attention. Soon after, a woman burst through the door and announced that she had an appointment for her female, along with a stud to be tested for breeding compatibility. Once she had the attention of the room, she went to retrieve her dog. She returned with a large, black Great Dane at her side. Major took one look at the Dane and dropped to the floor in a submissive position. He did not move until she had walked through the lobby and out the other side.

I wondered if Major was intimidated by the Dane's size. Perhaps he only liked dogs that were of similar size and shape. My wondering ceased as the male walked in. He was a foot taller at the withers (shoulders) than the female. He was a massive dog walking beside an elderly woman. If he wanted to attack, his owner would have had no control. I glanced down at Major. He remained calm. As the Dane passed by, both dogs calmly sniffed in each other's direction before the Dane continued through the waiting room and out the same door that the female had gone through moments before. It wasn't size. So what was it?

Finally, a pair of yellow Labrador retrievers entered the room. They seemed happy to be coming to such a fun place. One of the dogs saw Major and pulled so hard that his collar broke. He darted toward Major who showed no reluctance. Instead, his tail quivered as it had with the little fluffy dog. When they met, they greeted, sniffed, and rubbed against each other as though they were long lost friends.

Dogs have the ability to read the energy levels of other dogs. They can smell anxiety or happiness. They can read aggressiveness or stability. Dogs know when to approach and when to stay away. They know when to submit, when to avoid eye contact, and when to advance. It is amazing to watch animals interact intelligently even though they have never met.

In human terms this ability is called discernment. We could also use the words judgment, or sensitivity. God wants us to use good judgment, to be sensitive to those around us, to discern their spirit. 1 John 4:1 says, "My dear friends, don't believe everything you hear. Carefully weigh and examine what people tell you. Not everyone who talks about God comes from God. There are a lot of lying preachers loose in the world" (*The Message*). Paul wrote, "For God is my witness, how I long for you all with the affection of Christ Jesus. And this I pray, that your love may abound still more and more in real knowledge and all discernment, so that you may approve the things that are excellent, in order to be sincere and blameless until the day of Christ" (Philippians 1:8–10).

There are times when we can be excited about a relationship. At other times, we must avoid aggressive people. In very difficult times we must do everything we can to lay low until trouble has passed us by completely. What dogs do naturally we must cultivate so that we may remain strong in the love of Jesus.

> Make your ear attentive to wisdom, incline your heart to understanding; for if you cry for discernment, lift your voice for understanding; if you seek her as silver and search for her as for hidden treasures.
>
> Proverbs 2:2–4

Saturday: "Our Witness" Prayer Day

Prayer That We May Be a Good Witness

Ask a people why they are unwilling to give their lives to Jesus, and you might hear stories about how Christians caused them to stumble. The hypocrisy of Christians seems to be the most common reason for people not attending church. While it is an easy excuse, we would still be wise to take their argument seriously. Is it possible that you are the reason why someone has turned away from Christ? It is a sobering thought, especially when we consider that we will be held accountable for our actions.

In 1936, J. Edwin Orr was sitting in a revival meeting in New Zealand and was inspired to write this prayer, which was later put to music. The hymn known as *Search Me, O God* is still a great prayer. Use this hymn today as your own prayer. Take time to pause where you are so moved and allow God to commune with you.

Search me, O God, and know my heart today;
Try me, O Savior,
Know my thoughts, I pray.
See if there be some wicked way in me;
Cleanse me from every sin, and set me free.

I praise Thee, Lord, for cleansing me from sin;
Fulfill Thy Word and make me pure within.
Fill me with fire, where once I burned with shame;
Grant my desire to magnify Thy Name.

Lord, take my life, and make it wholly Thine;
Fill my poor heart with Thy great love divine.
Take all my will, my passion, self and pride;
I now surrender, Lord—in me abide.

O Holy Ghost, Revival comes from Thee;
Send a revival, Start the work in me.
Thy Word declares Thou wilt supply our need;
For blessings now, O Lord, I humbly plead.[4]

Week 13: Meeting the Needs of Others

Monday: Working with the Master to Serve Others

When Lisa took Kessie into her household, the chocolate Lab's life really began. When they are together, they are inseparable. They visit their friends at the park regularly, keep each other company, and practice their obedience training. Though Kessie is still a puppy, she is well on her way to becoming an obedience champion. Lisa and Kessie have a great relationship—one that other dogs would give anything to have.

What takes their relationship from good to great is that they use their relationship to serve others. On this day, Lisa and Kessie joined forces with the Petco Foundation in a 5K to help rescue dogs in need. It seems only fitting that they should help others to find the kind of relationship that they have together.

God has called us into a loving relationship through the blood of Jesus Christ. He knows what we need and he wants to bless us with those things. He asks us to "seek first His kingdom and His righteousness." This comes with the promise that "all these things will be added to you" (Matthew 6:33). Wow, what a promise! Jesus took our sins, died the death we deserved, and replaced it with eternal life and the promise that he will meet our needs.

Your relationship with Jesus moves from good to great as you partner with him to help rescue others in need. Special blessings come to those who obey Jesus' Great Commission: "Go therefore and make disciples of all the nations, baptizing them in the name of the Father and the Son and the Holy Spirit, teaching them to observe all that I commanded you; and lo, I am with you always, even to the end of the age" (Matthew 28:19–20).

As partakers of grace, it seems only fitting that we embrace the call of Jesus to go into all world and become disciple makers. Helping others find the kind of relationship that we have with Jesus brings great joy. Remember, he has promised to walk with us on this journey, and he has given us this promise: "Now to Him who is able to do far more abundantly beyond all that we ask or think, according to the power that works within us" (Ephesians 3:20).

Tuesday: Doing for the Least

Koda is an interesting dog. She is a cross between a dachshund father and a mother who is a Labrador and pit bull mix. That by itself makes Koda a unique dog. Though she has the facial expression of a dachshund, she has an amazing five-foot vertical leaping ability. But there is more to Koda's history that makes her a very unique dog.

Shortly after Koda was born, her mother began rejecting her. Sensing the rejection, her brothers and sisters began pushing her away. Koda found herself as an outcast in her own whelping box. The longer she was separated, the weaker she became. That was when Kirsten came into the picture. One look and Kirsten knew that she needed to save this little puppy.

They tried a bottle, but Koda wouldn't take it. They tried formulas, but nothing worked. They were losing the battle to keep Koda alive and they didn't know what to do. One day, Kirsten opened a can of tuna to feed her daughters for lunch. The odor of the tuna appealed to Koda. From four weeks on, Koda lived on tuna.

Koda's life reminds us of a story Jesus told about judgment day:

Then the King will say to those on His right, "Come, you who are blessed of My Father, inherit the kingdom prepared for you from the foundation of the world. For I was hungry, and you gave Me something to eat; I was thirsty, and you gave Me something to drink; I was a stranger, and you invited Me in; naked, and you clothed Me; I was sick, and you visited Me; I was in prison, and you came to Me." Then the righteous will answer Him, "Lord, when did we see You hungry, and feed You, or thirsty, and give You something to drink? And when did we see You a stranger, and invite You in, or naked, and clothe You? When did we see You sick, or in prison, and come to You?" The King will answer and say to them, "Truly I say to you, to the extent that you did it to one of these brothers of Mine, even the least of them, you did it to Me."

Matthew 25:34–40

There are far too many human Kodas in this world. Those who, by all rights, should care for them have rejected them. As a result they are spiritually hungry and thirsty. They are emotionally naked and they are imprisoned by sin. They may even be physically rejected, broke, hungry, and thirsty. They need us to save them from their rejection and sin. They might need something as simple as a can of tuna—or complete spiritual makeover—but we are God's hands and feet to meet the needs of a broken, lost, and rejected society.

Koda knows that she has been saved. As a result, she is fiercely loyal to her savior, Kirsten. She is supportive and protective because she was once lost, but now she has been found.

Who does the work of ministry for Christ? The job is given to those who were lost, but now have been found. We know what it is means to be saved so we know what it's like to lift others up. What we do naturally in ministry becomes the tuna that others need to find salvation.

Remember, the passage continues with those who were rejected by Christ. What was the reason given for their rejection? To paraphrase Jesus, "You saw me naked and hungry, thirsty and poor, and you left me in the corner of the box to die. You didn't do it to the least of my brothers, so you didn't do it to me."

Wednesday: Filling in the Gaps

Sophie is a beautiful little girl with her mother's eyes, a personality all her own, and a curious sense of adventure. She is her mommy's pride and joy. But like most of us, Sophie has her own set of needs. There are things she is blessed with in abundance, and things she wishes she had more of. To help fill her own sense of need, Sophie found her own little puppy, wrapped him in her blanket, and took her home.

Zero is warm and loving. He helps fill the void when Sophie doesn't feel well or is lonely. He is not real family, but he has a special ability to make Sophie feel loved. She chose him, and he is tuned in to what she needs and does his best to meet this needs. Because of this, they have become real companions.

Many of us live with our own set of unique needs. We have lost a family member, or we live far away from those we love most. We have lost a job and don't know where to turn. Our friend of many years is no longer around. Whatever the need is, we all have an empty place in our lives that needs to be filled.

The Bible describes the church with several familial terms. The word "adoption" is used five times in the New Testament. For example, Paul said, "For you have not received a spirit of slavery leading to fear again, but you have received a spirit of adoption as sons by which we cry out, 'Abba! Father!'" (Romans 8:15). The family name "brother" is used ninety-five times. Jesus said, "For whoever does the will of God, he is My brother and sister and mother" (Mark 3:35), and Paul wrote, "But that you also may know about my circumstances, how I am doing, Tychicus, the beloved brother and faithful minister in the Lord, will make everything known to you" (Ephesians 6:21). Jesus wasn't talking about actual, physical, brothers, but spiritual ones. The same is true with Paul, and so many others who used the word. "Sister" is a word used 16 times in the New Testament. For example, 2 John 1:13 says, "The children of your chosen sister greet you." Again, the writer was not talking about a physical sister but a spiritual one. The children were spiritual children.

The issue here is that the church is a place where we who are adopted into the family of God can go and fill in the gaps. We can find spiritual brothers and sisters, fathers and mothers, to help fill the void in our own lives. They may not be the family born to us, but as the adopted family of Christ they have the ability to recognize our needs and care for us in very unique ways.

I have one physical brother, but I've had many tremendous spiritual brothers. I have one physical sister, yet I can name a number of spiritual sisters who have been there in my times of need. My father passed away many years ago, and since that time I have enjoyed the fellowship of several spiritual fathers. I have not always been on the receiving end. I have been a brother and a father to others who had a gap in their own lives.

God did not use those family-type words by accident. He created the church so that we would have a place to go, to feel like we are a part of something. He gave us people who, if we allow them into our lives, will fill the gaps left by those who are no longer near us. When we are sick, they will be there to care for us. When we laugh, they will be able to laugh with us. When we cry, they will be compassionate toward us. In short, they will fill the gaps in our lives and help us to feel complete.

No wonder, Paul offered this prayer: "For this reason I bow my knees before the Father, from whom every family in heaven and on earth derives its name, that He would grant you, according to the riches of His glory, to be strengthened with power through His Spirit in the inner man" (Ephesians 3:14–16).

Thursday: Pay It Forward

Jake was the runt of the litter. The breeder wanted to put him down because he was not a perfect specimen. He was small and not very healthy and would probably have health problems anyway. But Jen fell in love with the little golden puppy and saved him from certain death. By six and a half months, the breeder's predictions came true. Jake became sick with AIHA, an autoimmune disease. He should have died then, but the skill of the doctor, and Jen's compassion, kept him alive. He was loved, and though he suffered greatly, Jen's comfort carried him through.

Four years later it was Jake's turn to share love and compassion with his master. Jen was going through a very difficult time in her life, but Jake was there for her. He knew what it meant to be loved. He understood what compassion was like. He had experienced comfort when everything looked hopeless. Because he had experienced these things himself, he was able to give it to others.

Recognizing his ability to give comfort, Jen and Jake enrolled in a therapy-dog training class. As a Therapy Dog International team member (TDI) they visited the head trauma unit at a local hospital, local nursing homes, a mother/child refuge home (working with the children of abuse), and made house calls for people who were immobile or in hospice care.

Jake shared compassion, offering comfort and assurance to those who were sick as well as those who were dying. Soon, Jake became sick once again. He became weak, and he struggled to keep his level of energy. He was under doctor's care almost continually for two years. Yet, he never gave up comforting others. In fact, he continued his work of compassion until the very end of his life.

Jake's life illustrates an important principle. Second Corinthians 1 says, "Blessed be the God and Father of our Lord Jesus Christ, the Father of mercies and God of all comfort, who comforts us in all our affliction so that we will be able to comfort those who are in any affliction with the comfort with which we ourselves are comforted by God. For just as the sufferings of Christ are ours in abundance, so also our comfort is abundant through Christ" (vv. 3–5). According to this passage, we are to take what we received in our own time of need and give it to others. We received comfort, so we pay it forward to those who are in similar need.

The apostle Paul continues with his own testimony, saying, "But God, who comforts the depressed, comforted us by the coming of Titus; and not only by his coming, but also by the comfort with which he was comforted in you" (2 Corinthians 7:6–7a). Titus was comforted by the church, which then sent him to comfort Paul in his time of need. This is the way the church works.

We have all experienced trials, whether sickness or heartache or loss. Having been through it, we understand what it means to be comforted. Our God desires us to take what we received in our suffering and share it with others. If you have suffered loss, find someone who is struggling now and minister to them. If you have had cancer, comfort a cancer patient. The needs are endless so the list could go on and on. The real question is, what have you experienced in your life and how can you pay it forward to someone who is currently in need? What has God given you that you can now use for His glory in the lives of others? Don't hold back. Don't keep it to yourself. You may be exactly the person that some sufferer needs. You may still be struggling but that does not excuse you from giving to others. I have often gone to the hospital to visit a dying brother or sister in Christ, only to find them in someone else's room witnessing for Christ.

You have experienced something that God can use. Pay it forward.

Friday: In the Deep End

Don't let the picture fool you. This is one amazing dog. Pluto is a Tennessee bluetick coonhound. Though he is a purebred, he is not your normal bluetick because he was born with none of the characteristic coloring of his breed. He is loyal to all of those who allow him to get close to their face. He needs a close up view and a good long smell of a person. Once the look and scent is in his mind, that person is his responsibility. He can track you no matter where you go.

One day his owner Nicole and my nephews were swimming. They were having a good time, and Pluto was off in the shade looking just like he looks in this picture. Nicholas, my nephew, was in the deep end, playing and splashing. All at once, Pluto sprang to his feet, ran toward the pool and jumped in. When his face surfaced from the water, he was next to Nic. Instinctively he grabbed Nic's hand in his mouth and began swimming toward the shallow end of the pool. Nic had little choice but to submit because these hounds are big dogs, with some of the largest paws in the canine world. They are powerful swimmers, so dragging Nic was not a difficult task.

Nic didn't know that he needed saving. He thought he was just having fun in the deep end of the pool. Pluto, however, recognized the splashing as a call for help and he knew the way Nic should go.

Consider the words of Ephesians 2: "And you were dead in your trespasses and sins, in which you formerly walked according to the course of this world, according to the prince of the power of the air, of the spirit that is now working in the sons of disobedience" (vv. 1–2). Here we were splashing around in the deep end of life, playing with our toys and having what we thought was the time of our life. We didn't know that we needed to be saved, but Jesus did. "But God demonstrates His own love toward us, in that while we were yet sinners, Christ died for us" (Romans 5:8). While we were in the deep end salvation was available, but we didn't see the need. Ephesians continues, "Among them we too all formerly lived in the lusts of our flesh, indulging the desires of the flesh and of the mind, and were by nature children of wrath, even as the rest" (2:3).

The good news is that Jesus knew what we could not see, and he came to our rescue. "But God, being rich in mercy, because of His great love with which He loved us, even when we were dead in our transgressions, made us alive together with Christ (by grace you have been saved), and raised us up with Him, and seated us with Him in the heavenly places in Christ Jesus, so that in the ages to come He might show the surpassing riches of His grace in kindness toward us in Christ Jesus" (2:4–7). Through the cross and an empty grave, Jesus brought us to the safety of God's love. Now that we are here we can look back on our "deep end" experiences and see that we were indeed splashing for help. We praise God for the fact that once we were dead, but now we are alive in Christ. But our story should not stop with our salvation.

"For by grace you have been saved through faith; and that not of yourselves, it is the gift of God; not as a result of works, so that no one may boast. For we are His workmanship, created in Christ Jesus for good works, which God prepared beforehand so that we would walk in them" (2:8–10). We are called to continue the work of saving those who are still in the deep end. This is the good work we are called to do: watching the deep end, reaching for those who are still splashing, and bringing them to the saving knowledge of Jesus Christ.

Pluto is no longer with us. He was killed at three years of age in a tragic accident. The memory of Pluto lives on in those he loved. They miss him very much. Jesus was tragically crucified at the young age of thirty. But he rose from the grave as a living Lord. He is still saving the lives of those who are in drowning. We cannot sit on the sidelines remembering a once crucified Lord. As those who have been saved, we must be obedient to our living Lord, who has called us to be his "Life Savers."

Your "deep end" experience is different than mine. You know what to look for and how to help others who have followed your path. In fact, each of us has unique "deep end" stories. Jesus wants to use our unique perspectives to bring all to salvation. Keep your ears open for the splash. Someone needs you today.

Saturday: "Meeting the Needs of Others" Prayer Day

Prayer That God Would Reveal Needs We Can Meet

The emphasis this week was on God's call to reach out to others in ministry. Paying it forward is doing for others what God has done for you. It is being willing to jump into the deep end for those in need. It is a lifestyle of ministry, one that lives the truth of Colossians 3:17: "Whatever you do in word or deed, do all in the name of the Lord Jesus, giving thanks through Him to God the Father."

In a world that continually asks, "What's in it for me?" God is calling us to live an "I'm-in-it-for-Jesus" life. The issue is that we hurry through life, missing opportunity after opportunity. Though we are challenged to live a Jesus-first life, we often can't even think of any needs to meet. We rarely notice what goes on around us. So pray today—and through all of next week—that God would open your eyes to see the things that he sees. Pray that your spiritual eyes would be open to the ministry he wants you to fulfill.

Week 14: Daily Struggles

Monday: Temptation

When the yard is large, and the toys are in view,
But the things that capture his attention are few,
What should a bored and lonely pooch do?
But to find a big hole to poke his tongue through! (FB)

Diana Krall sings a haunting jazz rendition of Tom Wait's "Temptation":

Dutch pink and Italian blue
He's there waiting for you
My will has disappeared
Now confusion is oh so clear
Temptation, temptation, temptation
I can't resist
Temptation, for love, temptation, temptation
I can't resist.

The word temptation, even without the visions it casts, is haunting. The apostle Paul tells the reason: "No temptation has overtaken you but such as is common to man" (1 Corinthians 10:13a). The key phrase here is that temptation is common to all men. The sources may vary, but the desire to stretch beyond our spiritual boundary is always present. We may not fully participate—merely sticking our tongue through the fence—but God does not deal in degrees. Jesus reminded us that even thinking a sin in our mind is unacceptable. The reason, James explains, is that temptation breeds lust, capturing our mind. This leads to sin, and, ultimately, to spiritual death.

The good news is that "God is faithful, who will not allow you to be tempted beyond what you are able, but with the temptation will provide the way of escape also, so that you will be able to endure it" (1 Corinthians 10:13b). Peter adds to our assurance that "the Lord knows how to rescue the godly from temptation, and to keep the unrighteous under punishment for the day of judgment" (2 Peter 2:9). Though God is able and willing to save us, there is a better way.

The psalmist desired not to hang around near the fence or peek through the holes. Instead, he chose to stay in the center of God's will. "But You, O Lord, are a shield about me, My glory, and the One who lifts my head" (Psalm 3:3). Using several pictures, David called God's protection a shield around him. He used other words as well. "The Lord is my rock and my fortress and my deliverer, My God, my rock, in whom I take refuge; My shield and the horn of my salvation, my stronghold" (Psalm 18:2). "You are my hiding place; You preserve me from trouble; You surround me with songs of deliverance" (Psalm 32:7). "As the mountains surround Jerusalem, so the Lord surrounds His people from this time forth and forever" (Psalm 125:2).

Whether we view it as a mountain range encompassing us, a place we are offered to hide, a shield, or the covering of the Spirit, we have been placed in God's protection. When we remain in the center of that place, we are far away from the hole in the fence where Satan eagerly waits. The air is not sweeter, the grass is not greener, the life of sin is emptier, and to borrow a few more words from Diana Krall:

> Well I know that she is made of smoke
> But I've lost my way
> He knows that I am broke
> But I must pay him
> Temptation, oh temptation, temptation, I can't resist.[5]

Let us cling to the assurance that God has a better plan. "Now He who establishes us with you in Christ and anointed us is God, who also sealed us and gave us the Spirit in our hearts as a pledge" (2 Corinthians 1:21–22).

Tuesday: Just Being on a Bumper Doesn't Make It True

The bumper sticker says, "He who dies with the most toys wins." Of course, when you see it, it's always mounted on a very expensive vehicle. I have never seen it on a car ready for the junkyard. It seems we look for validation wherever we can find it. Quite often we find it in our "stuff."

Dakota has found solace in the toys he gathered around him. Those toys are his "stuff." Each toy means something to him. Each has its own scent and its own purpose. Some are for snuggling, some are for chewing, while others are for chasing. Pulled all around him, the "stuff" becomes his security and peace of mind.

Yet toys come and go. They get old, fall apart, and become outdated. In the end we become a slave to "stuff." We call it maintenance, upkeep, or upgrades. We like our stuff, all shiny and new—but it never remains that way. Perhaps the bumper sticker should read, "He who dies with the most toys, dies exhausted." Fortunately, Dakota has so much more than a pile of toys. He has a master who cares very much and would do anything for him. Dakota is loved.

John wrote, "And I saw the dead, the great and the small, standing before the throne, and books were opened; and another book was opened, which is the book of life; and the dead were judged from the things which were written in the books, according to their deeds" (Revelation 20:12). This judgment will not be based on our toys or how much we have gathered. Instead, we will be judged by how much we have given.

Christ gave himself for us. He died with no toys to his name. What little he did have was gambled away at the foot of the cross. He gave everything for us, and he called us to lose our own lives to follow him. Paul testified, "I have been crucified with Christ; and it is no longer I who live, but Christ lives in me; and the life which I now live in the flesh I live by faith in the Son of God, who loved me and gave Himself up for me" (Galatians 2:20).

The old hymn says it well:

I'd rather have Jesus than silver or gold;
I'd rather be His than have riches untold;
I'd rather have Jesus than houses or lands;
I'd rather be led by His nail-pierced hand.

Refrain:
Than to be the king of a vast domain
And be held in sin's dread sway;
I'd rather have Jesus than anything
This world affords today.

I'd rather have Jesus than men's applause;
I'd rather be faithful to His dear cause;
I'd rather have Jesus than worldwide fame;
I'd rather be true to His holy name.[6]

Perhaps we need a bumper sticker that says, "He Who Dies with Jesus, Wins."

Wednesday: Why Does God Allow Evil?

Tell someone about Jesus and he or she is bound to ask the question, "If God is such a loving God, then why does he allow evil in this world?" To answer, we usually give a detailed explanation about free will. Sometimes they understand, and sometimes the discussion leads to more questions.

Couldn't God have just solved the problem in the beginning? If he had just got rid of Satan, we wouldn't be in this mess. But he didn't. And we find in the book of Job that God still had communications with Satan. So how do we explain sin and the presence of evil in a way all will understand?

Just outside of Parker, Colorado, is a large housing community that made the decision that the deer population would be protected within the borders of the community. This meant that within the borders of the community, man was not allowed to be a predator of the deer population. In addition they enacted rules to insure that predatory animals were kept out of the community.

With no natural predators the deer population expanded to four times the original population. The deer lost all fear of man and animal. They began foraging in planters and gardens, traveling in small herds. They paid no attention to people because they posed no threat. I was only four feet away from the deer in this picture. He just looked at me and continued munching on the bush in front of him.

Because all predators were eliminated, hoof disease, skin conditions, and other ailments began to show themselves. Limited amounts of food meant that the population often remained undernourished. So immune to fear were they that if you threw a rock at a deer, it would come over and smell it to see if it was edible. Without natural predators, animals suffer. The presence of predators keeps the animal population healthy and stable.

What does this story say about the presence of evil? Well, without a predator (evil) Christians become fat, spiritually diseased, and impervious to God's call. With no threat to our spiritual lives, why read the Bible, or pray, or even go to church? After all, nothing can harm us.

I am convinced that our society has declined, not because we have denied God but because we have denied the presence and power of evil. When that happens, it is only a matter of time before God becomes irrelevant. Don't believe this? Visit any major university campus and listen to the teachings of the professors. There is no sin, so we are free to ignore God and become our own source of power. And with that, our social values continue to decline.

God knows that we remain sharp when we understand the power of our predator: "Be of sober spirit, be on the alert. Your adversary, the devil, prowls around like a roaring lion, seeking someone to devour" (1 Peter 5:8). That sounds pretty predatory. This is why we are urged in Ephesians 4:27 not to "give the devil an opportunity." Instead we are to "put on the full armor of God, so that [we] will be able to stand firm against the schemes of the devil" (Ephesians 6:11).

James issues this challenge: "Submit therefore to God. Resist the devil and he will flee from you" (James 4:7).

Thursday: I Cannot Tell a Lie: The Cat Did It

Even great dogs make questionable decisions, especially when they are in the puppy stage. As a young boy, I remember our family dog cut his teeth on the footrest of an antique high chair. Puppies will pick through your shoes to determine the newest or the most expensive and then chew on that pair. One of our own puppies chewed a hole in wall-to-wall carpet in our house. What Dakota was looking for when he started in on Krista's feather pillow is anybody's guess. Like puppies, children go through periods where they make poor decisions and then lie about it. They will make up elaborate stories in their attempt to place blame on anybody but them self. As we grow, we move from childhood mistakes to various levels of sin. When we get caught we look for ways to assign blame. Unfortunately, this pattern of denial, blame, anger, and, finally, admission of guilt has brought down politicians, professional athletes, and even religious leaders.

The writer of Romans explored the concept of his own sin:

> So the trouble is not with the law, for it is spiritual and good. The trouble is with me, for I am all too human, a slave to sin. I don't really understand myself, for I want to do what is right, but I don't do it. Instead, I do what I hate. But if I know that what I am doing is wrong, this shows that I agree that the law is good. So I am not the one doing wrong; it is sin

living in me that does it. And I know that nothing good lives in me, that is, in my sinful nature. I want to do what is right, but I can't. I want to do what is good, but I don't. I don't want to do what is wrong, but I do it anyway. But if I do what I don't want to do, I am not really the one doing wrong; it is sin living in me that does it. I have discovered this principle of life—that when I want to do what is right, I inevitably do what is wrong. I love God's law with all my heart. But there is another power within me that is at war with my mind. This power makes me a slave to the sin that is still within me. Oh, what a miserable person I am! Who will free me from this life that is dominated by sin and death? Thank God! The answer is in Jesus Christ our Lord. So you see how it is: In my mind I really want to obey God's law, but because of my sinful nature I am a slave to sin.

Romans 7:14–25, NLT

It is interesting to hear Paul argue with himself as he wrestles to discover the truth about his own sin. Many times in reasoning through our own sin we make it to the "miserable-person-I-am" part, only to stop there. It is the wise person who moves on to the "who-will-free-me-from-this-life?" question. James would rather we not wait until we get caught: "Therefore, confess your sins to one another, and pray for one another so that you may be healed. The effective prayer of a righteous man can accomplish much" (James 5:16). James could give this encouragement because he witnessed it in practice in Acts: "Many also of those who had believed kept coming, confessing and disclosing their practices" (Acts 19:18).

We may not be the one who is struggling. If this is the case, we have responsibility to help others. Paul writes, "Brethren, even if anyone is caught in any trespass, you who are spiritual, restore such a one in a spirit of gentleness; each one looking to yourself, so that you too will not be tempted" (Galatians 6:1).

Chew as hard as you want on that pillow. You will never find anything more than tasteless feathers. There will be no substance. Your sin is empty. But Jesus is full of substance. He is able to free you from your bonds and fill you till you want no more.

Friday: Suffering for a Little While

Imagine a Toyota Prius packed with three adults, three dogs, one cat, some luggage and a pile of snacks. Take that full car and drive it through five states in two days. This was the scenario we experienced as we relocated from California to Colorado.

The cat rode in a carrier and suffered the experience of a leash at rest stops. Two dogs rode in the back with the cat. A pet barrier mounted behind the second row seat contained them. The third dog rode in the front with whoever rode in the passenger seat. With each stop, a different dog rotated to the front.

How do you convince animals that their temporary suffering will lead to a reward? They have no concept of a bigger yard, more freedom, wild animals to bark at, or miles of trails to explore. All they know is that they are stuck in a car having a miserable experience.

That experience has a parallel to the Christian life: "For to you it has been granted for Christ's sake, not only to believe in Him, but also to suffer for His sake" (Philippians 1:29). We are "children, heirs also, heirs of God and fellow heirs with Christ, if indeed we suffer with Him so that we may also be glorified with Him" (Romans 8:17).

It is so easy to get caught up in the ride. We struggle with personal struggles and withstand the judgment of others because of our faith. At times it feels like we are getting motion sickness from all the challenges we face in life. It is at these times when we peer through the cage at what seems like endless miles of struggle that we need to lift our eyes the heavens to recapture a vision of the hope that is before us. Paul said, "For I consider that the sufferings of this present time are not worthy to be compared with the glory that is to be revealed to us. For the anxious longing of the creation waits eagerly for the revealing of the sons of God" (Romans 8:18-19).

"But even if you should suffer for the sake of righteousness," wrote Peter, "you are blessed. And do not fear their intimidation, and do not be troubled" (1 Peter 3:14). There is a promise, made to those who endure the suffering of this present time. "After you have suffered for a little while, the God of all grace, who called you to His eternal glory in Christ, will Himself perfect, confirm, strengthen and establish you" (1 Peter 5:10).

The knowledge of a glorious future caused Paul to boldly proclaim, "For this reason I also suffer these things, but I am not ashamed; for I know whom I have believed and I am convinced that He is able to guard what I have entrusted to Him until that day" (2 Timothy 1:12).

Lift up your eyes. Catch a glimpse of the glory that is ahead. Remind yourself that God is not going to forget you. He will not let your down. The suffering of this life is but a moment compared to eternity with Jesus. "For a righteous man falls seven times, and rises again, but the wicked stumble in time of calamity" (Proverbs 24:16).

Saturday: "Daily Struggles" Prayer Day

Yielding our Struggles to God

"I don't make mistakes, I make catastrophes." Have you ever felt like this describes you? It is the feeling that you somehow acquired a special gift to make big messes. If anyone ever discovered your secrets, then no one would ever respect you again. If you feel like this sometimes—or all the time—then repeat these words slowly and with power: "Get behind me Satan."

You do not need to be bound by your struggles, nor should they define you. The path toward holy living is not a straight line, but a series of oval tracks. Picture a series of NASCAR tracks all linked together. A perfect top speed is determined for each oval, and the driver must achieve that speed before he can move on to the next track. It may take the driver one revolution of the track, or twenty. Once he has learned how to be successful on that track, he can drive to the next one.

If we struggle with a problem, burden, or sin, we are going in circles around the track. We have as many chances as we need to gain the victory, but we can't move on spiritually until we have been victorious. As we progress from track to track, we discover that it becomes easier to grow through the learning process. We don't struggle as much with each new oval, and we achieve our victory lap faster and easier.

So where are you on the path to spiritual growth? Have you memorized the scenery on this lap because you have been on it so long? It is time to begin your victory lap? Give it to God. You have struggled with this catastrophe far too long. There is so much more ahead for you, and the Lord is anxious for you to experience it. The only way you will grow through this is if you go through it successfully. That victory lap can start today.

Take the time—right now—to pray through that struggle, and start living your victory.

Week 15: More on Struggles

Monday: Trials

Our Australian terriers were bred for underground work. Taking care of rats, gophers, and other pesky animals comes natural to them. Jazzy, our female Aussie, has the ability to track the movements of an animal from above ground. She sniffs the ground and knows exactly where the animal is,

even though she cannot see it. So when we heard that earthdog trials were taking place just a few miles from our house, we were excited to see what our dogs could do.

Earthdog trials allow a dog to do what they have been bred to do. A caged rat is placed at the end of a tunnel under one of two trap doors (the cage is kept far enough away from the dogs that no harm comes to the rat). One trap door is for the rat, and the second trap door is used as a way of escape for the dog, should they experience trouble during the trial. A line of scent is placed at the entrance of the tunnel, and spread out in a line far enough that the dog can pick up the scent. The dog is supposed to pick up the scent, enter the tunnel, find the rat, and scratch and make noise for at least thirty seconds to pass the test. Jazzy picked up the scent right away. She ran to the entrance of the tunnel, looked in, and then jumped on top of the tunnel. She quickly chased the scent to the end of the tunnel from above ground to where the rat was being kept. Before the judge could move to protect the rat, Jazzy pried up the trap door with her nose, and jumped on top of the rat's cage. While I thought she was brilliant, she did not pass. She needed to go through the tunnel, not over it.

Earthdog trials are much like the trials that we face on a daily basis. God wants us to pass the test, and grow through our trials: "And we know that God causes all things to work together for good to those who love God, to those who are called according to His purpose" (Romans 8:28). We also know that each trial comes with "the way of escape . . . so that you will be able to endure it" (1 Corinthians 10:13). However, the growth of a trial comes as we go through it. The Psalmist wrote, "Even though I walk through the valley of the shadow of death, I fear no evil, for You are with me; Your rod and Your staff, they comfort me" (Psalm 23:4).

Wouldn't it be much easier to jump over that tunnel and go straight to the prize? The tunnel is dark, and the passage can be difficult. Surely we can just go around the trial and learn the same lesson. We should be able to walk around the valley and still win the victory. Yet this is not how we pass the test. We cannot outsmart the process and enter through a trap door at the end of the race. If we constantly avoid the tunnel, how will we ever know how God will use his rod and staff to comfort us? How will we ever come the place where we "shall not want" (Psalm 23:1)? Going through the trials brings us to the place where "goodness and mercy" is. Following the trial to its conclusion is how we gain the prize: "I will dwell in the house of the Lord forever" (Psalm 23:6).

Tuesday: Let Them Laugh

How do you respond when the world laughs at your faith? What do you do when others mock your ministry? Are you discouraged when people think you are foolish for serving Jesus?

Maybe your experience is like this photograph. Dodger, Krista's shih tzu, is in his wading pool attempting to stay cool. The top ring has popped, and what's left isn't perfect by any means. Dodger is taking his pool, and his attempt to swim, very seriously. Dakota, on the other hand, appears to be laughing so hard he can't stay upright. He is keeping his distance while mocking his friend's efforts.

When I announced that my book *The God Whisperer* had been published, a friend of mine broke into laughter. He joked to others about my belief in God. He poked fun at the book's title and mocked the idea that any God would want to do something for me. After the excitement about the book's publication subsided, my friend continued to mock me. Each time I am faced with a challenge, he says, "Your God doesn't seem to be whispering loud enough for you to hear him. Maybe he is not there at all. Have you thought about that?"

I am reminded of a story in the Gospels that illustrates this very situation. Jesus was called to the home of a synagogue leader whose daughter had just died. When Jesus arrived, the musicians and the mourners were in full swing. People were weeping to the death songs, as was the custom of the day. Jesus approached the crowd and told them to go home. He said, "Go away. The girl is not dead but asleep." But they laughed at him" (Matthew 9:24). Jesus is about to raise a little girl from the dead, and the crowd is laughing at him. We can only imagine the mockery that took place among the people as they dispersed toward their homes. "After the crowd had been put outside, he went in and took the girl by the hand, and she got up" (v. 25). Jesus took his task seriously in the face of the laughter. The very people he was about to die for were poking fun at His words.

David experienced this situation during his own life. This caused him to write, "The arrogant mock me unmercifully, but I do not turn from your law" (Psalm 119:51). Paul explained this mocking to the Corinthian church: "For the message of the cross is foolishness to those who are perishing, but to us who are being saved it is the power of God" (1 Corinthians 1:18). "For the foolishness of God is wiser than human wisdom, and the weakness of God is stronger than human strength" (1 Corinthians 1:25). Is it any wonder that John wrote, "Do not be surprised, my brothers and sisters, if the world hates you" (1 John 3:13).

So how do we respond to the scoffers of the world? We keep on wading in the rivers of life. We continue in our ministry. We follow through with the task at hand. We continue to call those who laugh our friend so that when they are ready we will be able to lead them to Christ. We continue to let our light shine in the darkness. We leave our light on the candle stand to shed light for the world to see. Those who would make fun of God do not discourage us. It didn't work with Jesus, and it can't work with us either. Why?

Take another look at the photograph of Dodger and Dakota. Which dog is free, and which one is on a chain? You see, the mockers don't even know how lost they are. They are bound by sin, unable to fathom the sweet release that could be theirs if they would give their life to Jesus. So let them laugh. Soon enough they will be crying, and we will be there to lead them to the living waters.

Wednesday: Laying It Down

Laredo has been a very active dog. He needs to be, since he has been to college, patrolled an almond ranch, and been through a wedding, several moves, and a whole host of other events. A person might be tempted to think that all a dog does is sleep (although I think dogs have that part right) but a dog's life is a busy life. Our own dogs keep watch on the house and make sure that no unfamiliar cars drive on our street without being noticed. They have an archenemy in a large crow that loves to taunt them. They have our grandkids to contend with. Reminding us of feeding time is a very important daily chore. Then they must make sure that we have our daily walk. Yes, a dog's life is busy indeed.

Recently Laredo began to limp. It was obvious that he wasn't feeling well. It pained him to complete his daily routine. He felt bad enough that staying in bed snuggled up under his blanket was all he wanted to do. Is it age? Maybe arthritis? Is the cold weather a problem? They let us know that they don't feel well, but they can't use words to tell us exactly what they are feeling. So, we guess, and wonder, and worry. Pain drains energy from their otherwise vibrant lives.

There are times when we all feel like Laredo. We hurt, and would rather just curl up under our own blanket. Some pain lasts a few days, but other pain lasts months and years. The other night I was taking part in worship with the members of our Bible study group, when a particular song drew me back to the picture of Laredo:

I'm trading my sorrow;
I'm trading my shame;
I'm laying it down
for the joy of the Lord.
I'm trading my sickness;
I'm trading my pain;
I'm laying it down
for the joy of the Lord.[7]

The chorus reminded me of the constant pain that was present in Paul. "Because of the surpassing greatness of the revelations, for this reason, to keep me from exalting myself, there was given me a thorn in the flesh, a messenger of Satan to torment me—to keep me from exalting myself!" (2 Corinthians 12:7). Though his pain was constant, he willingly laid it down. "And He has said to me, 'My grace is sufficient for you, for power is perfected in weakness.' Most gladly, therefore, I will rather boast about my weaknesses, so that the power of Christ may dwell in me" (2 Corinthians 12:9).

As we sang I thought of Laredo, and how much I can relate to his struggle. I identified with Paul's words: "We are hard pressed on every side, but not crushed; perplexed, but not in despair; persecuted, but not abandoned; struck down, but not destroyed" (2 Corinthians 4:8–9, NIV).

Arthritis, cancer, chronic pain, physical limitations, grief, loss, and a host of other issues attack our bodies leaving us to deal with constant pain. But we can still be "more than conquerors" if we keep our focus on the all-sufficient grace of the Lord. Our bodies may bend, but our spirits do not break because we have not been crushed. We may be hard pressed, but we have not been abandoned. We may be robbed of physical strength, but we need not give up our spiritual joy.

Take the time to rest, but never stop singing.

Yes, Lord, yes, Lord, yes, yes, Lord;
Yes, Lord yes, Lord, yes, yes, Lord;
Yes, Lord, yes, Lord, yes, yes, Lord.
Amen.

Thursday: Healing the Hurts of Everyday Life

Our friend Lisa brought Kessie, the chocolate Lab puppy, for a visit. Kessie is young and playful. As a puppy, she brought a whole new energy to the pack. All four dogs ran around the backyard barking and rolling and piling on top of each other. They were having such fun that it brought joy to our hearts.

In the midst of the fun, Satchmo stepped on something that sliced the pad of his foot wide open. The pads are thick and rough, providing protection from harsh terrain and extreme temperatures. Footpads even help regulate temperature since a dog perspires through the pads of their feet.

We were so caught up in the excitement of the afternoon that no one saw what happened. When things settled down we realized that Satchmo's right hind foot was resting in a pool of blood. What happened? They were all having so much fun. This was not the outcome we expected from a play date with our new puppy friend.

Pain comes when we least expect it. When our guard is down, and we are having a good time we are vulnerable to being hurt. A harsh word, a slight directed at you, a friend that turns on you, children who let you down, or someone you trust admits an indiscretion. Maybe the issue is physical. Your day was fine, and all of the sudden you are injured. There are times when we simply get caught through no fault of our own and we find ourselves wondering what went wrong? We get angry, complain that the situation is not fair, and look for someone to blame.

The reality is that things happen, our feet stumble, and we find ourselves in pain. "For we all stumble in many ways. If anyone does not stumble in what he says, he is a perfect man, able to bridle the whole body as well" (James 3:2). The point here is that only Jesus is perfect, so we should expect a degree of pain to come our way.

However, the Bible has some advice to live by: "But if anyone walks in the night, he stumbles, because the light is not in him" (John 11:10). "Therefore be careful how you walk, not as unwise men but as wise, making the most of your time, because the days are evil" (Ephesians 5:15–16).

"Consider it all joy, my brethren, when you encounter various trials, knowing that the testing of your faith produces endurance. And let endurance have its perfect result, so that you may be perfect and complete, lacking in nothing" (James 1:2–4). Pain helps pave the way for spiritual strength, bringing us to completion. Rather than question why God allowed this to happen to us, we should cultivate an attitude of rejoicing. We are being given the opportunity to grow.

"Therefore, since we have been justified through faith, we have peace with God through our Lord Jesus Christ, through whom we have gained access by faith into this grace in which we now stand. And we boast in the hope of the glory of God. Not only so, but we also glory in our sufferings, because we know that suffering produces perseverance; perseverance, character; and character, hope. And hope does not put us to shame, because God's love has been poured out into our hearts through the Holy Spirit, who has been given to us" (Romans 5:1–5). It is the pouring out of God's love that makes the difference in our growth. This is why we are called to unceasing prayer, bringing our requests to God.

If you have been hurt today, do not be discouraged. Have faith, pray, and look forward to the growth that will be yours. Remember the words of Proverbs 24:16: "For a righteous man falls seven times, and rises again. But the wicked stumble in time of calamity."

Friday: A Safe Place

When Kim and I brought our first Australian terrier into our home, the breeder urged us to use a kennel. Though we had never used a kennel before, we agreed to purchase one and train Jazzy to use it. We soon learned to appreciate the rewards of using a kennel. As other dogs were added to our pack, we increased the number of kennels in our house.

A kennel is like a doghouse, only made of wire. It can be covered or left open on all sides. Because it has a door, many view it as a cage. However, that is not how our dogs view their kennel. To them, it is a retreat when they are tired. It is the one place in the house that is completely theirs. They dig at their bedding, and push their blankets around to suit their own interests. It is their safe place, a retreat in times of trouble. It is where they go to be alone.

God calls us to retreat to our own safe place so that we can be alone with him. Isaiah wrote, "Come, my people, enter into your rooms and close your door behind you; Hide for a little while until indignation runs its course" (Isaiah 26:20). Jesus added to this idea when he said, "But you, when you pray, go into your inner room, close your door and pray to your Father who is in secret, and your Father who sees what is done in secret will reward you" (Matthew 6:6).

Where is your safe place? It doesn't matter if it is a bedroom, your favorite chair, or a closet. It only matters that you can be alone with God. When you are spiritually tired or experiencing times of trouble, this is the place God wants to meet you. Find that place and make it yours. Make a commitment that you will spend quality time with God. Let the world's indignation run its course. It is in that place where God will answer your deepest needs.

Saturday: "More on Struggles" Prayer Day

Continued Prayer to Yield our Struggles to God

God has promised that he will never give us more than we can handle. Yet, when you are in the middle of a problem that is being compounded by other issues, it is easy to feel like you are at your limit. Health issues can overwhelm us and social concerns envelop us. Spiritual trials can challenge us and family concerns engulf us. We need a safe place.

For Jesus that safe place was on the mountain, David retreated to a cave, and the disciples went to an upper room. "But you, when you pray, go into your inner room, close your door and pray to your Father who is in secret, and your Father who sees what is done in secret will reward you" (Matthew 6:6). So, where is your safe place where you can be alone with God?

Many people cannot name their safe place. This could be your struggle as well. There is no place to go where the kids, the animals, or your spouse are not already there. The television, the radio, and the cell phone serve as constant reminders that the world always wants your attention. Even God himself rested on the seventh day. (Although I doubt that he had any place to go. Where could he go where he wasn't already there?).

When you feel overwhelmed you need an emotional, spiritual retreat, a place where you can go to be alone with God. Notice, this is not just a place to be completely alone, but alone *with God*—a spiritual place. Your mind understands this concept because it has the ability to shut down, to zone out, to go blank whenever it is overloaded. If you allow your body and spirit to do the same, then you might discover that you're not actually at the end of your rope after all.

If you do not have a place of your own, then you have an assignment. Find your location, go there and pray. Try several spots until your body, soul, mind, and spirit agree that you have found your place. Then soak up God's love.

Week 16: Prepared For Ministry

Monday: Osmosis

Justine sat down to read a book one day. As she read, her cat became curious about what Justine was doing. What could be so interesting in that thing? Not fully understanding, the cat waited and watched as Justine continued to focus her attention on the book.

After a while Justine propped her book open to the page she was reading and went to another part of the house to get a drink. When she returned, the cat had taken over the book, choosing to lie down and take a nap on it. After all, the book was big, and had lots of words. Since cats are not known for their ability to read, perhaps the knowledge it contained could be learned by osmosis.

Far too many Christians treat the Bible in a similar fashion. We carry it around church, display it in prominent places at home, and proudly display it as a sign that we are believers. Many people write important dates in their Bible, stuff it full of church bulletins, or even stash money in it. But how often do we actually sit down and read it? We can't press it against our forehead hoping that the knowledge will sink into our brain without any effort. The truth is, there is no biblical osmosis.

The psalmist understood the importance of God's word: "Thy word is a lamp unto my feet, and a light unto my path" (Psalm 119:105, KJV). Ezra was a strong Old Testament character because he "set his heart to study the law of the Lord and to practice it, and to teach His statutes and ordinances in Israel" (Ezra 7:10).

It was when Moses "took the book of the covenant and read it in the hearing of the people" that they were able to say, "all that the Lord has spoken we will do, and we will be obedient!" (Exodus 24:7). Reading, hearing, speaking the words of Scripture out loud—this is what brings knowledge and conviction.

Paul urged Timothy to "be diligent to present yourself approved of God as a workman who does not need to be ashamed, accurately handling the word of truth" (2 Timothy 2:15). How can we accurately handle the word if we don't know what it says? We may be clothed in white, having been saved by the blood of Jesus, but if we have not grown from there, God is not going to be pleased. How can I say this? Well, look through the Gospels; count how many times Jesus asks the religious leaders of his day, "Have you not read . . .?"

"I didn't know," can't be our excuse for why we didn't read, meditate on, and follow God's word. For just when we try to use this phrase, Jesus will be sure to respond with, "Have you not read . . .?"

Tuesday: Be Still and Know

Dakota was a young basset hound when Krista and Jeff adopted him. Life in his new family would be fun and adventurous, but in the beginning there was a lot that he didn't know. The actions of his family assured Dakota that he was loved and wanted.

Some lessons would be learned through experience. Other lessons he learned by the direct instruction of his master. There were other lessons that could only be learned by watching and listening. For these lessons, Dakota would lie on his blanket and take everything in. He would remain perfectly still, moving only his eyes as he followed the movements of his new family. He learned what it meant to be a part of the family from the stillness of his blanket. He discovered how the family interacted. He watched the actions of the family shih tzu and learned how to be a part of his new pack. How many lessons Dakota learned while being still? This will never be fully understood, but had he not spent those quiet hours observing and listening he never would have become the wonderful dog that he is today.

The Bible makes many references about spending time being quiet. "Make it your ambition to lead a quiet life and attend to your own business and work with your hands, just as we commanded you" (1 Thessalonians

4:11). Paul continues this theme by writing, "Now such persons we command and exhort in the Lord Jesus Christ to work in quiet fashion and eat their own bread" (2 Thessalonians 3:12). The psalmist gave similar advice: "Know that the Lord has set apart his faithful servant for himself; the Lord hears when I call to him. Tremble and do not sin; when you are on your beds, search your hearts and be silent. Offer the sacrifices of the righteous and trust in the Lord" (Psalm 4:3–5).

The quietness we are called to is not designed to hide us from the world. We cannot use these verses as a call to withdraw from society. We are, instead, to focus our quietness on observing, listening, and learning what it means to be a part of God's pack. We listen to God; hear the word, observing others who have experience in the faith. We discover truths, and build our storehouse of knowledge; so that when we are in the world we know how to act, "so that the servant of God may be thoroughly equipped for every good work" (2 Timothy 3:17).

To this end God says, "Be still, and know that I am God; I will be exalted among the nations, I will be exalted in the earth" (Psalm 46:10). In that stillness you will learn just how much you are loved and wanted by the Lord. But use the stillness for other reasons as well. "Be still before the Lord and wait patiently for him; do not fret when people succeed in their ways, when they carry out their wicked schemes" (Psalm 37:7). Some of the best lessons, spiritual or otherwise, can be learned by observing what not to do.

Life can be like a busy intersection. You cannot merely stand on the corner and remain uninvolved. The crowd will push you along until you find yourself in a place where you never intended to be. To that end God calls us to find a place, on our own spiritual blanket, and be still. Learn and practice quietly until you are ready for ministry. Listen for the still small voice. Observe the success and struggles of others. Take in the fellowship of others as they show you what it means to be a part of God's pack.

Before you move away from this lesson, select a time and pick a location to be still, so that you too may know God in his fullness. It is easy to agree with the principles, but without making a firm commitment, you are still on that busy intersection.

Wednesday: Taking the Job Seriously

When Shimmy went to live with Elizabeth, we weren't sure that things would work out. Australian terriers are intelligent dogs and capable of adapting to many circumstances, but we were not sure if being a service dog for a disabled woman was within his capabilities. It was rough at first to fit in since a giant poodle named Daisy had been doing the bulk of the work. Shimmy wanted to do his part, but wasn't trained to take on the role.

Liz decided to change Shimmy's name to Dakota very early on. We were not sure why, but we accepted the change since Shimmy (I mean Dakota) was now Elizabeth's dog. Liz sent a picture of the snow in South Dakota and explained why she changed his name:

> Now you know in part why I named Dakota, Dakota. Phew! It takes lots of courage, strength and perseverance to live in this part of the country! The Dakotas match Dakota's ruff & rugged personality. Besides this, I know that truly God has named him for me.
>
> Dakota means "friend," and he is truly a friend to me. No matter what, he sticks by me. At night he snuggles next to me—I mean snuggles. Then he tops it off by putting his head on me. It's like he's guarding me or protecting me. I am so glad we kept him. His personality is like nothing I've ever known before in a dog. He is turning out to be the best Assistance Dog I, and many others, have ever known. He is even getting to be an expert at picking up dropped items for me. He doesn't hesitate like Daisy does. He picks up metal items like scissors, keys, & staplers with ease. This is hard for dogs because they don't like the metal feeling on their teeth.

The Bible calls us to be as committed to ministry as Dakota is to Elizabeth. "Guard, through the Holy Spirit who dwells in us, the treasure which has been entrusted to you" (2 Timothy 1:14). The idea of guarding the gospel does not mean to keep it from others or to hide it away. It means that we are to keep the message strong, not watered down. To that end we are urged, "Let us not lose heart in doing good, for in due time we will reap if we do not grow weary" (Galatians 6:9). "For consider Him who has endured such hostility by sinners against Himself, so that you will not grow weary and lose heart" (Hebrews 12:3).

As ambassadors for Christ we are to take our job seriously, guarding over those who have been entrusted to our care. The job can be difficult, and at times exhausting, but remember the model we have been called to follow. Paul explains, "That is why we never give up. Though our bodies are dying, our spirits are being renewed every day. For our present troubles are small and won't last very long. Yet they produce for us a glory that vastly outweighs them and will last forever! So we don't look at the troubles we can see now; rather, we fix our gaze on things that cannot be seen. For the things we see now will soon be gone, but the things we cannot see will last forever" (2 Corinthians 4:16–18).

There may times when we feel weary and the problems of the world feel like metal in our teeth. But stay the course, keep the faith, take your ministry seriously. You may face physical limitations, financial struggles, or time constraints. These issues, though they feel big now, are only temporary issues. The people you serve and the faith decisions they make are everlasting.

Thursday: Not Like Him

Meet Ruckus (foreground), who is pictured spending quality time with his best friend, Scooter. Whether Ruckus actually borrowed his owner's car or not is up in the air. However, they do seem comfortable in the driver's seat of the car. Kelli Ann posted this picture of Ruckus and Scooter online on *The God Whisperer* book page. I am sure that Kelli has a great relationship with Ruckus, but the picture itself brought a different picture to mind.

Dogs have become a very important part of the American landscape. Owners are known to identify then as babies and kids—as part of the family. People dress them up, dye their hair, and paint their nails. Owners take walks and push their dogs in baby strollers. Americans spend billions of dollars on their dogs every year all to make them a special part of the family. But no matter how much money is spent or how we try to make them into little people, one thing will remain true: they are still dogs.

This reality should cause us to think about mankind as well. God created the world and filled it with amazing plants and animals. Then He created man in His own image and placed him in the middle of the garden. He offered Adam and Eve the unique position of having dominion over every created thing. Then God extended a very unique gift—a special relationship demonstrated by the ability to walk the garden with Him. Yet, man did not want to be with God, or simply be in His image. We wanted to be equal to

God. The deceiver said, "For God knows that when you eat from [the tree in the middle of the garden] your eyes will be opened, and you will be like God, knowing good and evil" (Genesis 3:5).

The problem of wanting to be our own God was not isolated to the garden. It continued with each generation throughout the Old Testament. We find these words in Ezekiel: "Son of man, say to the leader of Tyre, 'Thus says the Lord GOD, "Because your heart is lifted up and you have said, I am a god, I sit in the seat of gods in the heart of the seas"; Yet you are a man and not God, although you make your heart like the heart of God'" (Ezekiel 28:2).

The same problem was described in the book of Romans: "For even though they knew God, they did not honor Him as God or give thanks, but they became futile in their speculations, and their foolish heart was darkened. Professing to be wise, they became fools, For even though they knew God, they did not honor Him as God or give thanks, but they became futile in their speculations, and their foolish heart was darkened" (Romans 1:21–22).

Here is a reality check: No matter how hard we try to put ourselves in the driver's seat, we will never be in control. We are not God. We are men. We are not the Creator but the created. "For this reason also, God highly exalted Him, and bestowed on Him the name which is above every name, so that at the name of Jesus every knee will bow, of those who are in heaven and on earth and under the earth, and that every tongue will confess that Jesus Christ is Lord, to the glory of God the Father" (Philippians 2:9–11).

When we believe we are capable of making our own decisions without seeking God, we put ourselves in His position. When we call every blessing "good luck," or believe that we deserve every good thing, we are putting ourselves in the driver's seat. Any time we insist on controlling our own lives without consideration of the Lord's will, we are trying to be our own God.

When our dog tries to control the family, chaos is often the result. The fact is that dogs need the leadership that a knowledgeable master can provide. They do not see what is ahead, and they have little memory of the past. In the same way, we have no idea of the depth of God's knowledge. He knows what is best for us, and He is able to bless us in ways we cannot comprehend. This is why we need to take ourselves out of the driver's seat, and yield to God's authority. "For this reason also, God highly exalted Him, and bestowed on Him the name which is above every name, so that at the name of Jesus every knee will bow, of those who are in heaven and on earth and under the earth, and that every tongue will confess that Jesus Christ is Lord, to the glory of God the Father" (Philippians 2:9–11).

Friday: In the World, Not of the World

What does it feel like to be in the world but not of the world? Honestly, most of us do not know. We have built-in support groups through family, church, and the workplace. We shop at familiar stores and travel the same streets every day. There is a comfort level that we experience because our routine helps us to feel comfortable. But, what would life be like if nothing that brings us comfort was in place?

Nicole is a new missionary in Madagascar. The streets are unfamiliar, as is the language. The people are different, and there is no family around. She did not go to Madagascar to work with churches, but to help start churches. Her job is to learn the language and customs by being immersed in the Malagasy culture. Her first year is designed for her to learn, not to do. The community needs to impact Nicole, so that she will be able to impact them later. I believe Nicole knows what it feels like to be in the world but not of the world.

This is where three Mastiff puppies named Shack, Rack, and Bennie come in. Nicole made a lifetime commitment to live, work, and serve in Madagascar. She invested everything to go there, but in the last several months she has discovered that the place she decided to move to is the place most people want to move away from. Many people Nicole has gotten to know have left Madagascar. Even missionary candidates Nicole moved to the country with couldn't handle the experience and moved back home. As a result, Nicole is living in a six-bedroom ministry house by herself.

Shack, Rack, and Bennie are named after Meshack, Shadrack, and Abednigo who were bold men of God in a pagan culture. They went through the fire, and came out untarnished. They believed God would be with them no matter what the circumstances indicated. When they were thrown into the fiery furnace, God provided angels to minister to them. In the world of Madagascar, Nicole needed her own ministering angels to give comfort, provide protection, and give her a familiar feel of what it was like at home. So she adopted three Mastiff puppies from missionaries who were bound for the states.

How do we treat those who serve the Lord full-time on the mission fields? How do we treat those who serve in the local church on a daily basis? Shack, Rack, and Bennie provide constant love, support, and encouragement. They will be there in the morning to help Nicole serve the Lord. They will keep her strong at noon and provide hugs when the day is done. When others leave, they will remain faithful. It reminds me of the time Moses led Israel to battle against Amalek. He stood on a hill overlooking the battle and raised up the staff of God. As long as the staff was held high, the battle tipped in favor of Israel. When Moses' arms dropped, the battle shifted to favor Amalek. The difference came with Aaron and Hur, who found a large rock for Moses to rest on. Then each man stood beside Moses supporting his arms until the battle was won and "Joshua overwhelmed Amalek and his people with the edge of the sword" (Exodus 17:13).

The only way the spiritual battle is going to be won is if we surround those who work for the gospel full time and support their arms. They cannot do the work without help. The burden is heavy, and their arms become tired. Nicole, like so many missionaries and Christian leaders, has given her life to serve Jesus. The Bible says that those who serve "are to be considered worthy of double honor, especially those who work hard at preaching and teaching" (Timothy 5:17).

What can you do for a full-time servant of God? You may be God's chosen one to minister to faithful men and women in the heat of a furnace. You might be the encourager that God has called to keep His workers strong. Show God's servants that you care. Stand beside them. Hold up their arms. The battle will be won when we all work together.

Saturday: "Prepared for Ministry" Day of Prayer

Dedication for Ministry

A children's song from the '60s and '70s said, "This world is not my home, I'm just a-passin' through. My treasures are laid up somewhere beyond the blue. The angels beckon me from heaven's open door, and I can't feel at home in this world anymore." It's a great song and still fun to sing. But wait a minute! We are not ready for that transition yet. Is it possible for us to be so heavenly minded that we are of no earthly good?

We all want to go to heaven and be with Jesus. That is not in question. What is in question is this: Are we looking so far ahead that we are missing the opportunity for ministry right now? Perhaps the better statement is, "This world is not my home, I'm just a-passin through. I'm taking people with me to heaven—how 'bout you?"

Heaven will be a great place, but will the people you know be there? Our job as believers is to capture as wide a swath as we can on either side of the path so that heaven is populated and hell is defeated. Your journey is different from anyone else's. Occasionally, spiritual paths cross, and we can get some help witnessing to someone, but what if you are the only believer someone ever really gets to know?

Today in your prayer time, make a list of the people you need to reach for Christ. Lift them up before Jesus and ask for guidance and support. Decide today that you are going to make a difference while you are on this earth.

Week 17: Spiritually Satisfied

RELAXING WITH THE PACK

HOW MANY DOGS DO YOU FIND?

Monday: The Leader of the Pack

Dogs have always been a part of our family. After a brief period without a pet, we were pleased when we added our first Australian terrier to the family. It wasn't long before we felt the need to add one more. Jazzy needed company during the day, so Satchmo was a logical addition. Everything beyond that just happened. We didn't start out to have a pack; we just ended up with one.

A balanced pack requires calm assertive pack leader. Dogs understand the chain of command within a pack. If you are not the leader then one of them will fill the spot. This usually includes skirmishes and tests of will to determine who will rise to the top. I am the leader of our pack, and as the leader I control the attitudes and actions of the pack.

Another requirement of a balanced pack is time spent together. Occasionally, I will drop to the floor and spend time at their level. I want them to know that I own their space and am comfortable occupying it with them. At other times, it is important to invite them into my space.

Inviting the pack into my space takes time. Each dog must exhibit a relaxed, submissive, attitude before it is allowed to enter my space. This doesn't happen all at once, but as a dog relaxes, that one is invited to join me. The purpose is to let them become comfortable in my space.

God followed the same plan. Jesus became a man so that he could occupy our space. Through his death, burial, and resurrection, Christ demonstrated his ownership of our space: "He made Him who knew no sin to be sin on our behalf, so that we might become the righteousness of God in Him" (2 Corinthians 5:21). "And Jesus came up and spoke to them, saying, 'All authority has been given to Me in heaven and on earth'" (Matthew 28:18). God wanted us to know that he owns our space, and as we submit our lives to his authority, then he invites us into his. This is why Peter wrote, "but sanctify Christ as Lord in your hearts" (1 Peter 3:15a).

When we become comfortable with God in our space, then we receive the promise that he wants us to enter his space. "Don't let your hearts be troubled. Trust in God, and trust also in me. There is more than enough room in my Father's home. If this were not so, would I have told you that I am going to prepare a place for you. When everything is ready, I will come and get you, so that you will always be with me where I am. And you know the way to where I am going" (John 14:1–4, NLT).

In order for us to be invited into God's space, we must first be comfortable with Jesus being Lord of our space. Your space includes your heart and mind, your home, possessions, job, and relationships. He must be your leader in all things here so that you will be invited into his space one day with these wonderful words: "Well done, good and faithful slave. You were faithful with a few things, I will put you in charge of many things. Enter into the joy of your master" (Matthew 25:21).

Tuesday: Pure Joy

Kessie celebrated her first birthday at the dog park where Lisa takes her. She has a whole bunch of friends that she spends time with several times a week. They run and fetch and play together. In Kessie's short life a great deal of learning has taken place because she was able to watch and imitate the behaviors she witnessed from other dogs. The idea that she was able to share her first birthday with her friends brought pure joy to her face.

What brings you pure joy? Chocolate or some other food might bring what you would call joy. The chance to spend a quiet Saturday with a book might bring joy as well. Each of these examples may bring joy, but it is only temporary joy. Pure joy goes beyond that to create feelings and behaviors that last well after a joyous event has taken place. I experienced pure joy at being named Kim's husband. It has changed my attitude and behavior for the last thirty-six years. Even now, I experience pure joy just to think about my relationship with her.

Think about how you felt the last time you experienced the kind of joy that is evident on Kessie's face. What event brought that joy? How has it changed you? Now let me ask another question: When was the last time you felt pure joy by being in church? That may be a tough question to answer, yet the Scripture is filled with examples of worship that brings pure joy. Psalm 59:16 says, "But as for me, I shall sing of Your strength; Yes, I shall joyfully sing of Your lovingkindness in the morning, for You have been my stronghold and a refuge in the day of my distress."

Psalm 98:4 reminds us that God's creation should bring us pure joy: "Shout joyfully to the Lord, all the earth; Break forth and sing for joy and sing praises." What God has done in our own lives should also bring pure joy. "Because Your lovingkindness is better than life, My lips will praise You. So I will bless You as long as I live; I will lift up my hands in Your name. My soul is satisfied as with marrow and fatness, and my mouth offers praises with joyful lips" (Psalm 63:3–5).

Peter wrote, "Though you have not seen Him, you love Him, and though you do not see Him now, but believe in Him, you greatly rejoice with joy inexpressible and full of glory" (1 Peter 1:8). Just knowing Jesus and being counted among those who will experience everlasting life should bring us pure joy.

But we still come back to the question of the last time we experienced joy in church. Like Kessie, who is still in her puppy stage, we need to be watching others, fellowshipping with the body, learning from believers around us, and growing in our relationship with Jesus. This is why Paul urged, "make my joy complete by being of the same mind, maintaining the same love, united in spirit, intent on one purpose" (Philippians 2:2). When we do this, then our joy will be complete also. Pure joy comes by making a commitment, shaping our behavior because of that commitment, and enjoying the fruit of that relationship.

Perhaps there is a better question to ask. Given all of this information, when will you next feel pure joy at being in church? "Now may the God of hope fill you with all joy and peace in believing, so that you will abound in hope by the power of the Holy Spirit" (Romans 15:13).

Wednesday: Happy Being Me

Libby is a terrific family companion. She is dedicated to Nancy in every way. She guards the home and makes sure the family is safe. But Libby has a passion that goes beyond her role as a family dog. She absolutely loves agility competition. In fact she is happiest when she is jumping through hoops and speeding through tunnels. She loves A-frames, the feel of the teeter-totter under her feet, and the rush of reaching the finish line first in her group.

Currently there are about forty-five different types of competitive activities that utilize the skills and instincts of dogs. We know about Frisbee-catching and confirmation because they are regularly showcased on television. There are fast-paced competitions like flyball and wiener racing, and slower competitions using scent and retrieval. Then there is the silence of obedience. Each competition is based on what a dog is good at, interested in, or instinctively drawn to.

What are you good at? What activities make you happy? What skills have you sharpened that bring you satisfaction? How can that skill be used in the Kingdom of God? "Do you see a man skilled in his work? He will stand before kings; He will not stand before obscure men" (Proverbs 22:29).

God is interested in your skill. He wants you to take that which makes you happy and use it for his glory.

"Let our lord now command your servants who are before you. Let them seek a man who is a skillful player on the harp" (1 Chronicles 22:15). "Let every skillful man among you come, and make all that the Lord has commanded" (Exodus 35:10). The skill that you have belongs to the Lord and came from the Lord. "He has filled them with skill to perform every work of an engraver and of a designer and of an embroiderer, in blue and in purple and in scarlet material, and in fine linen, and of a weaver, as performers of every work and makers of designs" (Exodus 35:35).

"Sing to Him a new song; Play skillfully with a shout of joy" (Psalm 33:3). What God desires, he desires in great numbers. "Their number who were trained in singing to the Lord, with their relatives, all who were skillful, was 288" (1 Chronicles 25:7).

All who bring their skill to the Lord will be like Jesse: "Then one of the young men said, 'Behold, I have seen a son of Jesse the Bethlehemite who is a skillful musician, a mighty man of valor, a warrior, one prudent in speech, and a handsome man; and the Lord is with him'" (1 Samuel 16:18).

Has it ever occurred to you that when you use your skill—the thing you are good at for the Lord—people will recognize that God is with you? So what if you are not gifted at speech. Most people are petrified of public speaking. God may be calling you to use your carpentry skills for His purpose. I have a friend who loves to go off-road with his Jeep. He leads a four-by-four ministry that targets outdoor enthusiasts. A retired friend loves to work with wood. He has started a movement of placing small wooden crosses in people's front yards. My love for dogs resulted in my writing a book. Another friend has mastered the bus schedule in order to get around. So he takes Christian tracts with him wherever he goes and witnesses for Christ. Yet another friend loves to sail. He now leads spiritual sailing camps for kids.

God asked Moses about the staff in his hand. He told him to throw it down on the ground and He would use it (Exodus 4:2, 3). In the same way, we are called to throw down our skills, talents, and interests so He can use them for His glory. "I have seen that nothing is better than that man should be happy in his activities, for that is his lot" (Ecclesiastes 3:22).

Thursday: Beneath the Shelter

When David and Joy spent a week on a houseboat this summer, Ben and Buffy went with them. The hot Arizona sun provided ample motivation to spend time in the cool waters of Lake Powell. Though Cavalier King Charles spaniels are not known for their interest in swimming, Ben seemed to enjoy the water.

After each swim, Ben would seek out his bright blue beach towel and snuggle beneath it. The towel became his refuge from the heat of the sun. When the hot, dry wind blew, Ben found a calm location under soothing fabric of his towel. The lake was a foreign place for a dog that spent most of his time in the forests of Colorado.

I am reminded of the old gospel song by Albert Brumley: "This world is not my home, I'm just a-passin through. My treasures are laid up somewhere beyond the blue. The angels beckon me from heavens open doors, and I can't feel at home in this world anymore." We believers live in a world that is foreign to us. The harsh winds can leave our spirits parched. The heat of our trials can burn our very soul. It is important then that we find a place of refuge. This refuge is described beautifully throughout the Psalms.

David prayed, "Let me dwell in Your tent forever; Let me take refuge in the shelter of Your wings" (Psalm 61:4). David knew that a refuge could always be found under the protective fabric of God's tent. "For in the days of trouble He will conceal me in His tabernacle; in the secret place of His tent He will hide me; He will lift me up on a rock" (Psalm 27:5).

The place of calm is not just for a king in a palace. The refuge is for all who come to Jesus. "But let all who take refuge in You be glad. Let them ever sing for joy; and may you shelter them, that those who love Your name may exult in You" (Psalm 5:11). God has a place for each of us when the trials of life blow against us. About that place David wrote, "You hide them in the secret place of Your presence from the conspiracies of man; You keep them secretly in a shelter from the strife of tongues" (Psalm 31:20).

When we are parched from the blazing heat of trials, where can we turn? When the scorching wind threatens to blow us off course, where do we find shelter? If we truly embrace the fact that we are just passing through this world, and heaven is our destination, we find joy in knowing that "God is our refuge and strength, a very present help in trouble" (Psalm 46:1).

If the struggles of life are pressing in, make the words of Psalm 17:8 your prayer: "Keep me as the apple of the eye; Hide me in the shadow of Your wings."

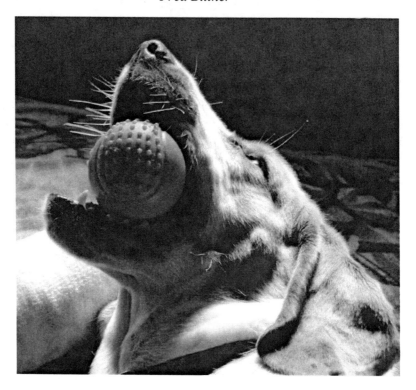

Friday: My Gift of Praise

What would be the highest honor a dog can bestow on its master? It might be to protect him or her in the face of danger, or to willingly surrender a prized possession. Perhaps Dakota is giving us a hint. This is another one of my friend Krista's incredible photographs of her basset hound, Dakota. The lighting is perfect as she looks up toward her master. She appears to be offering her favorite ball as a sacrifice of love. An unsettled dog will gather, hoard, and protect its possessions, and maybe become violent if someone gets too close. A balanced dog, on the other hand, will share with other dogs in the pack, and freely give back to the master who has given it everything.

Jesus said, "Do not store up for yourselves treasures on earth, where moth and rust destroy, and where thieves break in and steal. But store up for yourselves treasures in heaven, where neither moth nor rust destroys, and where thieves do not break in or steal; for where your treasure is, there your heart will be also" (Matthew 6:19–21). We all struggle with the desire to store up treasures. Entertainment parks count on it—when the exit for a ride goes right through the gift shop that sells trinkets from that ride. We have couched our desire for more in nice-sounding words like "accessorize," "upgrade," and "collect."

Jesus warned, "'Beware, and be on your guard against every form of greed; for not even when one has an abundance does his life consist of his possessions'" (Luke 12:15). It doesn't matter what fancy name you give it, Jesus still calls it greed.

How could God use what you have gathered? Draw close to Him, stand in His glorious light, and yield those things to the Lord. Make your gift a fragrant offering without strings. Give your toys to God simply because you love Him. And make the following statement, simplified in *The Message*, your fervent prayer:

> God, teach me lessons for living so I can stay the course. Give me insight so I can do what you tell me—my whole life one long, obedient response. Guide me down the road of your commandments; I love traveling this freeway! Give me a bent for your words of wisdom, and not for piling up loot. Divert my eyes from toys and trinkets; invigorate me on the pilgrim way. Affirm your promises to me—promises made to all who fear you. Deflect the harsh words of my critics—but what you say is always so good. See how hungry I am for your counsel; preserve my life through your righteous ways!
>
> Psalm 119:33, The Message

Saturday: "Spiritually Satisfied" Prayer Day

Rejoice in what God has done in our Lives

In the movie *Chariots of Fire*, a powerful story about Eric Liddell, British Olympic runner and, later, missionary to China, Liddell explains why he ran: "I believe God made me for a purpose. He also made me fast, and when I run, I feel his pleasure." His desire to run for the glory of God, made a huge impact on the outcome of those games. He won a gold and a bronze medal in the 1924 Olympic Games in Paris, forever sealing his testimony and making a big difference in the lives of many people.

Colossians 3:17, says, "Whatever you do in word or deed, do all in the name of the Lord Jesus, giving thanks through Him to God the Father." What can you give Jesus as your gift of praise? It may not come from a skill, but maybe from an opportunity which came out of a trial. I discovered after four major surgeries in three years, and a long-term disability, that writing became my gift of praise. To adapt Liddell's words—when I write, I feel his pleasure. This would not have been able to happen had it not been for years of physical pain.

But maybe you can't run or preach or write a sentence for the life of you. That's fine. What *can* you do? More than that, what are you passionate about? How can you use this for the glory of God? One special single mother struggled after the break-up of her marriage. She turned to couponing to make ends meet. She became a very successful coupon shopper, even teaching others how to shop this way. She discovered that she could turn couponing into a ministry. She now helps the Christian organization that reached out to her in her time of need. She provides food and health products to SECOR (Southeast Community Outreach) in Parker, Colorado, so that others can receive critical help. She does it all through coupons.

God made you who you are, and he wants you to be happy doing the special things that you can do. If social media has taught us anything, it is that we don't need to be geniuses to make an impact on the world. It only takes people being willing to put themselves out there, doing whatever it is that they can do. Often they want the glory for themselves. But what would happen if we said, "I believe God made me for a purpose. He also made me _____. And when I _____, I feel his pleasure."

Week 18: The Race Before Us

Monday: Run to Win

It is said that a picture is worth a thousand words. This picture of Laredo and my friend Renee running on the California beach brings several thousand words to mind. I am reminded of that great poem, "Footprints in the Sand." We walk this life with Jesus by our side. Sometimes, however, life gets rough. At those times, we understand that Jesus is still there, carrying us through the trial. Look behind you and recognize the footprints that belong to Jesus. Stay beside them and you will not go wrong.

My eyes are also drawn to the cirrus cloud formation in the blue sky. The name cirrus means locks of curly hair, creating a mental picture of the long hair of angels flowing in the breeze as they pass overhead. This reminds me that God is ever present. We are never alone as we are taunted by the turbulent waves of this world. Look toward the sky and glorify God for his daily provisions. He is still in control of His creation.

The ruggedness of the rocks shaped by the tides tells us that there may yet be trials ahead. The wind and the waves are still present and powerful. They can destroy us—or they can shape us into stronger, wiser Christians. As we face the storm with Jesus at our side, we are honed into something new. The old rough edges are knocked off and what is left brings glory to our God. This reminds me to constantly look ahead, knowing that each trial will make me a better person. Our God can still cause all things to work together for good.

Finally, my eyes are drawn to Renee and her yellow Lab. Laredo is running stride for stride with his master, but with one amazing difference: He is running with his head turned and his eyes on Renee. He is safe and secure because his master runs between him and the waves. He does not run ahead, or lag behind, but remains with Renee. The Scripture speaks directly to this point: "Watch out that you do not lose what we have worked for, but that you may be rewarded fully. Anyone who runs ahead and does not continue in the teaching of Christ does not have God; whoever continues in the teaching has both the Father and the Son" (2 John 1:8–9, NIV). "Do you not know that in a race all the runners run, but only one gets the prize? Run in such a way as to get the prize" (1 Corinthians 9:24).

"I instruct you in the way of wisdom and lead you along straight paths. When you walk, your steps will not be hampered; when you run, you will not stumble. Hold on to instruction, do not let it go; guard it well, for it is your life" (Proverbs 4:11–13, NIV). With the footprints of Christ behind us, and the presence of God before us, we can face the trials ahead and the waves that surround us. If we keep our eyes on Jesus and remain beside him, it will be well for our lives. This is God's promise.

"Therefore, since we are surrounded by such a great cloud of witnesses, let us throw off everything that hinders and the sin that so easily entangles. And let us run with perseverance the race marked out for us, fixing our eyes on Jesus, the pioneer and perfecter of faith. For the joy set before him he endured the cross, scorning its shame, and sat down at the right hand of the throne of God. Consider him who endured such opposition from sinners, so that you will not grow weary and lose heart" (Hebrews 12:1–3).

Tuesday: Where He Leads Me I Will Follow

Lisa and Kessie visited the dog beach recently. It was an incredible experience for Kessie as she experienced the ocean for the first time. She had been in a swimming pool a couple of times, but never anything as vast or as powerful as the ocean. At first the crashing of the waves and the corresponding undertow were a bit unnerving. With each frightening wave, Lisa assured her puppy that everything was all right.

As time passed, Kessie took her eyes off of the waves, trusting that her master was close at hand. She romped in the breakwater, rolled in the sand, dug holes, and fetched her favorite toy. How wonderful it was for master and lab to share the experience of the beach.

By the end of the day, both Lisa and Kessie were tired but very satisfied with their visit to the dog beach. Lisa packed up and gave Kessie the command, "Come!" Then turning, she began to walk toward the car. Without a leash and without any extra commands, Kessie followed closely behind the master she loves. It was so natural that Lisa nearly forgot that Kessie was only a few months old. Distractions could easily have drawn the puppy's attention. Other dogs or one last wave could have distracted her. But as attractive as those things might have been, Kessie knew that the one who said "Come!" was the most important loyalty in her life.

I am reminded of the story in Matthew 14 where Jesus sent his disciples on ahead of him at the end of a long day, across the Sea of Galilee. Jesus stayed behind to pray and be alone with his heavenly father. In the middle of the night Jesus walked across the water toward the disciples, intending to pass them by. The disciples thought they were seeing a ghost and were filled with fear. After Jesus assured them that it was he, Peter called out, "Lord if it is you, command me to come out onto the water with you." Jesus' response was short and to the point: "Come!" Peter stepped out of the boat and began to walk toward Jesus, but his fear of the wind and the waves quickly distracted him. As he sank, he cried out, "Lord, save me!" Jesus reached out, pulled him up and helped Peter back into the boat. It was there that Jesus said, "O you of little faith, why did you doubt?" (Matthew 14:22–31).

I don't know if the disciples said anything, but I sure could have come up with a list of reasons for doubting. Wind, waves, water in the boat, being tired and exhausted, not getting anywhere in three hours, being out on a stormy sea in the black of night—all seem like legitimate reasons for doubt. Until, of course, you realize that Jesus could conquer every one of those concerns. He had just fed five thousand people with one boy's lunch. And even now, he was walking on the surface of the water with no trouble. Sure the distractions were big, but God's power was bigger.

The picture of Kessie following Lisa reminds me of the chorus from an old hymn: "Where he leads me I will follow. Where he leads me I will follow. Where he leads me I will follow. I'll go with him, with him, all the way." We still have a God who says, "Come!" He is bigger than our waves, and bigger than the other distractions. He has led us through so many struggles. But do we have the faith to follow this time too?

Will you follow—not because you are bound with a leash, or because God is constantly barking commands at you—but because he simply said, "Come!" Don't ask God to command you to walk on any water if you are not willing to go with him all the way. There is no way that we want to hear, "O you of little faith, why did you doubt?" Remember, our Lord has overcome all distractions and is able to help you overcome yours as well. Do you have the faith to follow?

Wednesday: Observe to Be Observed

Jazzy, our Australian terrier, loves to be where the action is. If it's exciting, Jazzy wants in on it. Jazzy even wants to be a part of tedious tasks. She wants to be where the people she loves are, even if that means doing things that seem out of character. She enjoys swimming in the pool with us, straddling the seats between us on a long road trip, or curled up under our feet at the dinner table. Yet when Jazzy is involved in a new experience, she will find a place that is out of the way to observe.

On the day this picture was taken, the yard was alive with extended family members. She knew every one of them, but the experience was foreign to her. So she found a comfortable spot in a flowerbed, under an orange tree. From that location, Jazzy watched the excitement. She stayed under the tree until she was comfortable with the activities and had determined how to fit into the festivities. Once she was comfortable with the situation, she was ready to join in.

The prophet Isaiah was critical of the people around him. "You have seen many things, but you do not observe them; your ears are open but none hears" (Isaiah 42:20). To observe is to watch carefully and attentively, to take note of what has taken place. We may be in the presence of an event and miss its significance. We can watch someone perform a task right in front of us, and not be able to do the same task ourselves. We saw, but we did not observe.

The writer of Ecclesiastes wrote, "I said to myself, 'Behold, I have magnified and increased wisdom more than all who were over Jerusalem before me; and my mind has observed a wealth of wisdom and knowledge'" (1:16). Solomon's point is that he had gained wisdom and knowledge by carefully observing the people and events around him. Amazingly, others saw the same events and got nothing from them. The difference was that they saw, he observed.

How often do our children see us doing something only to hear them say, "I want to do it. I know how." So they try, but they have no idea what to do. They saw, but they did not observe. In the end they require a lot of help. They get frustrated, we get frustrated, and nobody has any fun. While talking about love in 1 Corinthians 13, Paul wrote, "When I was a child, I used to speak like a child, think like a child, reason like a child; when I became a man, I did away with childish things" (v. 11).

So what are we to observe? Paul helps us out here with these words: "Brethren, join in following my example, and observe those who walk according to the pattern you have seen in us" (Philippians 3:17). We need to observe godly people. Watch what they do, and how they do it. Then try it yourself. Learn from the actions of others. You will see common patterns in the lives of godly people. Practice those things. Don't just jump in thinking you've got it—become a disciple of someone you respect. And then observe, watch, and take note of the whats, hows, and whys of their actions.

We need to be observant, watching others and learning from them, because others are watching us. Peter exhorts, "Keep your behavior excellent among the Gentiles, so that in the thing in which they slander you as evildoers, they may because of your good deeds, as they observe them, glorify God in the day of visitation" (1 Peter 2:12). People will watch you today, observing your actions, determining whether your faith is significant or not. Will they see good deeds or childish behavior?

Observe and learn from others how to live a godly life. And when others observe you, may they see "Christ in you, the hope of glory" (Colossians 1:27).

Thursday: Put on Christ

Buffy and Ben, like most dogs, are happiest when their feet are firmly on the ground. There are, of course, certain breeds that will jump into any water they can find. But this is not the plight of the cocker spaniel. They are field hunters who can run long distances, tracking and retrieving for their master.

You can imagine the apprehensions the two dogs must have felt when they were placed on a boat for the first time. Sea legs must be acquired, and it doesn't get any easier just because they have four of them. From the time the boat pushed away from the shore their concern was evident. They huddled together drawing strength from each other, hoping against hope that their master knew what he was doing. What they did not understand was that they had been fitted with lifejackets to protect them should they fall into the lake.

As time progressed, they came to realize the protection they wore was like armor against the waves. Slowly they gained stability and learned to sway with the movement of the water. From there the dogs began to move freely around the boat, barking at birds and enjoying the experience. They became confident in the face of the waves because they trusted their master and relied on the lifejackets that protected them.

The Bible says,

Be prepared. You're up against far more than you can handle on your own. Take all the help you can get, every weapon God has issued, so that when it's all over but the shouting you'll still be on your feet. Truth, righteousness, peace, faith, and salvation are more than words. Learn how to apply them. You'll need them throughout your life. God's Word is an indispensable weapon. In the same way, prayer is essential in this ongoing warfare. Pray hard and long. Pray for your brothers and sisters. Keep your eyes open. Keep each other's spirits up so that no one falls behind or drops out.

Ephesians 6:13–18, *The Message*

We have been given the full armor of God to protect us from the storm: "As a result, we are no longer to be children, tossed here and there by waves and carried about by every wind of doctrine, by the trickery of men, by craftiness in deceitful scheming" (Ephesians 4:14).

When we begin the journey with Christ, we feel the movement of waves and see the effects of the wind around us. But we can have confidence in the face of the storm: "For we do not have a high priest who cannot sympathize with our weaknesses, but One who has been tempted in all things as we are, yet without sin. Therefore let us draw near with confidence to the throne of grace, so that we may receive mercy and find grace to help in time of need" (Hebrews 4:15–16).

So we are called to "be on the alert, stand firm in the faith, act like men, be strong" (1 Corinthians 16:13). Not only that, as we gain confidence in God's protection, we will be able to move about freely enjoying the companionship of our master. We have the promise that our lifejacket—the armor of God—will protect us on the way. "For I am confident of this very thing, that He who began a good work in you will perfect it until the day of Christ Jesus" (Philippians 1:16).

Friday: Keep Watch

Major is the youngest Australian terrier in our house. He is the last puppy born in Jazzy and Satchmo's litter. When he was about six months old, Major went to live with our son and his family. He had children to play with and a family to love him. He even had a kitty of his own. He grew attached to his family and the attention they gave him. A few months ago, however, Major rejoined our pack. It is the best of both worlds since he loves being around other dogs, and he still gets to see his family every day.

Major has very good ears and is incredibly inquisitive. He wants to be a part of everything that is going on around him. When he hears a noise outside, Major climbs to the top of the recliner in the living room. From the top of the chair he has a wonderful view of the front yard and the street. At these times he stands on the back of the chair with his eyes darting around the yard looking for the source of a sound. Once he locates it, he watches until the sound goes away.

Every afternoon, Major assumes a different posture on the back of the chair. He lays himself over the chair with back legs on one side and front legs on the other. In this posture he watches for our son to drive up with the kids. It must be a comfortable position because he can stay there for long periods of time. Major knows they will come, but he doesn't know when, so he keeps watch until his family appears. When they arrive, he wiggles and shrieks with excitement. His family is home and they are reunited.

Jesus tells us that we need to keep a fervent watch as well: "For this reason you also must be ready; for the Son of Man is coming at an hour when you do not think He will" (Matthew 24:44). "'But the exact day and hour? No one knows that, not even heaven's angels, not even the Son. Only the Father knows. The Arrival of the Son of Man will take place in times like Noah's. Before the great flood everyone was carrying on as usual, having a good time right up to the day Noah boarded the ark. They knew nothing—until the flood hit and swept everything away'" (Matthew 24:36–39, *The Message*).

Major remains flopped over the chair, nearly motionless, because he does not want to miss his daily reunion. It is the most important part of his day and he does not want to miss it. Are you ready for the coming of the Lord? Are you watching expectantly, not wanting to miss out? Is seeing the coming of the Lord and being a part of that great family reunion the most important thing in your life?

Paul writes, "Now concerning how and when all this will happen, dear brothers and sisters, we don't really need to write you. For you know quite well that the day of the Lord's return will come unexpectedly, like a thief in the night. When people are saying, 'Everything is peaceful and secure,' then disaster will fall on them as suddenly as a pregnant woman's labor pains begin. And there will be no escape" (1 Thessalonians 5:1–3, NLT).

Saturday: "The Race Before Us" Prayer Day

Run the Race with Endurance

"Watch out that you do not lose what we have worked for, but that you may be rewarded fully. Anyone who runs ahead and does not continue in the teaching of Christ does not have God; whoever continues in the teaching has both the Father and the Son" (2 John 1:8–9). "Do you not know that in a race all the runners run, but only one gets the prize? Run in such a way as to get the prize" (1 Corinthians 9:24).

We read this passage on Monday, and it was important to read it again. The easiest thing for a believer to do is to say, "I got this, Lord. I can handle it from here." While we may not say it with our mouth, we certainly say it with our actions. We pray for a door to open, and when God opens the door we run through it with the enthusiasm of a child. It is only when we get into trouble, or run out of ideas, or reach a fork in the road, or come to a dead end, that we remember to stop and look back to where we left God behind.

The focus this week was to "put on" Christ and keep watching for his prompting, following his lead, and running the race. People will be watching, that is a given, and when they do will they see a victorious Christian life, achieved because you put on the yoke of Christ and walked with him? Unique people are watched all the time. Those deemed attractive are always watched. Those with unique disabilities are also watched. The very tall and the very short, oversized and undersized, and people who live on the edge of social norms are all watched constantly. So, also, is the person who lives by grace in a graceless world.

Have you run past God? What areas of your life have you stopped praying over and started doing on your own. Your goal today is to turn those things back over to God. Make your prayer sound something like this: "Lord, I want you to shine through me. I want to live by grace so that when people look at me, they see you. Take this area of my life over once again. I desire to be yoked with you."

Week 19: Becoming God's Person

Monday: Old Bones

Recently, we gave our dogs some nice bones to enjoy. Each dog grabbed its bone and disappeared to enjoy the gift. Very soon, however, two of the dogs were back hoping for more. What happened to their nice juicy bones? They couldn't possibly have finished them, and yet their treats were nowhere to be found.

I decided to keep watch. If a bone showed up, I would take it and set it aside. Soon enough, Jazzy had a bone. I retrieved it and set it aside. Then Satchmo showed up with one and I set that one aside, too. Not to be outdone, Major showed up with his. We had to retrieve that one because Major's bone was creating conflict within the pack.

Within a few days we had gathered nineteen bones. Where they came from we have no idea. They were well hidden in locations only the dogs knew about. Though the house and yard looked perfectly normal, old bones were hidden under the surface.

Looking at the pile of bones, I realized that our lives could be very similar. We accept Christ and begin our Christian walk. On the surface things may look great, but if we get frustrated or depressed, we dig up the old bones of our former life. We may call them habits or vices. We don't want people to know where our sins are hidden because we're not sure we can give them up. We are content to keep them hidden, and we justify their existence. After all, it's just one vice. It's not hurting anybody. Besides, no one is perfect. Everybody does it. On and on the internal argument continues. But is this how God wants us to live?

The Bible has a lot to say about old bones. To the religious leaders, Jesus said, "Woe to you, scribes and Pharisees, hypocrites! For you are like whitewashed tombs which on the outside appear beautiful, but inside they are full of dead men's bones and all uncleanness" (Matthew 23:27). To believers Paul wrote, "Therefore consider the members of your earthly body as dead to immorality, impurity, passion, evil desire, and greed, which amounts to idolatry. For it is because of these things that the wrath of God will come upon the sons of disobedience, and in them you also once walked, when you were living in them" (Colossians 3:5–7).

We may have lived in these sins before, but since coming to Christ we have put aside our old self, and now we are to be dead to those old bones. "In reference to your former manner of life, lay aside the old self, which is being corrupted in accordance with the lusts of deceit, and that you be renewed in the spirit of your mind" (Ephesians 4:22–23).

God wants us to be "transformed by the renewing of your mind" (Romans 12:2). This renewal creates a new path, a new direction, for our lives. When we face frustration or discouragement, God wants us to run to Him, not to old bones. He wants us to clean out the whole house, giving those bones to Him. Remember, with every issue or temptation, we are promised a "way of escape" (1 Corinthians 10:13).

Are "dead men's bones" really worth holding on to? Is it worth the fear that someone will discover where we have stashed our old bones? There is freedom, growth, and a new spiritual feast that God has for us when we make the commitment to break old patterns and allow Him to give us new ones.

Tuesday: Just Not the Same

Several years ago, Lisa and a group of dog-loving friends decided to take over Virgil "Gus" Grissom Park and use it as a dog park. Every evening, between five and ten regulars bring their dogs to socialize and run. They chase balls, play, eat, drink, and draw closer to each other.

One day, unexpected visitors happened by to join the fun. Two sheep, walking on leash, fascinated the dogs. However, from the outset it was obvious that they were different. They didn't chase balls or romp around the field. They didn't bark like the members of the pack or do any of the things that the other dogs enjoyed. They were welcomed, and encouraged to come back any time, but the two groups weren't likely to see eye to eye any time soon. Just being a visitor at the dog park did not make them dogs. Unless they became new animals, they would never be dogs.

Jesus used word pictures to express the same idea. In fact, He spoke of it often, using several different pictures to make his point. He used sheep and goats in Matthew 7:18–20: "All the nations will be gathered before him, and he will separate the people one from another as a shepherd separates the sheep from the goats." In Matthew 3:12, Jesus used the fields to create another word picture: "His winnowing fork is in his hand, and he will clear his threshing floor, gathering his wheat into the barn and burning up the chaff with unquenchable fire." Both parts are found in the field, but one part has the precious grain and the other does not.

In John 15:5–8, Jesus looked to the vineyards to make the same point: "I am the vine, you are the branches; he who abides in Me and I in him, he bears much fruit, for apart from Me you can do nothing. If anyone does not abide in Me, he is thrown away as a branch and dries up; and they gather them, and cast them into the fire and they are burned. If you abide in Me, and My words abide in you, ask whatever you wish, and it will be done for you. My Father is glorified by this, that you bear much fruit, and so prove to be My disciples."

In each of the situations, both parts were together in the fields. Yet in the end they were separated out. "All the nations will be gathered before him, and he will separate the people one from another as a shepherd separates the sheep from the goats" (Matthew 25:32). "And then I will declare to them, 'I never knew you; depart from me, you who practice lawlessness'" (Matthew 7:23).

So, what does it take to be a part of God's pack? How do we know if we are one who bears fruit? Jesus answered the question by saying, "I am the vine, you are the branches; he who abides in Me and I in him, he bears much fruit, for apart from Me you can do nothing" (John 15:5). "If you keep My commandments, you will abide in My love; just as I have kept My Father's commandments and abide in His love" (John 15:10).

The key is found in the word "abide" (to stay or remain). It means to be focused on Jesus, and to draw your strength from him. That comes when you give your life to him and trust in God's word. "Just as the Father has loved Me, I have also loved you; abide in My love. If you keep My commandments, you will abide in My love; just as I have kept My Father's commandments and abide in His love. These things I have spoken to you so that My joy may be in you, and that your joy may be made full" (John 15:9–11).

Wednesday: Come to Him

Dogs, like children, can find very creative ways to get into messes. They dig holes in the yard and track their muddy feet through the house. They dig through the trash and drink from the toilet. They bring sticks into the house just to chew them into tiny pieces. They seem to bark without cause just in case something might be outside.

Shimmy was constantly finding a way to get into trouble. Whether it was climbing into the dishwasher, exploring the top of the dinner table, or walking across a window sill more than three feet off of the floor. One time, we found him on the kitchen counter, grabbing items and dropping to them to his brothers on the floor below. How he accomplished it all I have no idea.

As capable as Shimmy was at getting into trouble, he was equally skilled at showing love. One would be hard pressed to find a more affectionate dog willing to yield to his master. When he showed us how much he loved us, we were quick to forget his transgressions.

I can only imagine that we must look a bit like Shimmy to our Heavenly Father. Sin is so easy to accomplish. It is far too easy to be like the person described in Proverbs, with "haughty eyes, a lying tongue, hands that shed innocent blood, a heart that devises wicked schemes, feet that are quick to rush into evil, a false witness who pours out lies and a man who stirs up dissension among brothers" (Proverbs 6:17–19, NIV).

As worthy as we are to receive punishment, we have the promise that "if we confess our sins, He is faithful and righteous to forgive us our sins and to cleanse us from all unrighteousness" (1 John 1:9). Solomon assures us that, "He who conceals his transgressions will not prosper, but he who confesses and forsakes them will find compassion" (Proverbs 28:13).

The good news of the gospel is that when we come to Him in humility and love, our God is anxious to forgive us. He deeply desires to have fellowship with us. For God says, "My grace is sufficient for you, for power is perfected in weakness. Most gladly, therefore, I will rather boast about my weaknesses, so that the power of Christ may dwell in me" (2 Corinthians 12:9).

Thursday: Do Dogs Have a Bucket List?

In 2007 a movie hit the big screen called *The Bucket List*. In the movie Jack Nicholson and Morgan Freeman embark on an adventure to accomplish the list of things they wanted to do before they died. Since each of them had a brush with death, the list became a whirlwind story. The movie struck a chord with Americans because it put a catchy name to the way many people feel.

We are always looking for the next big thing, the adventure of a lifetime, a great opportunity, or the hope of a great future. It seems to be the American way to dream about events yet to come. The problem occurs when we become so fixated on the future that we become dissatisfied with the present.

Do dogs have a bucket list? Do they set goals and live for the future? Are they crushed when plans don't work out? This last week Ginger, the chocolate Lab, came home from the veterinary hospital. The doctor removed a cancerous tumor along with her spleen. The cancer cannot be cured. At best, the doctor can help Lisa buy some time. You wouldn't know it, however, by looking at Ginger. The incision is healing well, and Ginger is ready to go. She wants to play and get back to the dog park. She is a very happy dog.

Dogs live in the present. They don't worry about the future. Nor do they resent the problems of yesterday. They are happy with this day, and they will take tomorrow when it comes. Ginger was completely unaffected by the word cancer. The idea of chemo brings no fear. She just loves her master, and she trusts Lisa's judgment.

James writes, "Come now, you who say, 'Today or tomorrow we will go to such and such a city, and spend a year there and engage in business and make a profit.' Yet you do not know what your life will be like tomorrow" (James 4:13). Living for your bucket list has several drawbacks. It means that you must be in control of your own life, which throws the principle of "the love of Christ controls us" (2 Corinthians 5:14) right out the window. Living for your bucket list makes you unhappy with your present, and that discounts Hebrews 13:5, which urges us to be content with what we have. The bucket list can take our eyes off of the real prize and onto things that ultimately do not bring happiness.

James continues, "You are just a vapor that appears for a little while and then vanishes away. Instead, you ought to say, 'If the Lord wills, we will live and also do this or that'" (James 4:14–15). By this statement, James urges believers to live in the present. Focus on your relationship with Jesus and make pleasing him the most important thing in your life. Be content with what you have right now. Give God the glory for being in control. Seek his will and walk in his footsteps. If today brings him glory, then tomorrow will take care of itself.

"But seek first his kingdom and his righteousness, and all these things will be given to you as well" (Matthew 6:33, NIV).

Friday: Eagerly Waiting

Buffy and Ben live in Colorado, in a beautiful community without fences. It is the kind of place where wild animals roam from property to property looking for food. If other animals are able to roam freely, then it stands to reason that Buffy and Ben could wander off as well. Yet something much stronger than a fence keeps them close to home. These dogs have experienced the love of their masters, David and Joy.

One day, Joy let the dogs out into the backyard. Normally they stay close to the house so that Joy can keep track of their movement. On this day, however, she lost sight of them so she had to investigate. Since they were not in the backyard, Joy decided to try the front of the house. When she opened the front door, she found both dogs sitting at the edge of the driveway, waiting for David. They were watching for his coming, knowing that it was the right time of day for him to return home from the office. They sat motionless, staring down the driveway, looking for any sign of his return. Soon their wait paid off, for their beloved master came home to be with them.

The Bible tells us that we are to have the same vigilance toward the return of Christ. "But we are citizens of heaven, where the Lord Jesus Christ lives," affirms Paul. "And we are eagerly waiting for him to return as our

Savior. He will take our weak mortal bodies and change them into glorious bodies like his own, using the same power with which he will bring everything under his control" (Philippians 3:20–21, NLT).

"We know that the whole creation has been groaning as in the pains of childbirth right up to the present time," writes Paul in another place. "Not only so, but we ourselves, who have the first fruits of the Spirit, groan inwardly as we wait eagerly for our adoption as sons, the redemption of our bodies. For in this hope we were saved. But hope that is seen is no hope at all. Who hopes for what he already has? But if we hope for what we do not yet have, we wait for it patiently" (Romans 8:22–25, NIV).

We have the assurance that Jesus is coming again. He told his disciples of that day: "Do not let your hearts be troubled. Trust in God; trust also in me. In my Father's house are many rooms; if it were not so, I would have told you. I am going there to prepare a place for you. And if I go and prepare a place for you, I will come back and take you to be with me that you also may be where I am. You know the way to the place where I am going" (John 14:1–4, NIV).

Sure, we're free to roam, to follow the wild ways of others—but why would we do that? We belong to Jesus, who has promised that he is coming again. Our job is to be prepared for his return, and to wait, patiently, watching for signs of his coming. There is no need to fear, and no room for worry. "Let us hold fast the confession of our hope without wavering, for He who promised is faithful" (Hebrews 10:23).

"Therefore, my beloved brethren, be steadfast, immovable, always abounding in the work of the Lord, knowing that your toil is not in vain in the Lord" (1 Corinthians 15:58).

Saturday: "Becoming God's Person" Prayer Day

Lord, Make Me the Person You Want Me to Be

We live in a world of fallen heroes. We put our trust in political figures, and then find out that they have been unfaithful to their families, misused funds, and become engulfed in sin. We are constantly surprised at religious leaders who commit horrible acts of immorality. We put our support behind a boss who turns out to be defrauding the company. Every one of these people started their journey with good intentions. The issue was that in the midst of their good efforts they were hiding old bones.

Old buried bones have a way of working themselves back to the surface of our lives. No matter how often we re-hide them, they continue to plague us. Like alcoholism, drug addiction, sex, gambling, lying, stealing—whatever the addiction, stuffing it down will not make it go away. As soon as the pressure is on, we face those temptations once again.

Not getting caught is no victory either. Sneaking to another town to meet Mrs. Robinson will not make our lives any better. On the contrary, the truth will always come to the surface along with the old bones. So what is the answer?

God wants to do a thorough house cleaning in you today. You may not have succumbed to the old bones, but they still invade your mind and shatter your peace. Open up to God. Tell him about those old bones. He already knows about them anyway. He will take delight in the openness and will lead you through it. If you need help working through something, ask God to bring that help to you.

Today, commit yourself to becoming transparent, with nothing buried and nothing to hide. Your relationships will be better, your faith will be stronger, and you will live a more healthy life.

Week 20: Godliness

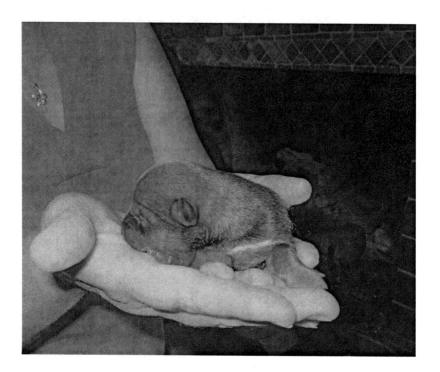

Monday: Growing Up

There is something special about a litter of puppies. They are so fragile at birth. Australian terrier puppies begin their life only five to six ounces in weight. You can hold one in the palm of your hand and feel its tiny heart beating against your palm. Like their infant human counterparts, puppies have their own unique smell. Snuggle up to a puppy and the smell becomes an unforgettable experience. Your memory may even bring that smell to mind by just reading this description.

As they grow, puppies learn to play. They roll around and wrestle with their siblings. They play tug-of-war with anything small enough to put in their mouth. They can be running one minute and asleep in your lap the next minute. They don't have a care in the world.

Dog owners often say that they would love it if their dog could remain a puppy its whole life. We remember the smell, the playfulness, and the excitement that it brought to the family. What we don't remember are the uprooted flowers from the garden, the chewed up pillows, or the accident stains in the carpet. As fun as that period was, a puppy must grow into a mature dog and fulfill its role as your pet and as a member of its breed. A puppy that doesn't grow is not healthy.

We know that growing up is an essential part of life. Every living thing grows, changes, and matures. Yet many people are satisfied to remain spiritual babies all their life. They are happy playing the part of a Christian without any thought of growing up to fulfill their roles as believers and responsible members of the church. The apostle Paul said, "Brethren, do not be children in your thinking; yet in evil be infants, but in your thinking be mature" (1 Corinthians 14:20). "As a result, we are no longer to be children, tossed here and there by waves and carried about by every wind of doctrine, by the trickery of men, by the craftiness in deceitful scheming; but speaking the truth in love, we are to grow up in all aspects into Him who is the head, even Christ" (Ephesians 4:14–15).

A puppy begins with milk, then soft food, and finally food fit for adult dogs. Christians must follow that same pattern in their spiritual lives. We must progress in the depth of our understanding, or the spiritual food we take in. God wants us to grow so he can use us in ministry. "But solid food is for the mature, who because of practice have their senses trained to discern good and evil" (Hebrews 5:14).

How is your spiritual growth? Are you mature, or are you stuck in spiritual infancy? God loves spiritual babies. He wants as many as he can get. But he has a purpose for each of us and does not want us to remain immature Christians. He has a ministry reserved for you and he is waiting for you to grow so that he can use you. "But you, be sober in all things, endure hardship, do the work of an evangelist, fulfill your ministry" (2 Timothy 4:5).

Tuesday: Reading Your Energy

This week I went to our local animal shelter to resolve a license issue for one of our dogs. Since I was there, I decided to try out a field trip that I recommend in my family devotional guide for *The God Whisperer*. I spent some time inside the shelter visiting the animals. As I walked the rows of cages, a profound thought occurred to me.

Several people, individuals and families, were milling around the shelter. They may have been looking for a lost dog or hoping to find one to adopt. Watching them, I noticed that the dogs barked, whined, and cried out. They were reading the energy of the families and matching human excitement with canine excitement. Many of the families I watched moved from cage to cage, discounting the possibilities of adoption because the dogs they observed were too energetic. Great opportunities were missed because the people did not understand their own energy.

As I walked the same rows of cages, dogs sat quietly with their eyes focused on my movements. I stopped at each cage and spoke to every dog in the shelter. I encountered only a single bark, but when I held out my hand and gave a gentle shush, he stopped and relaxed. What was the difference? Energy. I was calm, projecting confident energy in words and actions. Dogs that were considered out of control a few minutes ago were now sitting quietly in response to my energy. It was rewarding and alarming at the same time. Many of those misunderstood dogs will not make it out of the shelter alive. Some have been severely injured by humans, neglected and mistreated. Their condition was sad, but transformations could easily take place if the right people intervened.

The world is a lot like that shelter, filled with lost people who have been hurt and mistreated. They are held captive by sin and bound by their struggles. They need to be released by people who have the eyes and heart of Christ. All too often we look at the outside and judge their pain. Because of this we get back the same kind of energy. But when we approach them with the mind of Christ, then we have a whole new opportunity to share the love of Christ with them.

Consider these words of Paul:

> Don't lie to one another. You're done with that old life. It's like a filthy set of ill-fitting clothes you've stripped off and put in the fire. Now you're dressed in a new wardrobe. Every item of your new way of life is custom-made by the Creator, with his label on it. All the old fashions are now obsolete. Words like Jewish and non-Jewish, religious and irreligious, insider and outsider, uncivilized and uncouth, slave and free, mean nothing. From now on Christ defines everyone, everyone is included in Christ. So, chosen by God for this new life of love, dress in the wardrobe God picked out for you: compassion, kindness, humility, and quiet strength, discipline. Be even-tempered, content with second place, quick to forgive an offense. Forgive as quickly and completely as the Master forgave you. And regardless of what else you put on, wear love. It's your basic, all-purpose garment. Never be without it."
>
> Colossians 3:11–13, *The Message*

Wednesday: A Lot to Smile About

This is Basey. He is an interesting dog. He doesn't normally look this way—he looks like a normal Australian terrier. He only looks this way when he smiles. He smiles if you tickle him, or if he is particularly happy about something. His smile is one of Basey's more endearing qualities. I was reminded of this picture when Hardy (my daughter's black poodle) came over for the weekend. Hardy and Major are great play buddies. A few times over the weekend, I saw Hardy smile like this at Major.

Researchers know that dogs have a full range of emotions. They become angry, melancholy, and even depressed. They also become happy. We generally pay attention to their tail, which can wag wildly or be tucked between the legs depending upon how they feel. We use it as a gauge to interpreting the mood of a dog. Yet the more you get to know your dogs, the more you see the difference in their facial expressions as well. Dogs smile differently depending on their breed and the structure of their jaws. But make no mistake, there are times when they look at you and smile.

Someone once said, "Smile, it makes the world wonder what you have been up to." Ecclesiastes 3:4 says that there is "a time to weep and a time to laugh; a time to mourn and a time to dance." Believers are well known for their seriousness, but how well are we known for smiling and laughing? Here is how Israel reacted to God: "When the Lord brought back his exiles to Jerusalem, it was like a dream! We were filled with laughter, and we sang for joy. And the other nations said, 'What amazing things the Lord has done for them.' Yes, the Lord has done amazing things for us! What joy!" (Psalm 126:1–3, NLT).

Psalm 100:1–2 offers this encouragement: "On your feet now—applaud God! Bring a gift of laughter, sing yourselves into his presence" (*The Message*). The gathering of believers is an exciting event. "Come, let's shout praises to God, raise the roof for the Rock who saved us! Let's march into his presence singing praises, lifting the rafters with our hymns!" (Psalm 95:2, *The Message*). Peter said, "You never saw him, yet you love him. You still don't see him, yet you trust him—with laughter and singing. Because you kept on believing, you'll get what you're looking forward to: total salvation" (1 Peter 1:8–9, *The Message*).

We have a lot to smile about because we have a God who loves us, who sent His Son to pay the price for our sin. We are forgiven, and have the knowledge that we are going to enjoy everlasting life. Your smile may be the best evangelism tool that you have. So, if smiling makes people wonder what you have been up to, then by all means smile big, smile often, and smile with purpose. Smile for Jesus, and then tell them what you have been up to.

Smiling is infectious,
You can catch it like the flu.
Someone smiled at me today,
And I started smiling, too.

Thursday: It's All about the Walk

Jazzy and Satchmo love to go for walks. They know the sound of the specific kitchen drawer where the leashes are kept. Touch that drawer and the dogs are at our feet, ready to hit the road. Cesar Millan consistently points to the walk as the place where master and dog bond. It is the place where the master practices the pack leadership role, and the dog becomes comfortable following. Millan advises walking for a half hour with the dog beside you, focused on your movements and energy, before allowing it a break to sniff. In this way, you have established your role as the leader—and the free roaming time as a reward for a job well done.

"Walk with your dog next to you or behind you, never in front of you. If you haven't experienced the thrill of a dog (or more than one dog) walking next to you, totally in synch with your energy and your movements, then in my opinion, you haven't lived! If you have only been pulled on a leash by a dog tugging you from way in front, then you haven't enjoyed the true beauty and bonding that comes with correctly walking with a dog. Once you've done it right, trust me, you'll never want to go back to the old way!" [8]

The Bible has much to say about our walk as well. As a follower of Christ, we have been called to yield authority over to Christ: "For we are His workmanship, created in Christ Jesus for good works, which God prepared beforehand so that we would walk in them" (Ephesians 2:10). "And this is love, that we walk according to His commandments. This is the commandment, just as you have heard from the beginning, that you should walk in it" (2 John 1:6).

Are you running ahead of God, pulling away from his lead? Does it feel like you are dragging him along behind you? Do you move from one interest to another hoping that God will keep up with what you want to do? You need to decide whose plan you are following. You can tell by your walk. Are you in front, or by God's side, yielding to his prompting? You cannot walk in a worthy manner if you are missing God's gentle leading. Nor can you have a good relationship with Jesus if you refuse to walk with Him.

"Therefore as you have received Christ Jesus the Lord, so walk in Him" (Colossians 2:6). Once you've done it right, trust me you'll never want to go back to the old way!

Friday: Guardians

Family gatherings have become a very eventful experience at our house. When our three children come for a visit and bring our five grandchildren along with them we have quite a house full. The oldest grandchild is eight, and the youngest not quite a year. When they all converge on the house, it becomes an energetic celebration.

Jazzy takes these visits very seriously. She is incredibly gentle with the kids, even when they are rough with her. She watches over them, and makes sure that nothing goes wrong. She has appointed herself to be their guardian. She even acts as lifeguard when the kids are in the pool. No matter what is going on, Jazzy makes sure that everything is under control. She is serious about the role that she has taken on.

Isn't it great to know that our God is serious about watching over us? Paul had confidence in God's ability to care for him: "For this reason I also suffer these things, but I am not ashamed; for I know whom I have believed and I am convinced that He is able to guard what I have entrusted to Him until that day" (2 Timothy 1:12). We can feel secure knowing that God will not let us down. Every part of life that we yield to Him is kept safe under his watchful care.

In the same way, the Bible tells us that we are to be vigilant guardians, with the same intensity that Jazzy shows our grandkids. "So keep at your work, this faith and love rooted in Christ, exactly as I set it out for you. It's as sound as the day you first heard it from me. Guard this precious thing placed in your custody by the Holy Spirit who works in us" (2 Timothy 1:13–15, *The Message*). Timothy was reminded not to put his trust in wealth but to place his hope in God. Knowing that our God is watching over us, we are urged to do good, be rich in deeds, and be willing to share generously. Like Timothy, "guard what has been entrusted to your care" (1 Timothy 6:20).

We may be tempted to hide our treasure. If we don't tell anybody we're Christian, and if we hide the Bible in the back of the closet, then everything will be secure. Yet, that is not what we are called to do as guardians. Guardians keep their own faith strong, share that faith with others, and apply biblical principles to everyday life. Guardians let their light shine and look after those who are at risk of a spiritual drowning. They are ready in season and out of season to jump in and offer help where it is needed.

Jazzy does not act as guardian for all children, but she has taken on the role of guarding my five grandchildren. They are important to her because they are important to me. Since she is loyal to me, she is loyal to them. The Bible tells us that God desires that none should perish, but that all should be saved. Are you acting as God's guardian?

Saturday: "Godliness" Prayer Day

Prayer toward Godliness

To make sense of this week's readings, we need to go back to Tuesday's devotion, "Reading Your Energy." Dogs are amazing at reading energy. They can actually smell the fight or flight hormones that come with our fear. They know when we are upset or down. They know when an earthquake or storm is going to take place.

A tree trimmer relayed the story of a huge old tree that crashed through a house in a storm. The owner of the house had recently gotten a puppy. During that night, the dog sensed danger, jumped on his owner, and got him out of bed. Not more than three seconds later, the huge tree crashed through the wall, and crushed his bed.

People can read your energy as well. They also read your body language, mannerisms, and the tone of your words. They may not be able to predict a falling tree, or a seizure, but they can certainly tell when you are faking it. They know when you are afraid, or you don't believe the words that are coming out of your own mouth.

This is why your walk is so important. The way you walk with the Lord says a lot about you. Ephesians 5:15–16 says, "Be careful how you walk, not as unwise but as wise, making the most of your time, because the days are evil." Where we struggle is in the wisdom part of this statement. We do not view ourselves as wise.

The path to wisdom is found in God's word: "The law of the Lord is perfect, restoring the soul; the testimony of the Lord is sure, making wise the simple" (Psalm 19:7). If you know that God so loved the world that he gave his son, and that those who believe in him receive everlasting life, then you have wisdom. If you know that God has made you a part of his family, and his Holy Spirit lives inside of you, then you have wisdom. Psalm 111:10, says, "The fear of the Lord is the beginning of all wisdom." If you fear the Lord, then you are on your way toward wisdom.

All of us would like to know everything about God, but if we wait for that to happen, then nobody will ever again hear about Christ. Take what you do know and share it. The more of God you share, the more of God you will know.

Week 21: Serving Others

Monday: Friends

What is life without friends? A friend can make the difference in a happy and fulfilling life. Jazzy's best friend is a chocolate Lab named Ginger. She lives with my friend Lisa. Jazzy loves it when they have a play date. They are comfortable at our house or at Lisa's house, and they share each other's toys and even their favorite resting spots. They hold nothing back.

What is amazing about their friendship is that they are two completely different kinds of dogs. Their breeds are different, instincts are different, and they have very different shapes. They are colored differently, and have a six-year difference in age. One would not be surprised if they totally ignored each other. Yet, they are best friends, and love being together.

We have a God who offers to call us his friend:

"I've told you these things for a purpose: that my joy might be your joy, and your joy wholly mature. This is my command: Love one another the way I loved you. This is the very best way to love. Put your life on the line for your friends. You are my friends when you do the things I command you. I'm no longer calling you servants because servants don't understand what their master is thinking and planning. No, I've named you friends because I've let you in on everything I've heard from the Father."

John 15:11–15, *The Message*

With the declaration that we are God's friends comes the command to befriend others with his love. Those we are called to love will likely be different, with various challenges and a variety of needs. "Love prospers when a fault is forgiven, but dwelling on it separates close friends" (Proverbs 17:9, NLT). They may have different instincts, and likely a different heritage. We are not called to love only those who are just like us: "If you do good to those who do good to you," Jesus said, "what credit is that to you? For even sinners do the same" (Matthew 6:33). We are called to find value in people and to call them our friends. "Love never gives up. Love cares more for others than for self" (1 Corinthians 13:4, *The Message*).

So we return to our original question: What is life without friends? The friendship that you offer in Jesus' name may make an eternal difference for the people you invest in. Be a friend, love people, and hold nothing back. You represent the One who no longer calls you a servant, but a friend.

Tuesday: Compassion

Soon after he began to grow, we knew that Duke (one of Jazzy's puppies) was different than his three brothers. When the others were romping around, pouncing on each other, Duke sat quietly and watched the action. He was calm and relaxed—more interested in snuggling than playing. In addition, Duke was showing signs of a recessive trait. According to the American Kennel Club, Australian terriers' ears must be able to stand up on their own. Duke, however, had floppy ears. We were viewing Duke as breeders trying to raise champions and were convinced that it would be difficult to find Duke a good home. We were wrong.

A newly married couple called, asking if they could come see the litter. We were excited that one of the puppies might find a home. When they arrived, their attention went straight to Duke. They played with each of the puppies, but went back to Duke every time. He won their hearts and they could not imagine going home without him. As a result, Duke was not the last to go, but the first.

Paul wrote, "Therefore, as God's chosen people, holy and dearly beloved, clothe yourselves with compassion, kindness, humility, gentleness, and patience" (Colossians 3:12, NIV). All too often, we think of ourselves as unqualified to represent Jesus. We don't have the knowledge we think others have. We lack boldness to witness. We point to the flaws we think might prohibit us from being effective. But, God's priorities are different from ours. He places value on the quality of our character. He desires compassion, kindness, gentleness and patience. The Scripture's call is to "let your gentleness be evidence to all. The Lord is near" (Philippians 4:5, NIV).

The world is filled with lonely people. They are looking for compassion and support from someone who will show them a better way. They aren't interested in what we don't have; they need what we do have. It is through our weakness that God's strength shines through. We don't need to be perfect—just available for God to use. "But in your hearts set apart Christ as Lord. Always be prepared to give an answer to everyone who asks you to give the reason for the hope that you have. But do this with gentleness and respect," (1 Peter 3:15, NIV).

If you have a relationship with Jesus, then you may not be the last person who is sought out, but the first.

Wednesday: In the Right Place

Satchmo has developed an interesting behavior whenever Kim or I are working in the kitchen. He wedges himself in front of us, between our legs and the kitchen counter. It is Satchmo's place of security. He likes being pressed up against us in tight places. There is closeness and connectedness that comes with the touch. Even as a puppy, Satchmo would approach us from behind and press his face between our legs, the way a bashful child would hide from a stranger. Yet there is a greater hope for Satchmo when we're in the kitchen.

In this location Satchmo stays in front of us. The reason? He is putting himself in a place where he can receive the greatest reward. He is waiting patiently for something to drop from the counter onto the floor. When this happens, he looks up to gauge our reaction. If our reaction is hurried, he leaves the food alone. If our reaction is calm, he accepts the fact that our loss is his gain. Since there are two other dogs in the house, Satchmo has learned that putting himself in the place of greatest opportunity has its rewards.

Jesus met a woman while traveling through the region of Tyre. She approached Jesus with the special request to heal her daughter. Like

Satchmo, she placed herself in the place of greatest opportunity. She pressed herself against Jesus' feet. Jesus explained to the woman that he was sent to the Jews, "'Let the children be satisfied first, for it is not good to take the children's bread and throw it to the dogs.' But she answered and said to Him, 'Yes, Lord, but even the dogs under the table feed on the children's crumbs'" (Matthew 15:27–28). Jesus was moved by the woman's reply and granted her request that very moment. The blessing was hers.

What is it that you need most? Where can you go to receive God's blessing? The answer is simple. Put yourself in the place of greatest opportunity, pressed against the nail-pierced feet of Jesus. Humbly bring your needs to the Lord. Pray without ceasing, and wait patiently. God's blessings will fall on you. And you will be there to receive them.

Thursday: Overseers

When Marla's dog had puppies, Kristy was one of the first in line to adopt one of the cute little Labs. Chase has lived with Kristy and Joe for several years. During those years many changes took place in their household. Chase adapted to the birth of one son. Then came another son. The family of four is also a part of a much larger family group, all with kids.

While this may be a problem for other dogs, it was a blessing for Chase. If you in could interpret his bark, he would likely be saying, "Bring it on." He has become an overseer for the boys and all of their cousins and friends. Chase is a protector, an encourager, and a shepherd.

1 Timothy 3:1 says, "It is a trustworthy statement: if any man aspires to the office of overseer, it is a fine work he desires to do." In every congregation is a group of volunteers who have made the commitment to become overseers of the flock. They are the ones who look at the people coming through the doors and say, "Bring it on!" They are the ones who take seriously these words from Acts: "Be on guard for yourselves and for all the flock, among which the Holy Spirit has made you overseers, to shepherd the church of God which He purchased with His own blood" (Acts 20:28).

The overseers of your church deserve respect. They invest countless hours in the work of the church. Rarely do they receive recognition for what they do. Their sacrifice means less time for family, nights away from home, and responsibilities on weekends while others get to attend services and go home. At times they must take biblical stances, and make crucial decisions that add stress to their own lives, but they do it willingly because they have accepted the job of overseer. They also invest their time caring for those who cannot care for themselves. "Pure and undefiled religion in the sight of our God and Father is this: to visit orphans and widows in their distress, and to keep oneself unstained by the world" (James 1:27).

When was the last time you sought out the elders of your church and thanked them for the fine work they do? Honor has benefits for the overseer, and it has benefits for you. Following the leadership of someone you do not honor is much more difficult. Placing your trust in those who do the good work helps you follow their leadership. It also pleases God.

Friday: Becoming Like John

It was a boring, rainy day, and Casey was housebound. Without much that he wanted to do, Casey settled in to watch whatever television program might come on. Before long, Kahlua had joined Casey on the couch and took up residence on Casey's chest. There is a unique sense of peace that comes over us when we see a boy and a dog. On seeing this picture, my mind immediately pictured the apostle John.

John was just a fisherman. He was nobody special when Jesus met him. In fact, he wasn't even named first among the brothers, Zebedee. James got the first billing when they were called to become followers. Even as a disciple, John wasn't perfect. He was often more concerned about his position among the disciples, and his future role in the kingdom of heaven, than he was about the day-to-day work of Jesus. But as his three years of training progressed, John began to understand Jesus. The relationship deepened, and John took on a title that no other disciple could claim.

Jesus had gathered the disciples in the upper room for his last supper with them. At that time, Jesus announced that someone would betray him: "The disciples began looking at one another, at a loss to know of which one He was speaking. There was reclining on Jesus' bosom one of His disciples, whom Jesus loved. So Simon Peter gestured to him, and said to him, 'Tell us who it is of whom He is speaking'" (John 13:22–24).

Not only did he wear the title of "the disciple whom Jesus loved," he had the honored place next to Jesus and was granted full access to the bosom of his master. When the disciples questioned the betrayal, they may have been looking in Jesus' direction, but they were talking to John. He loves you, so you probably know more than we do. Tell us what you know.

How often do we wish that we could know the mind of Christ. We want more of him and his will. We desire to know him at a much greater level than our current knowledge. We can learn a great lesson from John. Don't get caught up in position, power, or politics around the church. Listen to Jesus. Go to the mountain with him and take in his glory. Follow the lessons that you are given through godly leaders and through your own study. Build a relationship of obedience and trust with the savior of your soul. As you do, you will know Christ more and more. Others will see you as a disciple whom Jesus loves. As you gain access to Jesus and rest in his bosom, others will begin to seek you out. You know Jesus. He loves you. Tell us what you know.

The process will be slow, and you may not even be able to determine when that growth took place, but be assured it will happen. When Jesus died, he gave the responsibility of caring for his mother to John. When it came time to reveal heaven to someone and tell about the end times, Jesus relied on John, the disciple whom he loved.

Want to know more? Love more. Want to grow more? Draw closer to Jesus. Don't proclaim that you are the disciple whom Jesus loves—become that person by climbing the mountain with him. Sit at his feet and learn from him, and the growth you desire will take place.

Saturday: "Serving Others" Prayer Day

Lord, Make Us Fit for Service

American advertisers have seized on the obesity epidemic. They are constantly telling us that we need to work out and go on a diet. While our health is certainly important (after all, our body is a temple of the Holy Spirit—1 Corinthians 6:19), God only told us to work out one time in the Bible: "So then, my beloved, just as you have always obeyed, not as in my presence only, but now much more in my absence, work out your salvation with fear and trembling; for it is God who is at work in you, both to will and to work for *His* good pleasure" (Philippians 2:12–13).

Our body may need exercise, but our relationship with God needs a serious workout.

> For this reason I bow my knees before the Father, from whom every family in heaven and on earth derives its name, that He would grant you, according to the riches of His glory, to be strengthened with power through His Spirit in the inner man, so that Christ may dwell in your hearts through faith; and that you, being rooted and grounded in love, may be able to comprehend with all the saints what is the breadth and length and height and depth, and to know the love of Christ which surpasses knowledge, that you may be filled up to all the fullness of God."
>
> Ephesians 3:14–18

Spend time today praying for strength, and for the courage to work out your salvation.

Week 22: Our Relationship with God

Monday: Never Leave Us

Puppies, like children, grow up with their own personality. While they share common traits as Australian terriers, the four puppies from Jazzy's litter have unique characteristics as well. Basey, is inquisitive. He wants to be a part of everything going on around him. He is also very intelligent, able to make connections quickly.

While Basey lived with us, he discovered what a suitcase meant. When Kim pulled one out and packed her clothes, Basey understood that she was going to disappear for a few days. He still had other dogs around during the days, and I was home in the evenings, so we never understood how much of an impact a suitcase had on him.

Last year around Christmas time, Basey went to Idaho to live with our long-time friends. He fit into the family quickly, enjoying the attention he received in Don and Bobby's home. But when they pulled out suitcases to pack for a trip, Basey's reaction was completely unexpected. Bobby packed what she could in the bedroom and then went to the laundry room to retrieve other items. While there, she heard Don exclaim, "Basey, what are you doing?" Basey was on the bed unpacking her clothes one piece at a time and throwing them on the floor. He obviously did not want her to leave.

Basey punctuated his understanding of the suitcase with Amy, their daughter, who stayed at the house while they were gone. One morning while Amy was busy, Basey unpacked the contents of her suitcase—but instead of dropping them on the floor, he dragged her clothes through the doggy door and into the backyard. Though he loved Amy, he wanted her to go home so that his master would come home.

The good news of the Scripture is that God doesn't have a suitcase. He has no intention of leaving you alone. He will stand with you in every circumstance. In the Bible we are told, "'Be strong and courageous, do not be afraid or tremble at them, for the Lord your God is the one who goes with you. He will not fail you or forsake you'" (Deuteronomy 31:6). The psalmist adds, "For the Lord will not abandon His people, nor will he forsake His inheritance" (Psalm 94:14).

"'For I know the plans I have for you,' says the Lord. 'They are plans for good and not for disaster, to give you a future and a hope'" (Jeremiah 29:11, NLT). He does not need to take a vacation from you. He does not give up, or turn away. "For I am confident of this very thing, that He who began a good work in you will perfect it until the day of Christ Jesus" (Philippians 1:6).

Tuesday: Rest

Dogs can be pretty laid back. They sleep an average of thirteen to eighteen hours each day depending on their size. A dog can lie down and be asleep almost instantly. We have all watched our favorite pet nodding off in a sitting position. Their eyes get droopy and their head slowly lowers until they can't hold it up anymore.

Satchmo is one of the best sleepers that I have ever witnessed. He will use someone's foot as a pillow if he doesn't have access to an actual pillow. He knows how to get comfortable. One of Satchmo's favorite sleeping positions makes him look more human than canine. He will climb into an available chair and throw himself back into a sitting position. Then he will place one of his front legs on the armrest of the chair to stabilize himself. He will sit there peacefully at first and watch whatever we happen to be doing. Very soon, however, Satchmo will drift off to sleep in his seated position. Sometimes I take a nap with him—Satchmo sitting back in one chair, and me sitting back in another. From that position, the world is a wonderful place.

God wants us to rest. He modeled it for us when he worked six days and rested on the seventh. He made us to desire rest and to enjoy rest. In our busy world it is hard to find the time to get proper rest. We are always in a hurry, working hard, on the move, and over-committed. It seems like rest gets squeezed from both ends. We go to bed later and get up earlier in hopes of getting our daily list accomplished. Yet when we get the time, our body really enjoys being able to rest. Perhaps this is why God spoke of a day of rest that is still to come: "Now if Joshua had succeeded in giving them this rest, God would not have spoken about another day of rest still to come. So there is a special rest still waiting for the people of God. For all who have entered into God's rest have rested from their labors, just as God did after creating the world. So let us do our best to enter that rest. But if we disobey God, as the people of Israel did, we will fall."

This rest will be the most satisfying of all, and God wants us to be ready for it. To ready ourselves we must be in the Word. "For the word of God is alive and powerful. It is sharper than the sharpest two-edged sword, cutting between soul and spirit, between joint and marrow. It exposes our innermost thoughts and desires. Nothing in all creation is hidden from God. Everything is naked and exposed before his eyes, and he is the one to whom we are accountable."

Once we are in the Word, we need to trust what it says without wavering. "So then, since we have a great High Priest who has entered heaven, Jesus the Son of God, let us hold firmly to what we believe." And finally, we need to trust in God's grace. "This High Priest of ours understands our weaknesses, for he faced all of the same testings we do, yet he did not sin. So let us come boldly to the throne of our gracious God. There we will receive his mercy, and we will find grace to help us when we need it most." Scripture quotes are from Hebrews 4:8–16, New Living Translation)

If we focus on these three things, then we will not only receive the rest, which is yet to come, but we will enjoy much better rest here and now.

Wednesday: Looking Intently

Jazzy, our female Australian terrier, has an incredible ability to fix her gaze on me. She picks a location within a few feet of where I am, sits perfectly still, and focuses her complete attention on me. I am not even sure that she blinks. She wants to know what I am doing. She studies my movements and tracks the motion of my hands. At times I wonder what she finds so interesting to watch. At other times I am struck by her devotion and how much she desires to witness my every move.

When Jesus was taken into the clouds, as recorded in Acts chapter one, the disciples looked intently into the sky as he was going. They were very interested in what was happening to their Lord. They wanted to witness His movement as Jesus rose into the sky. They stood with their complete attention on the one who died to set them free. So fixed was their gaze that they failed to notice the arrival of two men dressed in white.

The disciples were energized by what they saw in the physical clouds. We are called to gain strength from spiritual clouds. "Therefore, since we have so great a cloud of witnesses surrounding us, let us also lay aside every encumbrance and the sin which so easily entangles us, and let us run with endurance the race that is set before us, fixing our eyes on Jesus, the author and perfecter of faith who for the joy set before Him endured the cross, despising the shame, and has sat down at the right hand of the throne of God" (Hebrews 12:1–2). Our constant encouragement is to do the work, live the Christian life, and serve the Lord. It is what we are called to do as believers. Yet the key to running the race is our ability to fix our eyes on Jesus. James tells us that we are to have the same focus. "But the one who looks intently at the perfect law, the law of liberty, and abides in it, not having become a forgetful hearer but an effectual doer, this man will blessed in what he does" (James 1:25).

It is difficult to fix your eyes on something when you are already moving. The key is to gain your focus before starting. When you do, movement becomes easier. The activity of running the race must begin by fixing our eyes on Jesus, gazing intently at his word, focusing on his ministry, and gaining strength from his love.

Take some time to sit before the Lord. Fix your gaze on Him. Learn his commands. Absorb his teaching. When you come to know the way he moves, your life will better reflect his love. When you do, you can claim the promise that you will be blessed in what you do.

Thursday: What Others Do Not See

My friend Laura has an African pygmy hedgehog for a pet. His name is Emile (after a hedgehog in a movie), and he has been with Laura for nearly four years. An African pygmy hedgehog is not an animal that many would consider keeping as a pet. After all, they have sharp quills that make the hedgehog difficult to snuggle with on the couch. Yet, there are people who value the hedgehog greatly.

Laura became interested in hedgehogs when she read a book of Christmas stories. A couple of the stories included a hedgehog family. From that point, Laura was hooked. Watching them roll up into a tight little ball is fun, and they have great personalities, but could one have a hedgehog as a pet?

When Laura and her husband moved to Colorado, she discovered a hedgehog society that puts on hedgehog shows, much like dog shows. The curiosity was much too great, so she went to see what it was all about. At the show she met a breeder, and it was just a matter of time before Emile became a part of the family.

You and I can be a lot like African pygmy hedgehogs. Our personalities can be prickly at times, and others may have a hard time recognizing the value in us. When we look in the mirror, we see negative areas in our lives that resemble sharp quills. It can be overwhelming, and all we want to do is to curl up in a ball like the hedgehog and hope that nobody sees how flawed we really are.

The good news is that there is a rescue society that values you. They look past the quills and see the hidden qualities of your heart. This rescue society is called the church, and it is filled with others who are just like you. Jesus Christ—who loves us so much that he left heaven, put on our life of prickly quills, and suffered alongside us—heads the church. He died and rose again for us. "But God demonstrates His own love toward us, in that while we were yet sinners, Christ died for us" (Romans 5:8).

God values us and wants to make us loveable. He wants to turn our quills into things of beauty. Through Paul, God said,

> Consider the members of your earthly body as dead to immorality, impurity, passion, evil desire, and greed, which amounts to idolatry. For it is because of these things that the wrath of God will come upon the sons of disobedience, and in them you also once walked, when you were living in them. But now you also, put them all aside: anger, wrath, malice, slander, *and* abusive speech from your mouth. Do not lie to one another, since you laid aside the old self with its *evil* practices, and have put on the new self who is being renewed to a true knowledge according to the image of the One who created him—*a renewal* in which there is no *distinction between* Greek and Jew, circumcised and uncircumcised, barbarian, Scythian, slave and freeman, but Christ is all, and in all.
>
> Colossians 3:5–11

As we grow in our relationship with God, each of our quills is reshaped into something he can use for his glory. He reveals the hidden qualities of our heart and makes us a valuable part of his family.

No matter how prickly you see yourself today, the society called the church is longing to take you in and help you become the person Jesus wants you to be. Then you, too, will be able to sing the praise song, by Dennis Cleveland:

Beautiful, beautiful
Jesus is beautiful
And Jesus makes beautiful
Things of my life.
Carefully touching me
Causing my eyes to see
And Jesus makes beautiful
Things of my life.

Friday: Biting Off More Than You Can Chew

Fred is a Chihuahua mix puppy that was rescued by a shelter in Washington. When Norma set eyes on him, she knew that he was going to be her dog. As soon as she adopted him, Fred's name was changed to Pepe. Pepe was the name of a stuffed donkey that Norma owned when she was a child. Pepe kept Norma company, absorbed her tears, heard her stories, loved her through her problems, and was always there for her. Pepe the puppy has taken on the role vacated by the old donkey.

Pepe seems to understand that he has been rescued and that Norma has become his savior and master. He wants nothing more than to please his new master. He gets excited every time she enters the house. He runs through the house, dives under the couch, slides to the other side, and runs back around the house. He ends up diving under the ottoman. After a few heavy breaths, he goes through the routine again. He loves to sit in Norma's lap and be close to her. He would do anything for Norma. Unfortunately, Pepe doesn't understand his size and ability and at times he bites off more than he can chew.

Moses bit off more than he could chew when he tried to defend his people from the Egyptians. Saul bit off too much when he tried to kill David. David bit off too much when he took a walk on the roof of his palace and spied on a bathing woman. Peter bit off more than he could chew when he tried to defend Jesus by cutting off a guard's ear, and then again when he denied Jesus three times. Saul/Paul caused problems when he persecuted the believers. John Mark bit off too much and abandoned the missionary journey. You get the point, but do you understand the lesson? Every one of these individuals bit off more than he could chew—but God restored them and used them mightily.

We were condemned to death and needed rescuing. Jesus Christ became our Savior and Master. He has taken us in and wants to share his mysteries with us. It is easy for us to think we can go after the big stick from the beginning. When we find that we have bitten off more than we can chew we withdraw and question ourselves. But Paul wrote, "If anyone supposes that he knows anything, he has not yet known as he ought to know" (1 Corinthians 8:2).

"Let no man deceive himself. If any man among you thinks that he is wise in this age, he must become foolish, so that he may become wise. For the wisdom of this world is foolishness before God. For it is written, 'He is the One who catches the wise in their craftiness'" (1 Corinthians 3:17–19). Our faith is not based on the ability to leap tall buildings or catch speeding bullets. It is not about our greatness. It is about our weakness. It is what Paul said when he wrote, "And He has said to me, 'My grace is sufficient for you, for power is perfected in weakness.' Most gladly, therefore, I will rather boast about my weaknesses, so that the power of Christ may dwell in me. Therefore I am well content with weaknesses, with insults, with distresses, with persecutions, with difficulties, for Christ's sake; for when I am weak, then I am strong'" (2 Corinthians 12:9–10).

When you find you have bitten off more than you can chew, don't beat yourself up. Learn from it. Allow your weakness to shine through. Be the person Jesus died to save. That person is the one Jesus saw who needed rescuing. He wants to love us and share his secrets with us. He will take those big sticks and grow you into them as you learn from your challenges.

Saturday: "Our Relationship with God" Prayer Day

Desire a Growing Relationship with God

The good news of this week is that God does not expect you to wear a cape, jump tall buildings, or stop speeding bullets. He is not calling you to be a super hero. Nor is he focusing on spiritual giants.

God does not give you an insurmountable task and then sit idly by to watch you fail. Anything God asks you to do, he will also give you the ability to do. Super strength is not a prerequisite. Psalm 51 says that God isn't really interested in big gifts, big sacrifices, or big offerings. What he really wants are the shattered lives and broken egos of those who are ready to sit at his feet and be loved.

The psalmist goes on to say that when we come to him in brokenness, then he is delighted and builds us into the person he wants us to be. When that happens, our worship becomes powerful. That is when God is delighted.

Have you bitten off more than you can chew? Do you feel a little prickly and not very loveable? Maybe you just feel like you have been left out in the cold. Come to Jesus and sit at his feet. Pour out your brokenness at the foot of the cross and let him build you into a strong tower.

Week 23: Point of View

Monday: Seeing Eye-to-Eye

Sometimes it takes a little work for dogs to see eye-to-eye. Sometimes dogs aren't willing to get to know others. They growl and the hair stands up on the back of their necks as they project their foul temper to other canines that get too close. Then there are shy dogs that fear any attempt to become friends. They withdraw and hide under anything they can find, all the while quivering uncontrollably.

Friendly dogs are eager to get to know other dogs around them. Sure they smell each other, but that is their way of learning about each other, as they come to understand who they are, what they do, and what they eat. They pick up the scent of the other dog's master, and they smell how nervous or willing the other dog is to engage in the conversation. The more they get to know each other, the more willing they are see each other eye-to-eye.

Bella is a poodle and Chihuahua mix. She is small and quick in her movements. She is excitable and likes to be involved with her surroundings. She is a vital part of Sarah and Daniel's life. Sadie, on the other hand, is a German shepherd owned by Sarah's parents. Shepherds tend to like calm, order, and control. The only things Belle and Sadie share in common are that they are both canines, with the same family ties. They only get together occasionally, and when they do they need to reestablish their relationship. But, once that happens, the relationship is strong. Sadie drops her head and Bella stands up tall so they can look each other in the eye and enjoy their united relationship.

The church is filled with people with two things in common. We are all believers, and we share the same family name (Christian). We have different backgrounds, jobs, experiences, and levels of maturity. We look different, think differently, and express ourselves in different ways. At times we might like to growl and chase others off. Other times we would rather retreat under a chair and hope that people leave us alone.

God speaks clearly about this thing called the church, of which we are all a part. "Behold, how good and how pleasant it is for brothers to dwell together in unity!" (Psalm 133:1). To achieve this unity, we need to be open with each other. We need to communicate, and take an interest in other believers. "Beyond all these things put on love, which is the perfect bond of unity" (Colossians 3:14).

Reaching the point where we see eye-to-eye with the body of Christ is important, "for the equipping of the saints for the work of service, to the building up of the body of Christ; until we all attain to the unity of the faith, and of the knowledge of the Son of God, to a mature man, to the measure of the stature which belongs to the fullness of Christ. As a result, we are no longer to be children, tossed here and there by waves and carried about by every wind of doctrine, by the trickery of men, by craftiness in deceitful scheming" (Ephesians 4:12–14). How do we do this? Paul explained it in earlier verses. We are to act "with all humility and gentleness, with patience, showing tolerance for one another in love, being diligent to preserve the unity of the Spirit in the bond of peace. There is one body and one Spirit, just as also you were called in one hope of your calling" (Ephesians 4:2–4).

Seeing eye-to-eye takes work, understanding, and, at times, compromise of our own desires. However, the benefits of spiritual growth, unity of spirit, and impact on the unbelieving world far outweigh the risks of letting others into our personal space. Whether you need to stand up and be counted—or sit down and be loved—the body of Christ has a ministry to perform in you. The body of Christ also has a ministry to be performed *by* you. That will only happen when we all commit to seeing eye-to-eye.

Tuesday: I Just Like Stuff!

Alba's cat has an almost Garfield-ian quality. The orange cat we have all come to know is overweight and lazy. His response to things is laced with cynicism. He likes his stuff and he protects it with the tenacity of an addict. Odie had better not look too intently at Garfield's stuff, or there is trouble ahead.

This cat is content to lie on her back amid the games, food, snacks, and possessions. She may look docile, but don't try to touch her stuff or the claws will come out! She will be more than happy to let you hang around. She may purr and reach out to you for affection—as long as you don't delve into her dependency on her stuff. Whether it is good for her or not, she will not tolerate anyone butting into that part of her life.

God knows about all of the stuff we would rather not talk about. He knows that we protect our stuff, not allowing others to discuss what they already know is there:

Now the deeds of the flesh are evident, which are: immorality, impurity, sensuality, idolatry, sorcery, enmities, strife, jealousy, outbursts of anger, disputes, dissensions, factions, envying, drunkenness, carousing, and things like these, of which I forewarn you, just as I have forewarned you, that those who practice such things will not inherit the kingdom of God. But the fruit of the Spirit is love, joy, peace, patience, kindness, goodness, faithfulness, gentleness, self-control; against such things there is no law. Now those who belong to Christ Jesus have crucified the flesh with its passions and desires. If we live by the Spirit, let us also walk by the Spirit. Let us not become boastful, challenging one another, envying one another.

Galatians 5:19–26

"When do we challenge each other?" you might ask. Challenges occur when someone points out the stuff we are trying to protect. "It is my life, and I can do what I want!" we might say, "And it isn't a problem. I can stop anytime I want too." We can be just as addicted to anger, lust, and idolatry as we are to drugs and alcohol. Laying it down is never easy, but pretending it isn't there will damage our soul.

Therefore, since Christ has suffered in the flesh, arm yourselves also with the same purpose, because he who has suffered in the flesh has ceased from sin, so as to live the rest of the time in the flesh no longer for the lusts of men, but for the will of God. For the time already past is sufficient for you to have carried out the desire of the Gentiles, having pursued a course of sensuality, lusts, drunkenness, carousing, drinking parties and abominable idolatries. In all this, they are surprised that you do not run with them into the same excesses of dissipation, and they malign you; but they will give account to Him who is ready to judge the living and the dead. For the gospel has for this purpose been preached even to those who are dead, that though they are judged in the flesh as men, they may live in the spirit according to the will of God.

1 Peter 4:1–6

Is the stuff you hide really worth the damage it is causing? Make Romans 13:13 your goal today: "Let us behave properly as in the day, not in carousing and drunkenness, not in sexual promiscuity and sensuality, not in strife and jealousy."

Wednesday: Security

Molly Mae had a rough beginning. She was unloved, mistreated, and devalued as a pet. She was unwanted was in need of rescue. Fortunately for her, a rescue society existed that saw her for what she could become. They took her in, cleaned her up, and made her available for placement with a loving family.

Today, Mollie Mae is happy, healthy, and secure. She has a great family and she is very much loved. She has become the dog the rescuers knew she could be. In her new family, Mollie Mae values her security. She loves pleasing her masters, and is totally comfortable in their presence. Through her, other dogs are getting the chance to be rescued from their old lives as well.

We live in a very rough world. Millions of people are unloved, mistreated, and devalued as human beings. They feel completely unwanted and are in need of rescue. Fortunately, there is a rescuer named Jesus who sees us for who we can become. He reaches out to us, saves us, makes us clean again, and places us in his church so that we can feel the security of being a part of a family. All of us came from that old life: "for all have sinned and fall short" (Romans 3:23). Some had it harder than others, but all of us were in the same situation: "And you were dead in your trespasses and sins, in which you formerly walked according to the course of this world, according to the prince of the power of the air, of the spirit that is now working in the sons of disobedience. Among them we too all formerly lived in the lusts of our flesh, indulging the desires of the flesh and of the mind, and were by nature children of wrath, even as the rest" (Ephesians 2:1–3).

Once this security in Christ has been received, many forget their old path. They ignore the fact that there are still millions out there who need rescue. Instead they become comfortable in their new habits, and even become self-righteous and judgmental of those who are still lost in sin. They completely ignore the fact that "all these things are from God, who reconciled us to Himself through Christ and gave us the ministry of reconciliation" (Ephesians 5:18). With one hand we are to reach to God, and with the other we are to reach out to others who need rescue.

Pay close attention to these words from the apostle Paul: "Now may our Lord Jesus Christ Himself and God our Father, who has loved us and given us eternal comfort and good hope by grace, comfort and strengthen your hearts in every good work and word" (2 Thessalonians 2:16–17). Why did God give us this security, comfort, hope, and strength? So that we may offer good words as we work on his behalf.

"Remember those who led you, who spoke the word of God to you; and considering the result of their conduct, imitate their faith" (Hebrews 13:7).

Thursday: In His Image

Grover is a pretty special dog. He has lots of personality and he takes delight in making people happy. So when his birthday came around, Grover was honored with a party of "mini me" cupcakes. Each little treat was created to reflect the image and personality of Grover. Each one looks different, but all capture an aspect of who Grover is.

Grover and his cupcakes are an excellent example of the creation story in Genesis: "Then God said, 'Let Us make man in Our image, according to Our likeness; and let them rule over the fish of the sea and over the birds of the sky and over the cattle and over all the earth, and over every creeping thing that creeps on the earth.' God created man in His own image, in the image of God He created him; male and female He created them" (Genesis 1:26–27)

Every one of us was created to be a unique reflection of God. We do not look alike, nor do we think alike. Our skillsets are different, and we have differing gifts. Yet each of us reflects the unique nature of God. We began our life as God's creation, and His goal for us is to grow into a more accurate reflection of who God is.

"And we know that God causes all things to work together for good to those who love God, to those who are called according to His purpose. For those whom He foreknew, He also predestined to become conformed to the image of His Son, so that He would be the firstborn among many brethren; and these whom He predestined, He also called; and these whom He called, He also justified; and these whom He justified, He also glorified" (Romans 8:28–30).

No matter what we go through, God wants to use it to shape us, mold us, and make us into what he wants us to be. "But whenever a person turns to the Lord, the veil is taken away. Now the Lord is the Spirit, and where the Spirit of the Lord is, there is liberty. But we all, with unveiled face, beholding as in a mirror the glory of the Lord, are being transformed into the same image from glory to glory, just as from the Lord, the Spirit" (2 Corinthians 3:16–18).

To reflect the image of God we need to cleanse ourselves of ungodly things. Once we do this, Paul urges us to "put on the new self who is being renewed to a true knowledge according to the image of the One who created him" (Colossians 3:10). The more we surrender the old sinful self, the more we gain in our understanding of God. The more we understand, the more we can grow and reflect the image of our God.

Friday: A Healthy Dose of the Word

Grover has the very interesting habit of taking over Stacy's Bible whenever she is not looking. We would consider it an accident if it happened once, but it seems to happen consistently. Grover is very interested in what is in the Word of God. When Stacy's Bible is not available, Grover goes for her journal. What is it that Grover sees? Why is he so interested in the Bible?

We may never know why he does this, but we do know what we can get when we focus on the Bible. "But one who looks intently at the perfect law, the law of liberty, and abides by it, not having become a forgetful hearer but an effectual doer, this man will be blessed in what he does" (James 1:25). When we look intently at God's Word, and abide in that Word, we are blessed. But, what does it mean to look intently at the perfect law?

James urged us to put aside "all filthiness and all that remains of wickedness, [and] in humility receive the word implanted, which is able to save your souls" (James 1:21). Thinking about an implant, we recognize that it is something that is placed inside of us. A pacemaker is a device which is placed in a person's chest to keep the heart beating properly. The Word implanted does not mean we cut open our head and stash a Bible in there. We must take it in one word, one verse, and one chapter at a time. The psalmist declared, "Your word I have treasured in my heart, that I may not sin against you" (119:11).

In the same psalm the writer tells us how he builds the treasury of the Word in his heart: "My eyes anticipate the night watches, that I may meditate on your word" (119:148). Put simply, he studies every night. In fact, he can't wait for evening to come so that he can be in fellowship with God. So, how important is your interaction with God's word?

When we make a dedicated effort to spend time with God, amazing things happen. We begin to comprehend the mind of God and how he wants to transform us. "For the word of God is living and active and sharper than any two-edged sword, and piercing as far as the division of soul and spirit, of both joints and marrow, and able to judge the thoughts and intentions of the heart" (Hebrews 4:12).

You have a standing appointment to join in fellowship with God. His Word is ready, and he is waiting for you to desire a healthy dose.

Since you have in obedience to the truth purified your souls for a sincere love of the brethren, fervently love one another from the heart, for you have been born again not of seed which is perishable but imperishable, that is, through the living and enduring word of God. For, "all flesh is like grass, and all its glory like the flower of grass. The grass withers, and the flower falls off, but the word of the Lord endures forever." And this is the word which was preached to you.

1 Peter 1:22–25

Saturday: "Point of View" Prayer Day

Prayer that we share God's Point Of View

In the 1840s and '50s, there was a political party that was referred to as the "Know Nothings." It was made up of several secret societies dedicated to keeping newcomers out of America, and especially to keep them out of the mainstream of society. If confronted about the party, members would say, "I know nothing."

The church is not an exclusive club designed to keep newcomers out. Christians are not a bunch of know nothings. Paul, however, had a vastly different view about knowing nothing. He said, "For I am determined to know nothing among you except Jesus Christ, and Him crucified" (1 Corinthians 2:2). To know nothing but Christ is not exclusive but inclusive. It does not discriminate, but accepts all who come. Instead of being hateful, it loves and welcomes. It is not secretive, but open and vulnerable because the love of Christ indwells us.

Do you share God's point of view? Where does your view need to change? Today in your prayer time, discuss this area with God, and resolve to know nothing but Christ and Him crucified.

Week 24: Who Is My Neighbor?

Monday: Abused

They call him Sparky, but to look at him you may not be sure why. Sparky was found on the streets, hungry, emaciated, filthy and abused. The shelter estimates that he is approximately nine years old—although it is difficult to tell after all he has been through. Once he was rescued, washed, and groomed, Sparky became a different dog. The shelter found an obvious spark in his eyes. After he was deemed healthy, Sparky was made available for adoption in a loving home.

If you saw Sparky on the street, it would not be unrealistic to grab your children, cross the street and hope that no airborne disease wafted off of his body. We may say something like, "Somebody ought to do something about that dog." It brings to memory a story found in Luke 10 about a lawyer who approached Jesus one day with a question: "'Teacher, what shall I do to inherit eternal life?' [Jesus] said to him, 'What is written in the Law? How does it read to you?' And he answered, 'You shall love the Lord your God with all your heart, and with all your soul, and with all your strength, and with all your mind; and your neighbor as yourself.' And He said to him, 'You have answered correctly; do this and you will live'" (Luke 10:25–28).

The lawyer would have been wise to leave the discussion there, but he just had to argue the point. So he asked,

"And who is my neighbor?" Jesus replied and said, "A man was going down from Jerusalem to Jericho, and fell among robbers, and they stripped him and beat him, and went away leaving him half dead. And by chance a priest was going down on that road, and when he saw him, he passed by on the other side. Likewise a Levite also, when he came to the place and saw him, passed by on the other side. But a Samaritan, who was on a journey, came upon him; and when he saw him, he felt compassion, and came to him and bandaged up his wounds, pouring oil and wine on *them*; and he put him on his own beast, and brought him to an inn and took care of him. On the next day he took out two denarii and gave them to the innkeeper and said, 'Take care of him; and whatever more you spend, when I return I will repay you.' Which of these three do you think proved to be a neighbor to the man who fell into the robbers' *hands*?" And he said, "The one who showed mercy toward him." Then Jesus said to him, "Go and do the same."

Luke 10:25–37

Jesus took the whole law and whittled it down to two statements. But, what if Sparky was your neighbor? Would you be the one who shows mercy? Can we love the Lord our God with all our heart, soul, mind, and strength without loving the Sparky's around us? Can we look past the matted hair, the dirt, and the abuse and see the spark in the eyes of lost people? They are the neighbors we are called to love.

Tuesday: Distressed

M. Scott Peck, began his book, *The Road Less Traveled*, with three powerful words: "Life is difficult." It has been difficult since the beginning of Genesis in the garden. Trying to sort out why people suffer, get cancer, have accidents, or suffer at the hands of others is a question for which there are no good answers, except that life is difficult.

Charlie is a loving, friendly dog who enjoys going on walks and snuggle with his owner. Unfortunately, at the time this picture was taken, Charlie had no owner. He began his life in Mexico as a healthy puppy. While he was still young, however, someone decided to take out his anger on the world by shooting Charlie with a gun and watching him die. The bullet severed his spine, leaving him paralyzed in the back half of his body.

As a dog in distress, Charlie was treated and fitted with a kind of canine wheel chair. Once strapped onto his wheels, Charlie gets around well by pulling himself along. He struggles with bumps, thick carpets, wet surfaces and rocks, but he does everything in his power to live his life as a normal dog.

When you look at Charlie's picture, what do you see? Are you fixed on the wheels? Or do Charlie's warm, loving eyes draw you in? The fact is, most people see the disability and not the dog. But Jesus looked past the disabilities, the questions, and the desire to place blame. He looked at the heart.

As Jesus entered Capernaum, a centurion approached Jesus asking for help. His servant was paralyzed. Jesus responded by saying "I will come and heal him" (Matthew 8:7). No hesitation, just concern for the servant and the love of this soldier.

There is a wonderful account in Luke 5 of Jesus' healing of the paralytic:

> One day He was teaching; and there were some Pharisees and teachers of the law sitting there, who had come from every village of Galilee and Judea and from Jerusalem; and the power of the Lord was present for Him to perform healing. And some men were carrying on a bed a man who was paralyzed; and they were trying to bring him in and to set him down in front of Him. But not finding any way to bring him in because of the crowd, they went up on the roof and let him down through the tiles with his stretcher, into the middle of the crowd, in front of Jesus. Seeing their faith, He said, "Friend, your sins are forgiven you." The scribes and the Pharisees began to reason, saying, "Who is this man who speaks blasphemies? Who can forgive sins, but God alone?" But Jesus, aware of their reasoning, answered and said to them, "Why are you reasoning in your hearts? Which is easier, to say, 'Your sins have been forgiven you,' or to say, 'Get up and walk'? But, so that you may know that the Son of Man has authority on earth to forgive sins,"—He said to the paralytic—"I say to you, get up, and pick up your stretcher and go home." Immediately he got up before them, and picked up what he had been lying on, and went home glorifying God. They were all struck with astonishment and began glorifying God; and they were filled with fear, saying, "We have seen remarkable things today."
>
> Luke 5:17–26

Jesus saw people. He saw sin. He recognized need and knew that he could meet those needs. Yet, the percentage of people who have disabilities, and attend church is very small. Perhaps we need to focus more on their eyes, and less on their wheels.

Wednesday: Not So Lucky

What would you call a person in chains, with a small area in which he can move freely, isolated from society, and forced to live in solitude? Chances are, the word that comes to mind is "prisoner." This is how we treat criminals who have committed crimes against society. The difference between most prisoners and this dog is that the prisoner will eventually be set free.

His name may be Lucky, but there is nothing lucky about his life. He cannot run or play. He has no visitors, and his space is nothing more than dirt and roots. His chain forces him to remain in solitude, even though his heart desires to be in fellowship with people.

One can almost hear the voice of Joe Cocker coming through the barks and howls of this dog:

I'm under your spell
Like a man in a trance
You know darn well that I don't stand a chance
Unchain my heart let me go my way
Unchain my heart you worry me night and day
I live a life of misery
And you don't care a bag of beans for me
Unchain my heart set me free.[9]

We live in confidence that God keeps his promises. "For You will not abandon my soul to Sheol; Nor will You allow Your Holy One to undergo decay" (Psalm 16:10). We pray, "Do not hide Your face from me, Do not turn Your servant away in anger; You have been my help; Do not abandon me nor forsake me, O God of my salvation!" (Psalm 27:9). We trust that our chains have been broken and we are truly free. But what about those who are still bound by sin?

All around us are people who are chained to alcohol and drugs and a host of other addictions. There are those who are abandoned and abused. There are people in the middle of every crowd who feel completely alone and unloved. They are the Luckys of the world, and they need help to find the freedom that you are trusting in today. You may not have the answers, but you hold the key to the padlock, which, when unlocked, will enable them to get started in the right direction. They want to be free, but they need our help. Like Lucky, they desire to run, and love, and be free. Right now they are weak, but they can become strong.

God has called us to help those bound by sin to understand what real freedom is like. "Yet those who wait for the Lord Will gain new strength; They will mount up with wings like eagles, they will run and not get tired, they will walk and not become weary" (Isaiah 40:14).

Thursday: In Season and Out of Season

As dogs age they tend to gain weight and slow down. We often say during those times that our dogs are past their prime. The reality is that active dogs can remain lean and healthy well into their mature years. Hershey is a great example of what it means to be lean and healthy. If there were an ounce of fat, you'd be hard pressed to find it. Hershey is poised and ready at all times for whatever might come her way.

Believers are called to remain poised and ready for whatever comes our way. Paul exhorted Timothy to "be ready in season and out of season; reprove, rebuke, exhort, with great patience and instruction" (2 Timothy 4:2). Every season seems to have issues. It rains too much, snows too deep, gets hot, or cold, or both in the same day. Hurricanes have their season; tornadoes have a season as well. What is true about weather is also true of spiritual seasons. We need to be ready: "You therefore, beloved . . . be on your guard so that you are not carried away by the error of unprincipled men and fall from your own steadfastness" (2 Peter 3:17).

It is interesting to notice how the words "be on your guard" are used in the New Testament. In this passage, we are to be on our guard against the errors of unprincipled men. Here are five more occasions where the phrase is used in the New Testament:

- Be on guard for yourselves and for all the flock, among which the Holy Spirit has made you overseers, to shepherd the church of God which He purchased with His own blood. (Acts 20:28)
- Be on guard, so that your hearts will not be weighted down with dissipation and drunkenness and the worries of life, and that day will not come on you suddenly like a trap. (Luke 21:34)

- Be on your guard! If your brother sins, rebuke him; and if he repents, forgive him. (Luke 17:3)

- Beware, and be on your guard against every form of greed; for not even when one has an abundance does his life consist of his possessions. (Luke 12:15)

- But be on your guard; for they will deliver you to the courts, and you will be flogged in the synagogues, and you will stand before governors and kings for My sake, as a testimony to them. (Mark 13:9)

Guarding the flock, not letting our hearts be weighed down, watching out for our brothers, watching for greed and the need for possessions, and guarding against those who would drag us to court: Is it any wonder that Paul called these events "seasons"? We cannot slow down and become spiritually fat, because the seasons of life never give up.

Keep watching and praying that you may not enter into temptation; the spirit is willing, but the flesh is weak.

Matthew 26:41

Friday: Show Them Your Good Side

The boxer is one the most graceful species of the canine world. My first experience with them came at a dog show. They walk majestically and can glide across an area without making a sound. In spite of their size, the boxer is a very graceful animal. That does not, however, mean that they are the perfect pets.

Boxers love their owners and are tolerant of children in the family, but they are not generally very social. They can be very temperamental around other dogs, even within the same household. Boxers' uniquely shaped nose means that they are loud sleepers. Their impressive looks are brought about by the efforts of their breeders. Their ears and tail are cropped to meet the breed standard.

Betsy belongs to my friends Phil and Donna. She has all of the qualities of a boxer. Yet even with all of the challenges of the breed, Betsy is a beautiful example of a boxer. It's as though she understands she isn't perfect, so she does everything possible to show us her good side.

Christians aren't perfect, either. We are only complete because our sin has been trimmed and Jesus Christ has shaped our lives. On our own, we are still very adept at sinning. Paul confessed in 1 Corinthians 15:31 that he died daily to the imperfections of his human nature. He suffered from the same temptations that we face, but he was committed to representing Christ by showing the world his good side. We might even say that Paul was committed to showing the world his "God side."

Jesus said, "Let your light shine before men in such a way that they may see your good works, and glorify your Father who is in heaven" (Matthew 5:16). Our job is to show the world our good side. Why? Because "we are [God's] workmanship, created in Christ Jesus for good works, which God prepared beforehand so that we would walk in them" (Ephesians 2:10).

Have you ever noticed that when we are tempted to sin, we look around to make sure there is nobody who might recognize us? We don't want to get caught doing the wrong thing. This is not God's way. He wants us to be caught doing good things: "Instruct them to do good, to be rich in good works, to be generous and ready to share" (1 Timothy 6:18).

Sure, we are not perfect, but we are complete in Jesus Christ. So show others your good side. Show them your *God* side so that they might glorify your Father in Heaven.

Saturday: "Who Is My Neighbor?" Prayer Day

Prayer for Our Ministry to Our Neighbors

One of the biggest issues the church may have ever faced is not the style of its music, the color of the carpet, or even its basic doctrine. The issue that has been difficult to resolve is the question, "Who is my neighbor?" The lawyer asked Jesus about it and wasn't happy with the answer. He was much happier loving people who were just like him. To think that Jesus viewed a Samaritan as more righteous than the finely dressed Jewish lawyer was disturbing.

The early church struggled with the question of neighbors. We see in the book of Acts how the church had to invent a special ministry for the widows and orphans who were coming to Jesus. James found it necessary to redirect the church about how they treated the rich and the poor. Gentiles were told they needed to become Jews before they could be real Christians.

We can see the shortfalls of the early church, but are we any better today when we don't even know the people on our street? Do we love our neighbor when we give money to feed the poor we do not know, and ignore the poor who are right before our eyes?

God has called us to see the Sparky in everyone, beginning in our neighborhood, community, city, and all the way to the ends of the earth. Go meet your neighbors, show them your good side, and be ready to give an account for the hope that is in you.

Week 25: Matters of Faith

Monday: Crossing Over

Duke is the perfect companion for Jean. He loves to take long walks on the beach, and enjoys watching the sunset. Jean prefers Balboa Island in California as the location. Duke is a three-year-old chocolate Lab. He is loyal and attentive to his master, so walks like this are regular events.

After a nice long walk around the island, Jean decided to take the ferry back to the mainland. On this particular day Jean and Duke were the only passengers on the ferry. It was the perfect reminder of the years Jean spent sailing in the same area. The two sat quietly, taking in the mist of the salt water, feeling the breeze on their faces. Crossing over was a wonderful experience.

Paul loved his work as an apostle, but he also struggled with his desire to leave this world and be with the Lord:

> But I am hard-pressed from both directions, having the desire to depart and be with Christ, for that is very much better.

Philippians 1:23

For I am already being poured out as a drink offering, and the time of my departure has come. I have fought the good fight, I have finished the course, I have kept the faith; in the future there is laid up for me the crown of righteousness, which the Lord, the righteous Judge, will award to me on that day; and not only to me, but also to all who have loved His appearing.

2 Timothy 4:6–8

Therefore, being always of good courage, and knowing that while we are at home in the body we are absent from the Lord—for we walk by faith, not by sight—we are of good courage, I say, and prefer rather to be absent from the body and to be at home with the Lord. Therefore we also have as our ambition, whether at home or absent, to be pleasing to Him. For we must all appear before the judgment seat of Christ, so that each one may be recompensed for his deeds in the body, according to what he has done, whether good or bad.

2 Corinthians 5:6–10

As much as we enjoy our own walk around the island, life will end before we know it. We will all cross over. The question is, where will we be going? What is your destination? The only way to know for sure is to follow the words of Jesus:

"Do not let your heart be troubled; believe in God, believe also in Me. In My Father's house are many dwelling places; if it were not so, I would have told you; for I go to prepare a place for you. If I go and prepare a place for you, I will come again and receive you to Myself, that where I am, there you may be also. And you know the way where I am going." Thomas said to Him, "Lord, we do not know where You are going, how do we know the way?" Jesus said to him, "I am the way, and the truth, and the life; no one comes to the Father but through Me."

John 14:1–5

Tuesday: Follow the Leader

The term "here comes trouble" fits Tiki well. She is an active little shih tzu who lives with my friend Maxine. She is curious about everything, and is willing to try just about anything. Each day as Tiki watched Maxine get ready for the day, she observed how Maxine put on her make-up. "Any confident dog could do that," Tiki must have thought. So when Maxine was not looking, Tiki grabbed a bright colored lipstick and did her best to look like her master.

Jesus said, "I gave you an example that you also should do as I did to you" (John 13:15). "Follow the Leader" is not just a game. For Christians it is a way of life. The disciples observed the example of Jesus and did their best to follow their leader. Later on, the apostle Paul said something similar about himself: "Brethren, join in following my example, and observe those who walk according to the pattern you have in us" (Philippians 3:17).

Our task is to follow the example of Jesus and the apostles—who themselves were following the example of Jesus. Paul repeated this concept to the church in Thessalonica: "For you yourselves know how you ought to follow our example, because we did not act in an undisciplined manner among you" (2 Thessalonians 3:7).

What is the example we are to follow? Godliness, holiness, and the fruit of the spirit are a few things we must follow. "Likewise urge the young men to be sensible; in all things show yourself to be an example of good deeds, with purity in doctrine, dignified, sound in speech which is beyond reproach, so that the opponent will be put to shame, having nothing bad to say about us" (Titus 2:6–8).

But we are also called to suffer for Christ: "For you have been called for this purpose, since Christ also suffered for you, leaving you an example for you to follow in His steps" (1 Peter 2:21). Of all the "example" passages we find, perhaps this is the one we would most like to avoid. Yet, we can suffer in many ways as believers. Sometimes we suffer at the hands of others, but more often we suffer by our own frailty. We suffer in our rebellion from Christ, and at times we stumble in our attempts to be like Christ. As it happened with Tiki, we try to be like our master and fail in our attempts. The results are often written all over our face.

No matter how weak we are, or how many times we struggle in our attempts, there is still no better life than to follow the example of Jesus. We grow through the losses and we celebrate the successes. With each step we are becoming more like the Christ, "who has called [us] out of darkness into His marvelous light" (1 Peter 2:9).

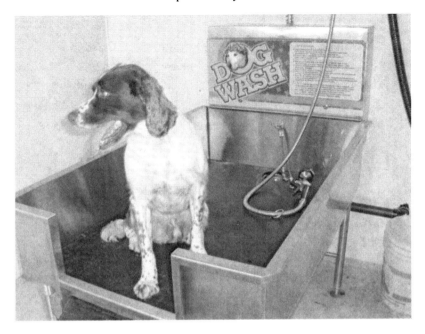

Wednesday: I Will Do It All for Jesus

Jim and Claudia live in Ontario, Canada, where they are serving one of the largest churches in the country. They are also involved in church planting in Canada, as well as in Europe. They are busy people, but never too busy to enjoy life in Canada. Murphy makes sure that their life is full.

On this particular day, Murphy took part in something new. Claudia took him to a public dog-wash facility. Such a washing was new to him, but he went through it because it was what Claudia wanted. He trusted his master, and was willing to do whatever she asked.

This picture reminds me of a passage in 1 Peter:

> For Christ also died for sins once for all, the just for the unjust, so that He might bring us to God, having been put to death in the flesh, but made alive in the spirit; in which also He went and made proclamation to the spirits now in prison, who once were disobedient, when the patience of God kept waiting in the days of Noah, during the construction of the ark, in which a few, that is, eight persons, were brought safely through the water. Corresponding to that, baptism now saves you— not the removal of dirt from the flesh, but an appeal to God for a good conscience—through the resurrection of Jesus Christ, who is at the right hand of God, having gone into heaven, after angels and authorities and powers had been subjected to Him.

1 Peter 3:18–22

Today's church culture seems polarized over the concept of baptism. Each group seems to have their own passage of Scripture to use when it comes to salvation. But, before you go to the next page, let's look at the passages that talk about being saved. I will underline how each passage describes how we are saved.

> For <u>by grace</u> you have been saved through faith; and that not of yourselves, it is the gift of God.
>
> Ephesians 2:8

> Who has saved us and called us with a holy calling, not according to our works, but <u>according to His own purpose and grace</u> which was granted us in Christ Jesus from all eternity.
>
> 2 Timothy 1:9

> He saved us, not on the basis of deeds which we have done in righteousness, but <u>according to His mercy</u>, by the <u>washing of regeneration and renewing by the Holy Spirit</u>.
>
> Titus 3:5

> Now I make known to you, brethren, the gospel which I preached to you, which also you received, in which also you stand, by which also you are saved, if you <u>hold fast the word</u> which I preached to you, unless you believed in vain. For I delivered to you as of first importance what I also received, that Christ died for our sins according to the Scriptures.
>
> 1 Corinthians 15:1–3

> For <u>the word of the cross</u> is foolishness to those who are perishing, but to us who are being saved it is the power of God.
>
> 1 Corinthians 1:18

> If you <u>confess with your mouth</u> Jesus as Lord, and <u>believe in your heart</u> that God raised Him from the dead, you will be saved.
>
> Romans 10:9

> For in <u>hope</u> we have been saved, but hope that is seen is not hope; for who hopes for what he already sees?
>
> Romans 8:24

> They said, "<u>Believe in the Lord Jesus</u>, and you will be saved, you and your household."
>
> Acts 16:31

Someone may ask, "Well, if all of those passages are true, then at what point am I saved?" While we would like to make the answer difficult, the truth is found in a much simpler question. Will you give your all to Jesus? You see, it's not about the minimum amount due (like on our credit card statements). It's about surrender. If I love Jesus, I will do all of these things, and anything else God asks me to do.

Do we dare say, "I don't think I need to do this or that?" If it's in the Bible, can we relegate it to a position of unimportance? The Bible isn't written in a step-by-step owner's manual format. This is why we need to read the whole thing and follow everything in it. Can we call it "surrender" if we are only willing to do part of what the Bible says to do?

I am not all that interested in the "minimum amount due." So I will read the Word, believe in my heart, confess with my mouth, place my hope in Jesus, trust in God's grace, call upon his mercy, and be baptized as well. True surrender says, "I will do it all for you Jesus. Bring it on."

"Now why do you delay? Get up and be baptized, and wash away your sins, calling on His name" (Acts 22:16).

Thursday: God's Right Hand

New puppies are great fun. They are excited to learn, they love attention, and are very active. Since they are just starting out, they don't always have control of their body. They fall, run into things, and lose control because their muscles can't keep up with what their mind wants to do.

Max got to spend some play time with Stella, Gini's new puppy. Stella will be small as a full grown dog, so she is tiny as a puppy. It would be easy for Max to get carried away and injure the tiny little puppy. Yet Max understands that she is delicate. Max has freely offered his right hand for Stella to chew on, play with, and be shielded by. That hand is a symbol of acceptance, love, and protection. As long as Max's hand is present, Stella is secure.

The Bible has a lot to say about God's right hand in our lives. For example, "He trains my hands for battle, so that my arms can bend a bow of bronze. You have also given me the shield of Your salvation, and Your right hand upholds me; and Your gentleness makes me great. You enlarge my steps under me, and my feet have not slipped" (Psalm 18:34–36).

God's right hand is the place where we can take refuge (Psalm 117:7). The psalmist says, "You have also given me the shield of your salvation, and your right hand upholds me; and your gentleness makes me great" (Psalm 18:35). "My soul clings to you; your right hand upholds me" (Psalm 63:8).

God's right hand is mighty, exalted, and strong (Psalm 89:13). The right hand of the Lord is exalted and does valiantly (Psalm 118:16). For those who oppose God, the right hand deals a crushing blow, and to those who love him, the right hand is a shield of protection.

We dare not spend our lifetime outside of the hand of God. We do not need to rely on the craftiness of our own intellect. That will very easily get us crushed by the world. But the hand of God will raise up the weak. It's no wonder that Paul said, "Therefore I am well content with weaknesses, with insults, with distresses, with persecutions, with difficulties, for Christ's sake; for when I am weak, then I am strong" (2 Corinthians 12:10)

Surely we stumble and fall. We are spiritually uncoordinated at times. But God wants us to be counted among those who place their trust in the protection of God's mighty right hand.

Friday: So Great a Cloud

Murphy is an English springer spaniel. He comes from a well-documented bloodline of champions. Who he is, is a reflection of those who have gone before him. The way he carries himself, his retrieval instincts, his coat, and appearance all speak to the quality of the dogs up his bloodline.

Murphy is comfortably lounging on a quilt that was likely made by some member of her family. Many of us have such a quilt in our homes. Each piece of fabric has a history of an event, or a time period. A favorite garment, a dress from a first date, or something shared with a friend can provide the material that is sown together into a single blanket that reminds us of our past. Those memories, and our history, make up who we are today. We are reflection of those who went before us.

New Testament writers describe a faith bloodline that comes down from a vast spiritual family: "But you are a chosen race, a royal priesthood, a holy nation, a people for God's own possession, so that you may proclaim the excellencies of Him who has called you out of darkness into His marvelous light" (1 Peter 2:9). The bloodline of Christ, which all believers share, is filled with spiritual champions who have changed the world. We are able to walk and talk the gospel because of what those before us have accomplished.

The writer of Hebrews expanded on this by painting an emotional picture of the quilt that led to the church. He speaks of Abel, Enoch, Abraham, Sarah, Esau, Jacob, Joseph, and Moses. He spoke of the faith of those who marched around Jericho, of Rehab, and Samuel, and the amazing acts of faith which came through the prophets. Each gave a piece of him- or herself to make up the spiritual quilt on which we now rest. Is it any wonder that the writer could boldly proclaim, "Therefore, since we have so great a cloud of witnesses surrounding us, let us also lay aside every encumbrance and the sin which so easily entangles us, and let us run with endurance the race that is set before us, fixing our eyes on Jesus, the author and perfecter of faith, who for the joy set before Him endured the cross, despising the shame, and has sat down at the right hand of the throne of God" (Hebrews 12:1–2).

Don't think for one minute that you are all alone. Never allow Satan to place the negative thought in you that you are not important. God has included you in his royal priesthood, and he is sewing you into the quilt of his mighty church. He has called you to help create today's spiritual platform that believers of the future will build upon. You can make a difference today.

Saturday: "Matters of Faith" Prayer Day

Sold Out for Jesus

Be counted among those who are sold out for Jesus. Sold-out believers keep their eyes on the prize of the upward calling of God, they are obedient to the Word of God, and they remain under the direction of God's right hand. They know they are following Jesus because of the testimony of the "great cloud of witnesses" who have led the way. Sold-out Christians place no limits on obedience to Christ.

This book has covered many spiritual subjects and backed them all up with Scripture. The goal of this day is to take a spiritual survey of the things you have learned, the ways you have grown, and the areas where you still need to be sold out. Take a pen and write that list somewhere in this book. Then pray through it. Celebrate your victories, rejoice in your growth, and commit to work on those areas that have been a struggle.

Don't close this book until you create your list. God wants to hear from you.

Week 26: Holidays

Monday: Where Size Matters

Countless stories have been written about boys and their dogs. Lassie comes to mind, as does the classic book *Old Yeller*. There is something magical about the relationship between a boy and the animal he loves. Such is the case with Micah and his dog Chase.

From the time that Micah came home from the hospital, Chase has been loyal to his young master. In fact, when Kristy and Joe struggle to settle Micah down, Chase is able to do the trick. They just love being together. Sure, Chase is massive next to his tiny master. It is also true that Chase could easily overpower Micah. But he doesn't. Instead he is tender and nurturing. Chase is perfectly willing to accept that Micah may grab a handful of hair or an ear once in a while. He knows that Micah is still learning how to be a good master. Yet he doesn't mind, because in spite of the size, age, and maturity difference, Micah is the master.

Sometimes we feel like Micah: small, untrained, and unable to defend ourselves. The cares of the world may look like Chase: ominous and intimidating. If you share those feelings then you need to shift your focus to the place where size really matters. You see, the size of your God matters.

"You, dear children, are from God and have overcome them, because the one who is in you is greater than the one who is in the world" (1 John 4:4, NIV). "And there is salvation in no one else; for there is no other name under heaven that has been given among men by which we must be saved" (Acts 4:12).

The size of your trust matters as well. "For I am confident of this very thing, that He who began a good work in you will perfect it until the day of Christ Jesus" (Philippians 1:6). Do you believe the words of this verse? If so, then you understand why the size of your trust matters. This is also true with the size of your faith: "And the Lord said, 'If you had faith like a mustard seed, you would say to this mulberry tree, 'Be uprooted and be planted in the sea'; and it would obey you'" (Luke 17:6). Perhaps the best news of all is that the size of our hope matters: "For this reason I also suffer these things, but I am not ashamed; for I know whom I have believed and I am convinced that He is able to guard what I have entrusted to Him until that day" (2 Timothy 1:12).

It's easy to take our eyes off of these truths and place them on the huge teeth of the world. Daniel could have done that when he was thrown into the lion's den. But he trusted his God. He had faith that God would keep His promises, and his hope kept him safe. He was outsized and outnumbered, but he was still the master—not because of who he was, but *whose* he was.

Before moving on to the next item on your daily agenda, find your Bible and read Romans 5:1–5. That passage will remind you of where size matters.

Tuesday: Find Christ This Christmas

Now in those days a decree went out from Caesar Augustus, that a census be taken of all the inhabited earth. This was the first census taken while Quirinius was governor of Syria. And everyone was on his way to register for the census, each to his own city. Joseph also went up from Galilee, from the city of Nazareth, to Judea, to the city of David, which is called Bethlehem, because he was of the house and family of David, in order to register along with Mary, who was engaged to him, and was with child. While they were there, the days were completed for her to give birth. And she gave birth to her firstborn son; and she wrapped Him in cloths, and laid Him in a manger, because there was no room for them in the inn.

In the same region there were some shepherds staying out in the fields and keeping watch over their flock by night. And an angel of the Lord suddenly stood before them, and the glory of the Lord shone around them; and they were terribly frightened. But the angel said to them, "Do not be afraid; for behold, I bring you good news of great joy which will be for all the people; for today in the city of David there has been born for you a Savior, who is Christ the Lord. This will be a sign for you: you will find a baby wrapped in cloths and lying in a manger." And suddenly there appeared with the angel a multitude of the heavenly host praising God and saying,

"Glory to God in the highest,
And on earth peace among men
With whom He is pleased."

Luke 2:1–14

May the Christ of Christmas become your refuge and strength.

Wednesday: For Those Who Look

For dogs to be completely obedient to their master they must gain control of all their senses. A dog must hear the master's commands, watch the master's movements, sense the master's presence, and tune in to the master's emotions. To do this, we must teach them to focus ears, nose, and eyes on their master.

Teaching a dog to look begins by holding a treat out so the dog can see it. As he looks at the treat, he receives it. Next, move the treat in front of your face and say "Look." He will look straight at the treat, and your face behind it. As he develops the skill to look at the treat in front of your face, you can now begin to eliminate the treat, leaving the dog to look straight at your face. The look command takes time and conditioning, but it's a vital connection between dog and master.

The Bible is full of examples of those who looked for Christ. During the Christmas season, we remember one man who looked for Christ's coming: "At that time there was a man in Jerusalem named Simeon. He was righteous and devout and was eagerly waiting for the Messiah to come and rescue Israel. The Holy Spirit was upon him and had revealed to him that he would not die until he had seen the Lord's Messiah. That day the Spirit led him to the Temple. So when Mary and Joseph came to present the baby Jesus to the Lord as the law required, Simeon was there. He took the child in his arms and praised God, saying, "Sovereign Lord, now let your servant die in peace, as you have promised. I have seen your salvation, which you have prepared for all people. He is a light to reveal God to the nations, and he is the glory of your people Israel!" (Luke 2:25–32 NLT).

The city was filled with people, and the temple was hopping with those eager to perform their rituals. Yet none of them noticed Jesus. Why? They weren't looking. Only Simeon and Anna noticed the presence of the one born to save the world from sin. While everyone else was busy doing their own thing, Simeon and Anna were looking for the fulfillment of the Scripture.

How many of God's blessings are you missing out on simply because you are not looking? We pass by focused on our own pursuits as someone else stands in awe of God's gift. How did we miss it? Why did the blessing pass us and reach them? Is it because they were looking and we weren't? Fixing our attention on Christ is a biblical principle that we can't ignore. We must train ourselves to look for His presence, will, and blessings. "But according to His promise we are looking for new heavens and a new earth, in which righteousness dwells. Therefore, beloved, since you look for these things, be diligent to be found by Him in peace, spotless and blameless, and regard the patience of our Lord as salvation; just as also our beloved brother Paul, according to the wisdom given him, wrote to you" (2 Peter 3:13–15).

The one who is blessed is the one who looks intently into the law of liberty, according to James 1:25. The goal of looking caused the Hebrew writer to write these words:

> Do you see what this means—all these pioneers who blazed the way, all these veterans cheering us on? It means we'd better get on with it. Strip down, start running—and never quit! No extra spiritual fat, no parasitic sins. Keep your eyes on Jesus, who both began and finished this race we're in. Study how he did it. Because he never lost sight of where he was headed—that exhilarating finish in and with God—he could put up with anything along the way: Cross, shame, whatever. And now he's there, in the place of honor, right alongside God. When you find yourselves flagging in your faith, go over that story again, item by item, that long litany of hostility he plowed through. That will shoot adrenaline into your souls!
>
> Hebrews 12:1–3, *The Message*

Thursday: Wait for His Timing

The challenge of training a puppy is for the master to become more important than the sights, smells, and sounds that constantly bombard our pets. They hear sounds in frequencies we are incapable of detecting. As puppies, they haven't acquired the ability to filter out distractions and focus on one thing. This is why we must teach them to focus on us and trust our timing.

Kessie is proving to be a very special Labrador retriever. She is learning quickly, and Lisa is a wonderful teacher. Kessie comes on command, sits, and understands the down command. Now she is learning to wait. Lisa uses kibble, which, if Kessie is patient enough, Lisa will give to her. At times, Kessie forgets the command and jumps for the food. When she does, Lisa takes it away. Goodies will come, but in Lisa's timing. Kessie must learn that waiting has its rewards. All of the distractions mean nothing when Kessie's master holds out the kibble and gives the command to wait.

The Bible tells us that rewards are waiting for us as well. These rewards will be given to us in God's timing. This is why David wrote, "To You, O Lord, I lift up my soul. O my God, in You I trust, do not let me be ashamed; do not let my enemies exult over me. Indeed, none of those who wait for You will be ashamed; Those who deal treacherously without cause will be ashamed" (Psalm 25:1–3).

It is so easy to be caught up in the sounds and smells of Christmas. These distractions can block out the most important part of the season. For this reason we pause to remember the baby born of a virgin and laid in a manger. He is the one spoken of by the Isaiah: "For a child will be born to us, a son will be given to us; and the government will rest on His shoulders; and His name will be called Wonderful Counselor, Mighty God, Eternal Father, Prince of Peace. There will be no end to the increase of His government or of peace, on the throne of David and over his kingdom, to establish it and to uphold it with justice and righteousness from then on and forevermore the zeal of the Lord of hosts will accomplish this" (Isaiah 9:6–7). Having heard the promise, the people waited for the coming King. "But as for me," said Micah, "I watch in hope for the Lord, I wait for God my Savior; my God will hear me" (Micah 7:7).

The child-King, born in poverty and hung on a cross "at the right time" (Romans 5:6) has promised that he will come again. He said so in John 14:1–3: "Do not let your heart be troubled believe in God, believe also in Me. In My Father's house are many dwelling places; if it were not so, I would have told you; for I go to prepare a place for you. If I go and prepare a place for you, I will come again and receive you to Myself, that where I am, there you may be also." For this blessing we must watch and wait, knowing that Jesus will come again "at the right time."

Celebrate his birth and keep your focus on his blessing. "We know that the whole creation has been groaning as in the pains of childbirth right up to the present time. Not only so, but we ourselves, who have the first fruits of the Spirit, groan inwardly as we wait eagerly for our adoption to sonship, the redemption of our bodies. For in this hope we were saved. But hope that is seen is no hope at all. Who hopes for what they already have? But if we hope for what we do not yet have, we wait for it patiently" (Romans 8:22–25).

This Christmas, join with others who eagerly wait for the coming of the Lord. Make sure that Jesus is the reason for your season. And remember the words of Isaiah who said, "Yet those who wait for the Lord will gain new strength; They will mount up with wings like eagles, they will run and not get tired, they will walk and not become weary" (Isaiah 40:31).

Friday: Comfort and Joy

There is nothing like basking in the light of the sun with your best friend. Laredo has been there every day of Hunter's life, helping his growth, cleaning up the food Hunter dropped from his high chair, and watching over the crib as Hunter slept. Laredo was patient through the grabbing and pulling period, tolerated the "let-me-try-to-ride-you" period, and remained faithful to his little master every step of the way. Those experiences have created a bond between them that breeds a level of comfort that can only be understood by experiencing it first-hand.

The Bible uses a word that is often overlooked. The word is "comfort," which in its various forms occurs nearly 90 times in the Bible. Paul uses "comfort" ten times in only six verses at the beginning of Second Corinthians, and 19 times in the epistle altogether.

Grace to you and peace from God our Father and the Lord Jesus Christ. Blessed be the God and Father of our Lord Jesus Christ, the Father of mercies and God of all **comfort**, who **comforts** us in all our affliction so that we will be able to **comfort** those who are in any affliction with the **comfort** with which we ourselves are **comforted** by God. For just as the sufferings of Christ are ours in abundance, so also our **comfort** is abundant through Christ. But if we are afflicted, it is for your **comfort** and salvation; or if we are **comforted**, it is for your **comfort**, which is effective in the patient enduring of the same sufferings which we also suffer; and our hope for you is firmly grounded, knowing that as you are sharers of our sufferings, so also you are *sharers* of our **comfort**.

2 Corinthians 1:2–7 (emphasis added)

The concept of comfort must be defined from two directions to gain a complete understanding. It means to give hope and strength, but it also means to relieve grief and trouble. Our God relieves grief, takes pain on himself, and provides the way of forgiveness from sin. In its place He provides comfort, strength, and hope. He has also called those who have been comforted to become comforters, helping to relieve grief and provide hope to others. The picture of Hunter and Laredo basking in the sun is a perfect picture of the church. As we gather together to glorify Jesus, the Son of God, we find comfort in him and provide comfort to each other.

Now with Christmas being cleaned up, the decorations coming down, and the slow return to normal life, let's not forget the promise of the Christmas carol. The comfort promised has been delivered in the birth of Jesus the Christ. That promise does not go away with the decorations. If you are suffering with stress, worry, or grief, make it your goal to seek the comfort spoken of so often in the Scripture. It is there for the taking—and it is yours for the giving.

God rest ye merry, gentlemen;
Let nothing you dismay.
Remember Christ, our Savior,
Was born on Christmas day,
To save us all from Satan's power
When we were gone astray.
O tidings of comfort and joy,
Comfort and joy!
O tidings of comfort and joy![10]

Saturday: All Things to All People

Meet Tyler and Lauren, two very patient beagles. They belong to Nancy, who loves to dress them for every holiday. The dogs have outfits for nearly every season and are happy to show them off. Nancy has developed a slide show of her dogs to share with all of her friends. This begs the question: When is a dog not a dog? When he is wearing bunny ears, or a Santa hat, or a leprechaun costume.

I am reminded of the testimony of the apostle Paul:

> Even though I am free of the demands and expectations of everyone, I have voluntarily become a servant to any and all in order to reach a wide range of people: religious, nonreligious, meticulous moralists, loose-living immoralists, the defeated, the demoralized—whoever. I didn't take on their way of life. I kept my bearings in Christ—but I entered their world and tried to experience things from their point of view. I've become just about every sort of servant there is in my attempts to lead those I meet into a God-saved life. I did all this because of the Message. I didn't just want to talk about it; I wanted to be in on it!
>
> 1 Corinthians 9:19–23, *The Message*

Paul's approach matched the way Jesus lived his life: "Therefore, it was necessary for Jesus to be in every respect like us, his brothers and sisters, so that he could be our merciful and faithful High Priest before God. He then could offer a sacrifice that would take away the sins of the people" (Hebrews 2:17, NLT). The point here is that God wanted to develop a relationship with us, so Jesus set aside his equality with God. He put on skin and lived among us. Then Jesus took our sin onto himself and wore it to the cross. He put on a tomb and rose from the dead to provide the way of salvation for us.

When we enter into the Easter season, we must recognize that we are God's representatives to the world. Our job is to take the gospel into the world. If we sit back, expecting the world to come to us, the job will never get done. Our challenge is to follow the example of Jesus and the way explained by Paul. What can you do at Easter to make a difference in somebody else's life? If it means putting on bunny ears to become more like them, then by all means wear the ears. Just remember the goal—that we may win them to the resurrected Savior, Jesus Christ.

Notes

---

[1] Lyrics by William J. Gaither and Gloria Gaither. Copyright 1982 by Gaither Music and River Oaks Music Co.

[2] "Jesus Take The Wheel," songwriters: James, Brett; Lindsey, Hillary; Sampson, Gordie; Performed by Carrie Underwood on the album *Some Hearts* (November 2005) Arista Records, Nashville, TN.

[3] "I Just Want To Be Where You Are," Don Moen, Integrity Hosanna Music, A Division of David C. Cook (1989).

[4] Search Me O God, words by J. Edwin Orr, 1936, first published in the book, *All You Need*.

[5] "Temptation," written by Don Waits, sung by Diana Krall, Verve Music Group, 2004.

[6] "I'd Rather Have Jesus," written by Rhea F. Miller, 1922, Public Domain.

[7] "Trading My Sorrows," by Darrell Evans, Vertical Music, 2002.

[8] Milan, Cesar, and Jo Peltier. *Be the Pack Leader*. New York: Three Rivers Press, 2007.

[9] "Unchain My Heart," by Bobby Sharp, B. Sharp Music 1961, performed by Joe Cocker, Capital Records, 1978.

[10] "God Rest Ye Merry, Gentlemen," author unknown, published by William B. Sandys, 1833

Other Books
By Fred Bittner

The God Whisperer

The Kneeling Christian For Small Groups

The Pursuit of God For Small Groups

Galatians For Small Groups, A Study of Grace

Relational Discipleship

The Art of Worship (coming in 2013)

CPSIA information can be obtained at www.ICGtesting.com
Printed in the USA
LVOW05s1318070813

346759LV00003B/51/P

9 780985 699208